READER OF THE PURPLE SAGE

WESTERN LITERATURE SERIES

Reader of the Purple Sage

Essays on Western Writers and Environmental Literature

ANN RONALD

FOREWORD BY MELODY GRAULICH

UNIVERSITY OF NEVADA PRESS

RENO & LAS VEGAS

Western Literature Series

University of Nevada Press, Reno, Nevada 89557 USA

Copyright © 2003 by Ann Ronald

Manufactured in the United States of America

Library of Congress Cataloging-in-Publication Data

Ronald, Ann, 1939–

Reader of the purple sage : essays on Western writers

and environmental literature / Ann Ronald ;

foreword by Melody Graulich.

p. cm. — (Western literature series)

Includes bibliographical references and index.

ISBN 0-87417-524-0 (pbk. : alk. paper)

1. American literature—West (U.S.)—History and

criticism. 2. Natural history literature—West (U.S.)—

History. 3. Authors, American—Homes and haunts—West (U.S.)

4. West (U.S.)—Intellectual life. 5. West (U.S.)—In literature.

6. Nature in literature. I. Title. II. Series.

PS271 .R66 2003

810.9'978—dc21   2002012924

The paper used in this book meets the requirements
of American National Standard for Information
Sciences—Permanence of Paper for Printed Library
Materials, ANSI Z39.48-1984. Binding materials were
selected for strength and durability.

FIRST PRINTING

12 11 10 09 08 07 06 05 04 03

5 4 3 2 1

For Lois,
designated driver of the purple sage

CONTENTS

In the mid-1980s, I was on a plenary panel with Ann Ronald, then past-president of the Western Literature Association. We were supposed to speak informally for ten minutes on "Future Directions in Western Literary Studies." After Ann's speculative and humorous remarks, the final panelist rose to read a written text. He would begin, he said, with a list of the influential critics of western literature. He read five names, all men. Five more men followed. I don't remember how long the list went on, but when he finally concluded, without mentioning one woman, Ann and I simultaneously turned to smile ruefully at each other. The audience burst into laughter. I don't think he ever figured out what they were laughing at.

The audience, however, recognized that sitting next to him on the stage was a major voice in western American literature, the author of books on Zane Grey and Edward Abbey and numerous essays, many of them about her immediate region—Nevada and the Great Basin. Ronald was attracted to Abbey for good reason: though generally far more tactful, she too has a strong, iconoclastic, and always humorous voice. Literally and metaphorically, her voice welcomed dozens of young writers like me to the study of western literature, encouraging us to look beyond the familiar and to seek new subjects in places others overlook.

Even then Ann Ronald was hatching plans for one of the most significant "future directions" in literary studies. As an officer of the Western Literature Association, she would encourage the development of an entire organization—the Association for the Study of Literature and the Environment. As department chair and then dean at the University of Nevada, Reno, she would foster a new discipline, ecocriticism, by hiring faculty in joint appointments in literature and in the environment and by helping begin a graduate program in the field.

Ronald's own writing demonstrates her willingness and her eagerness to head off in new directions. The lively essays in *Reader of the Purple Sage* explore unexpected writers and topics, chronicling her evolution as an essayist as she scouted out the contours of two emerging fields. Hired as a young faculty member at Reno, she claimed her new homeplace by reading and writing about her precursors. *Reader of the Purple Sage* suggests how influential the move to the high desert was for Ronald, how her approach to reading and writing has been shaped by her life in the arid West. Thinking of writing a book about Nevada writers, she wandered the region, not only following Abbey and reading the state's most celebrated writer, Walter Van Tilburg Clark, but also researching unknown writers— women who homesteaded or were married to mine operators in Tonopah—and making her way to Reno and Las Vegas as well as into the desert. In these early essays Ronald did for the Nevada literary landscape what she would later do for the Great Basin ecosystem: lead her readers to look beyond their expectations for the spectacular, the dramatic, the grand, and instead listen for the sustaining seep of the small desert stream, let the eye adjust to gradation rather than contrast.

Ronald's Nevada, her Great Basin, is part of a larger region, itself part of the vast and varied American West. As she writes about Nevada's cultural traditions, she considers their relationship to the literatures and the cultures of the West, the most expansive subject of her critical essays. As her early work on two very different west-ern transplants, Grey and Abbey, suggests, throughout her career Ronald has explored both writers who popularize the romantic themes of the "Old West" and writers who warn us about the future directions of the "New West." She praises and critiques the masters of Western American literature, but, particularly in her essays, she has always been committed to introducing overlooked works to a general audience. She is acutely aware that texts present "interpre-tations" of western history and culture, and she draws our attention to those interpretations. The essays in the second section of *Reader of the Purple Sage* follow trail drives throughout the region created by a celebrated writer, Larry McMurtry, and a Colorado hike up Pike's Peak described by an English "lady" traveler, Isabella Bird. Two essays implicitly contrast a realistic portrayal of pioneering days in Montana with a mythic epic of western settlement. The fi-nal essay of part 2, "Stegner and Stewardship," in which Ronald presents an ecocritical reading of the environmental writings of a writer she much admires, is typical of her best work. She acknowl-edges and pays her respects to Stegner's environmental warnings but simultaneously reveals their shortcomings.

"Stegner and Stewardship" also serves as a transition into the third section. Ronald's work has increasingly examined the inter-play between place and writing, between, as she says, "the ways we live on the land and the ways we write about it." Initially focusing on the varied genres then collected under "nature writing" and searching for terminology to rethink the field, Ronald began to ex-plore how writers could convey their environmental knowledge and awareness broadly to their audiences. She replaces "awestruck" and "sublime" with "habitat" and "symbiotic," rhapsodic descrip-tions of emotional response with historical and scientific research and vocabulary. Throughout part 3, we see her walking new trails and defining new terms, new "taxonomies," new criteria for assess-ment, introducing new writers and new ways of looking at land-scapes.

The essays in this section tell the story of the growth of a new approach to studying literature, an approach Ronald helped pioneer. Her most recent essays on environmental writing, "Kingdom, Phylum, Class, Order: Twentieth-Century American Nature Writer" and "Raising the Bar," succinctly yet ambitiously map the complex ecology of a rapidly growing field.

As a critic and as a university administrator, Ann Ronald has nourished that growth. Appropriately, *Reader of the Purple Sage* concludes with Ronald setting out in yet another new direction, with what she calls her "own creative writing about the natural world." Once again she is in the vanguard of her field, both in *Earthtones: A Nevada Album,* her beautiful book about the Great Basin, and in *GhostWest,* an evocative exploration of historical and cultural echoes in landscapes throughout the Far West. Ronald's "nature" is not a pristine wilderness but always inflected with the resonances of human history. She is what I think of as a "place" writer, showing us how nature and culture; past, present, and future; memory and desire; story and history; human and nonhuman all together contribute to meaning.

In 1990, Wallace Stegner described what he thought the literature of the American West most needed. "It could use a little more confidence in itself," he said, "and one way to generate that is to breed up some critics capable, by experience or intuition, of evaluating western literature in the terms of western life," critics who could "read western writing in the spirit of those who write it." I'd say that Ann Ronald has provided all of us with that confidence. And she will continue to do so.

MELODY GRAULICH

ACKNOWLEDGMENTS

My thanks to all those who first published the essays included in *Reader of the Purple Sage*:

"Afterword." *Words for the Wild*. San Francisco: Sierra Club Books, 1987. 351–58.

"Company for a *Lonesome Dove*." *History and Humanities: Essays in Honor of Wilbur S. Shepperson*. Ed. Francis X. Hartigan. Reno: U Nevada P, 1989. 299–309.

"Environmental Journalism." *Halcyon: A Journal of the Humanities* 8 (1986): 81–91.

"Ghosts." *Earthtones: A Nevada Album*. Reno: U Nevada P, 1995. 79–97.

"Idah Meacham Strobridge: The Second Mary Austin?" *Weber Studies* 11 (Spring/Summer 1994): 97–105.

"Introduction." *A Lady's Life in the Rocky Mountains*. By Isabella Bird. San Francisco: Comstock Editions, 1987. xi–xviii.

"Introduction." *The Land Is Bright*. By Archie Binns. Corvallis: Oregon State UP, 1992. vii–xv.

"Kingdom, Phylum, Class, Order: Twentieth-Century American Nature Writer." *Western American Literature* 33 (Winter 1999): 384–402.

"A Montana Maturity." *South Dakota Review* 23 (Spring 1985): 89–98.

"The Nevada Scene Through Edward Abbey's Eyes." *Nevada Historical Society Quarterly* 27 (Spring 1984): 2–13.

"Raising the Bar." *Western American Literature* 34 (Spring 1999): 68–77.

"Reno: Myth, Mystique, or Madness?" *Halcyon: A Journal of the Humanities* 1 (1979): 87–101; reprinted in *East of Eden, West of Zion*. Ed. Wilbur Shepperson. Reno: U Nevada P, 1989. 134–48.

"*Shane*'s Pale Ghost." *New Orleans Review* 17 (Fall 1990): 5–9.

"Stegner and Stewardship." *Writers' Forum* 17 (Fall 1991): 3–16; reprinted in *Wallace Stegner: Man and Writer*. Ed. Charles E. Rankin. Albuquerque: U New Mexico P, 1996. 87–103.

"The Tonopah Ladies." *Nevada Historical Society Quarterly* 20 (Summer 1977): 90–100; reprinted in *Women, Women Writers, and the West*. Ed. Lawrence L. Lee and Merrill E. Lewis. Troy, NY: Whitson, 1978. 15–24.

"Walter Van Tilburg Clark's Brave Bird, 'Hook.'" *Studies in Short Fiction* 25 (Fall 1988): 433–39.

"Western Literature and Natural Resources." *Halcyon: A Journal of the Humanities* 11 (1989): 125–34.

"Why Don't They Write About Nevada?" *Western American Literature* 24 (November 1989): 213–24; reprinted in *Wilderness Tapestry*. Ed. Zeveloff, Vause, and McVaugh. Reno: U Nevada P, 1992. 97–109.

Each essay in *Reader of the Purple Sage* is replicated as it first appeared in its original publication. Because of this, some of the information may now sound dated. Living authors, for example, will have published more titles than perhaps are listed; certain environmental problems may have disappeared, while others may have been exacerbated by time. Despite the occasional imprecise detail, I trust that the overall observations are themselves timeless. I would also point out that the notes and bibliographical citations may be formatted differently in different essays. Within each individual essay, however, the documentation is internally consistent.

My literary imagination follows a Truckee River kind of route—beginning in the mountains, meandering down canyon, pausing in the city, culminating in the Nevada desert. There's been some rough water along the way, some evaporation, but also some deep pools for fishing and some very fruitful diversions.

I grew up in the Pacific Northwest, raised by an accountant father who enjoyed Plato and Herodotus for relaxation and a mother who devoured thick novels and political biographies. My favorite stuffed animal, a spindle-legged blue creature, was named Agamemnon, which suggests the kind of bedtime stories my parents must have read to me. Neither one of them attended college, but they surely aimed me in that direction. Books and magazines, often stacked double and triple on the shelves, covered every table and many of the chairs. By kindergarten, I could read, because that's what my family did in the evening, and I soon knew *Winnie the Pooh* by heart. In grade school, paper dolls slaked my thirst for narrative, along with Nancy Drew and *Little House on the Prairie*. We had no television, not until I graduated from high school and the University of Washington Huskies finally went to the Rose Bowl.

At the same time I was learning to read everything in sight, I also was growing up in the out-of-doors. Although wall-to-wall houses eventually surrounded my childhood home, the postwar-Seattle-building boom took awhile. Until I was in junior high, skyscraper evergreens grew north and west as far as I could see. As the only little girl in the neighborhood, I spent my early years climbing trees, building forts, and throwing sword ferns. When I felt more solitary than sociable, I made up stories. Every summer I went to camp on the Olympic Peninsula, where I discovered the wonders of canoeing and backpacking, and turned an affection for trite poetry into an enthusiasm for Edna St. Vincent Millay and then into an appreciation of T.S. Eliot and Bertolt Brecht. Now, looking back at my youth, my career and my fate seem inevitable—books and landscape, intertwined.

Like most teenagers, however, I didn't see the obvious direction. In college, I confess, I skied more often than I studied. I didn't even decide to major in English until the middle of my junior year, when I discovered I had more credits in the literature classes I was taking just for fun than in those courses that might lead me toward employment. When I finally wandered off to graduate school, my only purpose was to complete a Washington-state teacher's credential. At the same time, I took a couple of graduate English seminars, just for fun, and I was hooked. I quit my high school teaching job—I always had liked the books better than the bureaucracy—and got to work.

Once in graduate school, the career stream stopped overflowing the banks, though my path still cut some surprising new oxbows. I majored in the Victorians—today I teach mostly American Lit. I specialized in the novel—today I write nonfiction. I studied the onset of the Industrial Revolution—today I ponder its environmental legacy. The constant seems to be a fascination for landscape, for sense of place, for the ways in which people interact with the earth. In that first graduate seminar, I wrote my final paper about the bone-chilling moors of the Brontë sisters. Next I studied Melville's Galapagos and Hawthorne's Rome, then George Eliot's Florence and Mrs. Gaskell's countryside. My dissertation? "Functions of Setting in the English Novel," with Charles Dickens's London and Lincolnshire comprising the final chapter.

And while I was writing all these pages and pages of graduate student prose, I was living in the Midwest, where the harsh January wind blew off Lake Michigan and froze my nostrils shut, and where humid Julys promised the Chicago Cubs a pennant that never materialized, and where I felt forever comfortable in the old-stone Gothic library but found the accompanying landscape relentlessly flat. Looking for college teaching jobs, I drew a line down the front range of the Rockies, promising myself I'd never live farther east again. When I graduated, I headed west. Not to my beloved western red cedar and Douglas fir, however, not to tangy saltwater smells and the indescribable taste of fresh-caught steelhead. Instead, I found myself at the University of Nevada in Reno. What have I done? I wondered, as I signed that first contract more than thirty years ago and then drove into a land of little rain, a city of trembling trees.

What I had done became obvious immediately. I had come to a place where the sun actually remained visible on umbrella-less winter days, where corrugated mountains and sand-swept basins ranged just beyond the city limits, where a pickup truck soon superseded my Chevy convertible, and where I never again fretted about the fortunes of the Washington Huskies or the misfortunes of the Chicago Cubs. I also had come to a place where the university library boasted a Special Collections department that specialized in wrinkled manuscripts and leathery books of the American West, and where primary sources on the Victorians were in scant supply. Quickly, I adjusted. Within six months, I knew I loved the desert. Almost as quickly, I learned to love literature about the desert as well, from Zane Grey's Technicolor canyons to Edward Abbey's solipsistic spaces, and beyond.

I soon began writing about authors and books that focus on red rocks and rabbit brush, that describe monoliths shaped by geology and wind, that explore pathless panoramas, and that muse about our human responses to an ostensibly inhospitable terrain. And while I was discovering the allure of western prose, other American writers were converging on the western landscape, too. Bookstore shelves suddenly were lined with natural histories and nature writing, with celebrations of and elegies for the natural world, with first-person accounts of wilderness in a modern age. Scholars suddenly were scrambling to read and critique and make sense of this literary cornucopia. My colleagues and I found ourselves defining a new genre called "environmental literature," pursuing "narrative scholarship" by situating our critical voices in our own outdoor experiences, and writing for a much wider audience than did literary critics of the preceding generation.

Nonetheless, many of our thoughts about the landscape of books languish in obscure journals and out-of-print collections. This volume brings together a selection of my own essays about the literary West and its practitioners. From Wallace Stegner to Idah Meacham Strobridge, from *Shane* to *The Land Is Bright,* from Las Vegas to Tonopah and from Glen Canyon to an unnamed Nevada playa, *Reader of the Purple Sage* demonstrates exactly what I have become since moving to Nevada—a reader of the purple sage.

READER OF THE PURPLE SAGE

PART I

Nevada Writers of
the Purple Sage

"Why Don't They Write About Nevada?" I once asked, wondering why nature writers focus on glamorous landscapes instead of more ascetic spots like the Great Basin. I was being facetious. In truth, many authors have made Nevada their literary home. Some have written about the state's unique high desert distances and its southern Mojave vistas. Others have fictionalized its history and imagined its stories. Once upon a time I actually contemplated writing a book of essays about Nevada literature, a book that would look at city landscapes as well as country roads, that would include unknown novelists and favorite sons, that would assess the breadth and depth of Nevada prose. I finished two chapters.

The first examines those novels that describe my adopted home when Reno was a mecca for divorcées, in the 1930s. This was a Reno I never knew, though some of its flavor lasted into subsequent decades. In 1970 I still could wander tree-lined streets where a new freeway was swallowing the old boardinghouses. I could stand on the very bridge where women happily had tossed their wedding rings into the Truckee River. I could hike up Peavine Mountain and find herds of deer instead of hoards of houses. I could well envision Walter Van Tilburg Clark's *City of Trembling Leaves.*

Even as I was learning about Reno's past, I was exploring the mining stories of Nevada, too. I read tales of the Comstock for an essay I never wrote, and I excavated the literature of Tonopah's boom and bust. The ladies of Tonopah turned out to be a fascinating collection of writers, women who either loved or loathed their days near the gold fields, and said so. Their stories, which I unearthed just as scholars were beginning to take pioneer women's writing seriously, became the foundation of a second chapter about Nevada literature. When I started reading novels about Las Vegas, however, I was disappointed. Too many pages of Mafia molls and mobster exposés. *My* Las Vegas sits in the midst of flaming red rock canyons, near a Valley of Fire, in the shadows of Mount Charleston and the Sheep Range and Wire Grass Springs. The popular vision

3

of Las Vegas took root somewhere else. No crap tables for me, I decided, after I compiled a titanic list of casino novels I would need to read. No book about Nevada, either. I completely abandoned my incipient project.

I never lost interest in isolated Nevada writers, however. Idah Meacham Strobridge, for example, was extolling the virtues of the Black Rock desert long before anyone thought it worthy of being set aside as a special wilderness area. She and her family home-steaded the property located where the Lassen-Applegate cutoff leaves the Humboldt River. She explored her surroundings as often as she could, even after tragedy took the lives of her sons and her husband during the 1889 flu epidemic. Like other women writers of the late-nineteenth- and early-twentieth-century West, she wrote about her surroundings to aid the family finances and to earn some extra cash. Strobridge pictures a desert free from the Conestoga horrors of the California Trail but not yet attractive to vacationing SUVers. While she herself loved the Black Rock, I'm not sure she would have been impressed by the recent psychedelic spectacles of the Burning Man.

Walter Van Tilburg Clark, perhaps Nevada's best-known novel-ist, found the region's desert and its creatures fascinating. His *City of Trembling Leaves* continues to be the most accurate and touching portrait of Reno's past. Among his short stories, I've always loved the tale of the hawk he calls "Hook." When *Studies in Short Fiction* asked its editorial board members to write special pieces for an an-niversary edition, I immediately thought of Clark's story, a proto-type of western American literature. As I consider Clark's accom-plishments, I also think of Robert Laxalt's. Although I wrote a review of his history, *Nevada,* before I knew Bob personally, and although I often read his manuscripts before they went to press, I never penned an essay about Robert Laxalt's fiction. Perhaps such a piece will highlight a second collection of essays from the purple sage?

Finally, among these meritorious Nevada writers, I come to Ed-ward Abbey. He wrote sparingly about the Silver State, from an outsider's point of view. But he did so with talent and insight and with an appreciation for our open spaces. While Washington, D.C., bureaucrats dreamed of an MX missile system, Edward Abbey vehemently objected. Those of us who savor eastern Nevada's bristlecone scenery ought to be grateful for his forthright honesty. Honesty, in fact, characterizes the words of all these Nevada writers of the purple sage. Yes, some writers *do* write about Nevada, and they do it very well.

CHAPTER ONE

Why Don't They Write About Nevada?

During the past century and a half, a distinctly American literary genre called "wilderness writing" has emerged. Henry David Thoreau introduced it; John Muir refined it; hundreds of followers now write variations on the theme. Such authors supposedly are addressing man's relationship to any environment largely un-touched by men, or at least that is the common perception. Of course anyone who knows Thoreau's work realizes that Walden Pond was only a couple of miles from Concord, and that Thoreau not only went to town regularly but spent much of his time in the company of other men. His most powerful prose, however, locates a narrator in the midst of an untracked, pristine landscape. Such is the pattern of Muir's work, too. His finest essays extol splendid isolation in the Sierra Nevada, but a quite different reality included the luring of hoards of tourists to Yosemite in order to preserve the valley.

So American nature writing, from its inception, has been charac-terized by paradox. One might even ask—since the mere presence of a narrator necessarily precludes the existence of true wilder-ness—whether the genre ever existed in the first place? This "falling tree in a silent forest" puzzle is not my real question, though. Rather, a more critical concern should focus on a different conundrum. Why, as wilderness writing has developed in the twentieth century, are so many authors writing about the same places? And, tangentially, why are they choosing locales that no longer resemble genuine wilderness? Do readers prefer only "wilderness" to which human beings can relate? Are contemporary nature writers actually as anthropocentric as those they would condemn?

Glen Canyon serves as a model. John Wesley Powell described it initially as a "curious ensemble of wonderful features—carved walls, royal arches, glens, alcove gulches, mounds, and monuments. From which of these features shall we select a name?" he asks himself. "We decide to call it Glen Canyon. Past these towering monuments, past these mounded billows of orange sandstone, past these oak-set glens, past these fern-decked alcoves, past these mural curves, we glide hour after hour, stopping now and then, as our attention is arrested by some new wonder."[1] Here is the first stage of wilderness writing—the Adamic naming of the place, the uniqueness of the perception, and the fresh language used to picture it. Once Powell framed this initial vision, no subsequent author can possibly have quite the same pristine opportunity to capture an untouched Glen Canyon in words.

Many will try, however. A variety of compelling paragraphs describing aspects of the canyon can be found in Eliot Porter's pictorial version, *The Place No One Knew,* where the photographer presents a visual montage accompanied by excerpts from appropriate wilderness writers. A typical voice is Charles Eggert's: "The face of the cliff was stained with long, black streamers from the water which cascaded over the rim in wet weather. It was an imposing sight, a gigantic backdrop—a motionless hanging tapestry."[2] Paging through similar passages reminds the reader that only a finite number of adjectives and nouns appropriately reveal the canyon's magnitude. "On one side above me the red and gold wall was streaked with organ pipes of black and rose and taupe, and on the other, a drift of fringed veil hung delicately purple across its topaz face."[3]

Even as fine a stylist as Edward Abbey, whose *Desert Solitaire* contains a chapter depicting his leisurely float through Glen Canyon's last days—"Down the river we drift in a kind of waking dream, gliding beneath the great curving cliffs with their tapestries of water stains, the golden alcoves, the hanging gardens, the seeps, the springs where no man will ever drink, the royal arches in high relief and the amphitheaters shaped like seashells"[4]—could not perceptibly improve upon Powell's "curve that is variegated by royal arches, mossy alcoves, deep, beautiful glens, and painted grottoes."[5] Arches, alcoves, glens and grottoes, walls and tapestries, curves and cliffs repeat themselves, repeat themselves, until the mid-1960s. Then, suddenly, Glen Canyon changed into a figment of the imagination.

"The place no one knew" became Lake Powell. In telling phrases, a Reno newspaper clipping[6] describes what happened—the dam that was completed in 1963, the subsequent 161,390 surface acres of water, the 1.1 million kilowatts of electricity shared by eight states, the 2,000-mile shoreline, the awesome power of a government that could transform the desert. "Thanks to that Congress, an area was born so different, so colorful, so surrounded by huge colorful monoliths, towering cliffs, spires and peaks that, to movie makers and others, it would take on the appearance of another planet." While most wilderness readers will be startled to learn of Congress's omnipotence, they should not be surprised to discover the prosaic kind of wilderness writing such a creation can engender. "Today, with its myriad colors, rugged rock formations and blue skies and colorful reflections, the crystal-clear lake and collection of canyons, buttes and mesas is a vacationer's Shangri-La, one of mother earth's most unusual spots." The lack of adjectival imagination found in this newspaper article is "colorfully" characteristic. Quoting from its single-sentence paragraphs plainly demonstrates what can happen when a so-called wilderness turns completely civilized. Even Gannett readers are attracted to the place.

On the other hand, not everyone succumbed to the newly wrought grandeur. Wallace Stegner, for example, boldly negates what has occurred. "In gaining the lovely and the usable," he explains, "we have given up the incomparable."[7] Twin essays, written seventeen years apart and later published side by side in Stegner's *The Sound of Mountain Water,* juxtapose the old Glen Canyon and the new Lake Powell. The first recounts a 1947 float trip past "the sheer cliffs of Navajo sandstone, stained in vertical stripes like a ro- man-striped ribbon and intricately cross-bedded and etched," past "the pockets and alcoves and glens and caves."[8] The second, "Glen Canyon Submersus," acknowledges that "Lake Powell is beautiful." But Stegner's twenty-year-old perception, while reporting that "enough of the canyon feeling is left so that traveling up-lake one watches with a sense of discovery as every bend rotates into view new colors, new forms, new vistas,"[9] poignantly concludes that "the pro- tection of cliffs, the secret places, cool water, arches and bridges and caves, and the sunken canyon stillness"[10] have been lost.

The language of this particular wilderness has not been lost, however, for even as canyon country authors were losing Glen Can- yon they were already branching into other hidden curves of water- stained red rock. Where John Wesley Powell and Everett Ruess once explored, Edward Abbey followed, trailed closely by Ann Zwinger, David Douglas, Rob Schultheis,[11] and countless others— so many others, in fact, that their terrain begins to look familiar and what once was wilderness has become commonplace. Using the imagery of their predecessors, they simply discover new arches, al- coves, glens and grottoes. One magnificent canyon may be gone but hundreds more remain, each waiting to be described by one intrepid explorer or another, each waiting to be pictured in the same words, more or less.

Perhaps the only wilderness left on the Utah/Arizona border is the wilderness of self. Anyone who has spent a waterless day under the hot sun may disagree, but from a literary point of view, at least, red rock wilderness is no longer a pathless way. In fact, its tracks are so well trodden that the only genuinely new terrain is some inexpli- cable spot where an inner landscape takes precedence over the outer. Ann Zwinger's solo hike down the Honaker Trail is typical. She begins by acknowledging her uneasiness, "a tinge of apprehension. I'm not quite sure what I expect, and now that my ride is long gone and it's too late and I'm committed, even why I wanted to do this. But here I am, quite alone, and I should start."[12] Her words could have been written by any one of two or three dozen recent Southwest narrators.

Gradually her discomfort eases, her pace slows, and the tone of her prose grows contemplative. Like many of her contemporaries, she ponders the meaning and context of her isolation. "This is what wilderness is to me," she decides, "being alone and knowing no one is within miles, and that although others may have passed here there is minimal, or no, trace of their passage."[13] Apparently she has forgotten what she wrote a few pages earlier, when she described walking past the large yellow letters and numbers left by a Shell Oil Company geological trip. She has not forgotten, however, the subconscious trappings of the civilized world. Again like so many other recent writers, Zwinger balances the wilderness and the city together, noting first "that the materialistic agenda of everyday life does not pertain here," and finally focusing on the self in relation to what she has left behind and what she has found. "Many of us need this wilderness as a place to listen to the quiet, to feel at home with ancient rhythms that are absent in city life, to know the pulse of a river, the riffle of the wind, the rataplan of rain on the slickrock."[14] Here, then, is the pulse behind so many portrayals of man in the wilderness—Thoreau's "We need the tonic of wildness,"[15] for example. The narrator, drawing sustenance from his or her experiences, communicates that physical and spiritual rejuvenation to the reader.

On the next page of her essay, though, Zwinger actually questions the genuineness of the twentieth-century wilderness experience. Does wilderness, in the true sense of the word, any longer exist? Or are the pressures of civilization encroaching irrevocably? Quoting an archaeologist, Dr. William Lipe, and referring specifically to Grand Gulch, she acknowledges that "we are moving into an era of managed remoteness, of planned romance."[16] She and Lipe refer to the physical overcrowding of the popular slickrock country, but she might well be talking about wilderness writing, too.

To call contemporary wilderness writing a genre of "planned romance," to consider its practitioners artists of "managed remoteness," levels a serious indictment against the very experience and the
attendant literature so many readers enjoy. Jokes—about whether
this genre exists or not—aside, a serious summary of its extant
qualities leads to some telling points. Thanks to the spectacular vistas of certain areas like the Sierra, slickrock country, or Cape Cod,
thanks to certain environmental confrontations, and thanks to the
potent pens of certain authors, many contemporary wilderness
writers retrace each others' steps. Glen Canyon, first described so
vividly by John Wesley Powell and later "rediscovered" by a host of
successors, is a model environment of a landscape literally over-
used. That it also has been the focus of man's unfortunate anthropocentrism, developing as it has into a metaphor for all the dam ills
in the West, only heightens the frequency of its invocations. If Glen
Canyon indicates a pattern prevalent in the twentieth century, then
no one really is writing wilderness essays about the wilderness at all.
Rather, contemporary authors are writing contemplative pieces
about "beautiful" places where the hand of man—at least the existence of men—has always been apparent. Or where, if the hand of
man is not obvious, the head of the narrator is.

The focus, no matter how splendid or how remote the terrain,
centers not on the landscape itself but on the man or woman who
visits there. As Everett Ruess's last letter reveals, "I have not tired of
the wilderness; rather *I* enjoy its beauty and the vagrant life *I* lead,
more keenly all the time. *I* prefer the saddle to the streetcar and star-
sprinkled sky to a roof, the obscure and difficult trail, leading into
the unknown, to any paved highway, and the deep peace of the
wild to the discontent bred by cities. Do you blame *me* then for
staying here, where *I* feel that *I* belong and am one with the world
around *me*?"[17] [emphasis added]. Everett Ruess, wanderer of slickrock country, disappeared near Escalante in November, 1934. Since
then, he has become a legend for those who would discard respon-
sibilities, journey alone into a wilderness, and write. His anthems
have taken on a kind of mythic quality, drawing others to the land-

scape he so admired. A source of inspiration, as much a metaphor as Glen Canyon, Ruess here epitomizes the ironic anthropocentricity of a man who most wanted to put away his man-centeredness. The final line of his well-known "Wilderness Song": "*I* shall sing *my* song above the shriek of desert winds."[18]

It appears that wilderness writers can be as egotistical as anyone else. Meanwhile, their essays repeatedly civilize the very landscape they mean to portray as untracked and unchanged by man. No matter what they write about or why they write, it is clear that the human response is key. And if a wilderness is aesthetically inhospitable to man, American nature writers lose interest. "Why don't they write about Nevada?" the title of this article asks facetiously. Some images and themes from essays about the Great Basin not only answer this question but point to some important conclusions about the choices wilderness writers seem to make.

Obviously they like Glen Canyon better. As one might surmise, not many Nevada essays exist.[19] Most of the early ones were written by soldiers, adventurers, and pioneers. Just as John Wesley Powell set a standard for the Colorado River country, so the explorer John Charles Frémont crisscrossed and then initially described the basins and ranges east of the Sierra mountains. Frémont's passages, however, are starkly impersonal. "I started out on the plain. As we advanced this was found destitute of any vegetation except sage bushes, and absolutely bare and smooth as if water had been standing upon it."[20] Even the discovery of a setting as spectacular as Pyramid Lake engendered only moderate effusiveness. "The shore was rocky—a handsome beach, which reminded us of the sea. On some large granite boulders that were scattered about the shore, I remarked a coating of a calcareous substance, in some places a few inches, and in others a foot in thickness."[21] Obviously Frémont lacked the poetic eye of a Powell—always the military man's prose is characterized by a matter-of-fact tone, with few adjectives, adverbs, or figures of speech—but he did respond to the country in a predictable way. When a landscape calls for grandiose terms, an author will find the appropriate words; when a scene is less majestic, lesser language will do.

Throughout the exploration years of the nineteenth century, Nevada scenery was pictured as anything but beautiful. "A terrific wind blew, threatening for hours to strangle us with thick clouds of sand," writes one of the few women to recount her wagon trip across the desert. "We had now nearly reached the head of Humboldt Lake, which, at this late period in the dry season, was utterly destitute of water, the river having sunk gradually in the sand, until, hereabout it entirely disappeared."[22] Terse, unemotional, relatively flat—Sarah Royce's diction is as unprovocative as Frémont's, and it typifies those pioneer accounts of the time. Arguably, pioneering was difficult work, and such men and women had little time or energy for the penning of graceful prose. On the other hand, John Wesley Powell must have had just as few leisurely hours and must have been just as scared. The red rock canyon country, far more than alkali flats and blackened sage, simply stirs the spirit more emotionally. Writers, male or female, want their wilderness to be beautiful and inspirational. That master of effusive prose, John Muir himself, proves the point.

Not many readers know John Muir's Nevada prose. Originally published in dated newspapers and magazines, collected only once in a hardcover edition long out of print (and not reprinted in the recent rush of Muiriana), the five Nevada essays show off few of Muir's pictorial skills. Even the titles—"Nevada Farms," "Nevada Forests," "Nevada's Timber Belt," "Glacial Phenomena in Nevada," and "Nevada's Dead Towns"—reveal the paucity of Muir's Nevada imagination. A comparison between some of these Great Basin descriptions and Muir's better-known portrayal of the Sierra Nevada demonstrates exactly how "this thirsty land," this "one vast desert, all sage and sand, hopelessly irredeemable now and forever,"[23] failed to inspire him.

Most aficionados of American nature writing are familiar with the more famous passages from *The Mountains of California*. A long one, found in "A Near View of the High Sierra," Muir draws from a palette and places in a frame: "one somber cluster of snow-laden peaks with gray pine-fringed granite bosses braided around its

base, the whole surging free into the sky from the head of a magnificent valley, whose lofty walls are beveled away on both sides so as to
embrace it all without admitting anything not strictly belonging to
it. The foreground was now aflame with autumn colors, brown and
purple and gold, ripe in the mellow sunshine; contrasting brightly
with the deep, cobalt blue of the sky, and the black and gray, and
pure, spiritual white of the rocks and glaciers." The paragraph concludes with the young Tuolumne River crossing the scene, "filling
the landscape with spiritual animation, and manifesting the grandeur of its sources in every movement and tone."[24]

Paragraphs about Nevada, on the other hand, rarely invoke the
metaphors of artistry and creation, rarely end on such a spiritual
note. "Viewed comprehensively, the entire state seems to be pretty
evenly divided into mountain-ranges covered with nut pines and
plains covered with sage," writes Muir, "now a swath of pines
stretching from north to south, now a swath of sage; the one black,
the other gray; one severely level, the other sweeping on compla-
cently over ridge and valley and lofty crowning dome."[25] Not a
single Silver State paragraph ends with an invocation, although one
does manage to suggest that a covering of snow can make spruce
boughs look like a painting. More of the passages, however, are
actually denigrating, as when the visitor from abundantly green
California "emerges into free sunshine and dead alkaline lake-levels
. . . a singularly barren aspect, appearing gray and forbidding and
shadeless, like heaps of ashes dumped from the blazing sky."[26]

Even worse are the ghost towns, scattered "throughout the
ranges of the Great Basin waste in the dry wilderness like the bones
of cattle that have died of thirst." Muir sees them as "monuments of
fraud and ignorance—sins against science"[27] with no redeeming
features. His interest in their decay, however, raises a telling point,
for he apparently cared more about Great Basin economics than
Nevada aesthetics. Four of his five Nevada pieces—the one about
glacial phenomena is the exception—concern themselves with the
profitability of the land. "Nevada Forests," for example, concen-
trates on the "nut pine," and judges that "the value of this species to

Nevada is not easily overestimated. It furnishes fuel, charcoal, and timber for the mines, and, together with the enduring juniper, so generally associated with it, supplies the ranches with abundance of firewood and rough fencing."[28] Subsequent paragraphs pursue first the white man's and then the Indians' use of the "crop."

When Ann Zwinger was thinking about the receding southwestern wilderness, she remarked, "I wonder if the increasing pressures of civilization, of economic exploration, will encroach until the only wilderness we have is that left by default, land that has no value to anyone for anything else for the moment."[29] Her comment, Muir's fascination with meager economic values, and the plethora of canyon essays compared to the paucity of Great Basin ones lead to several conclusions. First—and most obvious—genuine twentieth-century wilderness may indeed be only that landscape which appears to be unprofitable. Now that snowbirds and rafting yuppies have discovered the Southwest, now that the oil companies have found Alaska, spectacular untracked landscape is dwindling and only the economically and/or visually ordinary is left. Second, aesthetics may be a "cash crop," too. A doubter need only look to the national parks for confirmation. Third, if the scenery lacks both so-called conventional "beauty" and financial virtue, a desperate writer will probably home in on the economics. While it is difficult to aggrandize the former, it is quite possible to conjure up the latter. Certainly Muir managed to focus his Nevada essays that way. Fourth, if neither an aesthetic nor an economic option is available, few writers will concentrate on an area at all. That's why, alas, they don't write about Nevada.

Well, one cannot state absolutely that no one writes about Nevada. But the numbers of conventional nature or wilderness essayists who have either focused on or noticed the area in passing are few and far between. Even William Kittredge—whose *Owning It All* proposes to assess "that country of northern Nevada and southeastern Oregon [that] is like an ancient hidden kingdom,"[30] and purports to analyze why, when "we owned it all,"[31] the dreamland went wrong—cannot sustain his attention on the land. One chapter considers the landscape in depth, but the remainder contain few environmental descriptions and speak more of personalities than places. A critic must not put words into Kittredge's mouth, or condemn him for not writing a different book. The point, though, is that he chose to exclude visual landscape, to include disparate settings even when the drift of the book dictates a kind of unity of place, and not to pen a collection of nature essays. The environment dictated otherwise. He leans toward an economic bias, too, explaining how well-intentioned ranching practices unfortunately wrecked the land. And he especially considers how his stories, retold, affect himself.

If a native son so transparently designs his prose, guests presumably will do the same. The most famous recent literary visitor is John McPhee. His well-known book, *Basin and Range,* documents a recognizably inhospitable Nevada landscape. That he does so in slightly different terms indicates only his style, not his innovation. Since McPhee's narrative voice tries for objectivity, it does not seek self or spirituality in the wilderness. Therefore, his figures of speech are measured, his point of view more photographic than painterly. "This Nevada terrain is not corrugated . . . like a rippled potato chip," he reports. "This is not—in that compressive manner—a ridge-and-valley situation. Each range here is like a warship standing on its own, and the Great Basin is an ocean of loose sediment with these mountain ranges standing in it as if they were members of a fleet without precedent, assembled at Guam to assault Japan."[32]

Even when McPhee considers some abstract qualities of the Great Basin, he holds them at arm's length. "Supreme over all is silence," he philosophizes. Instead of exploring the implications of such a sweeping observation, however, he refers to physicist Freeman Dyson on the subject. Deffeyes, the narrator's companion, finds pleasant "the aromatic sage";[33] the reader never learns what attracts McPhee. Much of the chapter is designed through the use of a distinctive literary device that lends distance—catalogue rhetoric—lists of empty valleys, lists of remote mountain ranges, lists of resident animals and birds, incremental repetitions that themselves replicate the apparent monotony of the basin and range terrain. And how does the central Nevada chapter end? Predictably. "More miles, and there appears ahead of us something like a Christmas tree alone in the night. It is Winnemucca, there being no other possibility. Neon looks good in Nevada. The tawdriness is refined out of it in so much wide black space. We drive on and on toward the glow of color. It is still far away and it has not increased in size. We pass nothing."[34] Emptiness and economics, not aesthetics and autobiography, juxtapose.

"We pass nothing." Thus an important American author passes judgment on Nevada. Many readers, I believe, would concur with his assumption, just as most wilderness writers have already agreed tacitly by not turning their eyes toward the landscape of basin and range. Or, when they have deigned to describe the Silver State, they have done so in somewhat deprecating fashions—either by focusing on its minimal economic returns or by comparing it unfavorably with its neighbors. John Muir may have found "delightful surprises . . . in the byways and recesses of this sublime wilderness," but at least he knew the sublimity was "scant and rare as compared with the immeasurable exuberance of California."[35]

He would probably have found no reason to favor Nevada over Glen Canyon, either. In direct contrast to what he professed, Muir—and indeed, most Americans—actually prefers wilderness to which human beings can relate. Arches, alcoves, glens and grottoes,[36] granite domes, cañons, peaks and valleys[37] are simply more appealing than "a gorgeous, fresh, young, active fault scarp."[38] Conventional aesthetics prevail. Furthermore, the very emptiness that defines wilderness and attracts wilderness writers apparently is the single most unappealing characteristic of Nevada. The irony remains unseen by most essayists.

It would seem that American wilderness writing is following the pattern of our westward movement, civilizing whatever can be touched or tamed while disdaining or ignoring what cannot. Just as settlers made their homes in verdant California long before they filtered permanently into the Great Basin—even today California's population far outnumbers the combined total of its neighboring states to the east—and just as photogenic scenery has always taken precedence over barren wastes, so nature essayists flock to intellectually appreciable locales rather than inhospitable sites. At worst this phenomenon leads to encroachment—whether industrial, economic, excursionary, or literary. At best, it results in some kind of overcrowding and aesthetic destruction. In its own way, then, American wilderness writing is destroying the very places it loves. To repeat, the irony remains unseen.

Glen Canyon and its surroundings have been humanized in prose as surely as in fact. One hundred or one thousand nature essays on a single subject can be almost as stultifying as a concrete hydroelectric edifice; either results in a kind of burial. By comparison, very little humanizing has taken place in the Great Basin. Not many industrial forays have successfully invaded the high desert— although the government keeps trying—and not many authors have been attracted to its desolate power. Thus the area is as much a metaphor for what has not happened in the twentieth century as Glen Canyon is a symbol for what has occurred. Men and women don't write about places like Nevada because traditional modes of appreciation are inappropriate there. Meanwhile, they torment themselves while describing the so-called beauty spots of the West. An unsolvable paradox, perhaps, but one that all wilderness enthusiasts should try to understand.

NOTES

"Why Don't They Write About Nevada?" was originally read at the First North American Wilderness Conference, Weber State College, February 1989. Now, with its third reprinting, the essay sounds even less inclusive than before. Recent scholars have hotly debated the human construction of the term "wilderness"; new pages by Nevada writers have been proliferating. Like every other essay in *Reader of the Purple Sage,* it would be quite possible to bring this one "up to date" by including the critical conversations of the past decade and by adding the words of current authors. However, I choose to let all these essays stand as they first were printed because the original versions best capture the particular historic moments of publication.

1. John Wesley Powell, *The Exploration of the Colorado River and Its Canyons* [1874] (New York: Penguin Books, 1987), pp. 232–33.

2. Charles Eggert, in *The Place No One Knew* by Eliot Porter, edited by David Brower (San Francisco: Sierra Club Books, 1968), p. 70.

3. Cid Ricketts Sumner, in *The Place No One Knew*, p. 72.

4. Edward Abbey, *Desert Solitaire* (New York: Ballantine Books, 1968), p. 187.

5. Powell, *Exploration of the Colorado*, p. 230.

6. Gannett News Service, "Consider scenic Lake Powell if you're looking for a dream vacation," *Reno Gazette-Journal* (11 December 1988), 17C.

7. Wallace Stegner, *The Sound of Mountain Water* [1969] (Lincoln: University of Nebraska Press, 1985), p. 128.

8. Stegner, *Sound of Mountain Water*, p. 117.

9. Stegner, *Sound of Mountain Water*, p. 126.

10. Stegner, *Sound of Mountain Water*, p. 136.

11. See, for example, David Douglas, *Wilderness Sojourn: Notes in the Desert Silence* (San Francisco: Harper & Row, 1987) or Rob Schultheis, *The Hidden West: Journeys in the American Outback* (New York: Random House, 1982); even though *The Hidden West* contains essays about inaccessible and less-traveled parts of the West, its best writing occurs in the chapter where the author hikes an obscure, distant, "beautiful" Southwest canyon.

12. Ann Zwinger, *Wind in the Rock* [1978] (Tucson: University of Arizona Press, 1986), p. 197.

13. Zwinger, *Wind in the Rock*, p. 210.

14. Zwinger, *Wind in the Rock*, p. 210.

15. Henry David Thoreau, *Walden* [1854] (New York: W. W. Norton & Company, 1966), pp. 209–10.

16. William Lipe, quoted in Zwinger, *Wind in the Rock*, p. 211.

17. Everett Ruess, quoted in W. L. Rusho, *Everett Ruess: A Vagabond for Beauty* (Salt Lake City: Peregrine Smith Books, 1983), pp. 178–79.

18. Ruess, in *A Vagabond for Beauty*, p. 181.

19. Two new entries, unavailable before this essay must go to the type-

setter, will be published by the time "Why Don't They Write About Nevada?" is in print. Ann Zwinger's *The Mysterious Lands* (New York: E. P. Dutton, 1989) promises to be a welcome addition to the current, necessarily sparse, collection of samples. Stephen Trimble's *Sagebrush Ocean*, due in fall, 1989, from the University of Nevada Press, promises the same. (My own *Earthtones: A Nevada Album* [Reno: University of Nevada Press, 1995] lies in the future.)

20. John Charles Frémont, *Narratives of Exploration and Adventure,* edited by Allan Nevins (New York: Longmans, Green & Co., 1956), p. 447.

21. Frémont, *Narratives of Exploration,* p. 339.

22. Sarah Royce, *A Frontier Lady* (New Haven: Yale University Press, 1932), pp. 39–40.

23. John Muir, *Steep Trails* (Boston: Houghton Mifflin, 1918), p. 154.

24. John Muir, *The Mountains of California* [1894] (Berkeley: Ten Speed Press, 1977), pp. 49–50.

25. Muir, *Steep Trails,* p. 167.

26. Muir, *Steep Trails,* p. 164.

27. Muir, *Steep Trails,* p. 203.

28. Muir, *Steep Trails,* p. 169.

29. Zwinger, *Wind in the Rock,* pp. 210–11.

30. William Kittredge, *Owning It All* (Saint Paul: Graywolf Press, 1987), p. 20.

31. Kittredge, *Owning It All,* p. 60.

32. John McPhee, *Basin and Range* (New York: Farrar, Straus, Giroux, 1980), p. 45.

33. McPhee, *Basin and Range,* p. 46.

34. McPhee, *Basin and Range,* p. 54.

35. Muir, *Steep Trails,* pp. 164–65.

36. See Powell, *Exploration of the Colorado,* p. 230.

37. See Muir, *Mountains of California,* p. 17, for example.

38. McPhee, *Basin and Range,* p. 49.

CHAPTER TWO

The Tonopah Ladies

Eighty years ago northern Nevadans spoke of "going down into the desert," implying that the lower half of their state was some kind of infernal region. Insufferably hot in summer, freezing in winter, windswept and nearly unpopulated, the land attracted only those few prospectors who still dreamed of another Comstock. Then one man's dream came true. On May 19, 1900, Jim Butler stumbled across a bonanza, and by the next spring a major mining rush was on, with people flocking to what had been the middle of nowhere—the new boomtown of Tonopah—hoping to find their fortunes in silver and gold. Some succeeded and others failed, while Tonopah and its sister city of Goldfield had success and failure too, first undergoing rapid growth and then years of slow abandonment. In short, Nevada's twentieth-century mining story differs little from thousands of others throughout the West.

Most of what we know about such booms and busts has come from the voices and pens of men. We have all listened to old-boy tall tales, read some factual histories, devoured some thrillers, and perhaps plodded through too many dry mineral statistics. About Tonopah and Goldfield, though, we can find out some different things. From these two towns comes a surprising amount of writing by women—first-person nonfiction narratives by Mrs. Hugh

Brown, Mrs. Minnie Blair, and Anne Ellis; third-person nonfiction accounts by Zua Arthur, Helen Downer Croft, and Lorena Edwards Meadows; magazine articles by Clara Douglas; novels by Zola Ross and B. M. Bower; even children's stories by Aileen Cleveland Higgins.[1] These works, some written in the midst of the boom and others reconstructed lovingly after the fact, some telling of firsthand experience and others drawing imaginatively from library research, suggest some important notions about how women in general saw themselves and how they perceived the quality of their lives while the West was being won.

By 1900 mining was attracting professional men—engineers, assayers, attorneys, bankers, stockbrokers—men "whose grubstake was the college diploma" (Brown, 38). They came from San Francisco and Philadelphia, from Stanford and Yale, and they brought their wives, ladies who were equally well educated and well traveled. Obviously, less advantaged women lived in Tonopah and Goldfield also, but since they weren't prominent we hear little about them or from them. Probably they were too busy at the time, and then less inclined to share their experiences later. Anne Ellis's *The Life of an Ordinary Woman* is the exception, but her title indicates a point of view quite different from her contemporaries' for, on the whole, women who came to southern Nevada thought of themselves as ladies. The *Oxford English Dictionary* defines the late-nineteenth-century "lady" as "a woman whose manners, habits, and sentiments have the refinement characteristic of the higher ranks of society," and this is precisely what Tonopah and Goldfield ladies had in mind. In fact, two of their book titles—*Lady in Boomtown* and *Tonopah Lady*—predicate that overriding concern. Being a lady was of the utmost importance.

Many amenities unheard of in the previous century encouraged such a posture. Tonopah, for example, had, in its first year, a weekly newspaper, a school, and church services; by 1902 (its second year), it had a piped water supply and electricity; by 1903, automobiles; by 1904, a railroad; and by 1907 some of the fanciest homes in the state stood where, only a decade earlier, had been nothing but sagebrush and sand. *Lady in Boomtown* highlights Mrs. Hugh Brown's life from early 1904 when she went to Tonopah as a young bride until twenty years later when she and her husband returned to California. Their first home was only a three-room cottage, but "thank goodness," she writes, it "had electric light and a telephone" (Brown, 17); that is, it was a place where she could be a lady. She reports that her mother had "insisted that no lady should ever be seen doing menial labor" (Brown, 56), but within a few days Mrs. Brown—as she always refers to herself—knows this is ludicrous in a three-room cottage in Nevada. Still, she confesses, she sent all her laundry to be done in Reno, a three-week round-trip. Furthermore, despite the inappropriateness of her trousseau, of her wedding presents, and of her furnishings, she emphasizes that she would never have traded her treasures for more practical things. "Tonopah was a community of city people," she explains, "who lived in roughboard houses and walked unpaved streets, but who dressed and acted as they would in San Francisco or New York" (Brown, 37); the lady from boomtown wanted it no other way.

Her fellow Nevadans, men as well as women, concurred. The weekly newspaper, for example, heralded Mrs. Brown as a "distinct acquisition to the social circle of Tonopah, being a lady of many accomplishments." And even more proprietary is the husband's point of view narrated by Minnie Blair, who joined the desert society after her 1909 marriage to a Goldfield banker. When she wanted to watch the formal shutdown of gambling in October, 1910, "Mr. Blair was quite shocked." He went downtown alone, but found that "just about all of [her] lady friends were there." The next day, when her devout Methodist neighbor remarked on her absence, Mrs. Blair, "with great humility," had to admit that she hadn't been allowed to go "because [her] husband said it wouldn't be any place for a lady" (Blair, 30). Half a century later, though, she still could quote his comment with pride.

The significance of being a lady in Tonopah occurred to another researcher too, Zola Ross, who fictionalized early-twentieth-century Nevada life in a novel she called *Tonopah Lady*. The heroine, a former vaudevillian seeking social status, marries and settles in Tonopah only to learn that her husband is both a bigamist and a fraud. "I'm going back to show business," she announces emphatically, "I'm all through pretending to be a lady" (Ross, 252). Ironically, neither a husband nor social position necessarily would have made Judith a lady; despite her theatrical career and her peculiarly unmarried state, she had always been one, as the denouement of the novel proves.

Not needing to overcome the stigmas of false marriages, or illegitimate children, but wanting to assure their reputations, the real-life Tonopah women found other ways to make themselves known as ladies. Their activities, quite different from those that occupied the men, were central to their writing. They formed sewing circles and women's clubs and built and decorated lavish homes, but they worked hardest to bring culture to their communities and to advance worthwhile causes. Mrs. Brown proudly tells of helping to establish the Tonopah public library, and later details her Red Cross achievements during World War I. Mrs. Blair mentions her war efforts too, while further indicating an interest in women's suffrage. Sometimes the ladies gather for strictly cultural reasons—to read Shakespeare aloud, to play the piano, to sing—but more often they filled the evenings with parties. In particular, they meshed their social life with the desert environment. For example, Mrs. Brown fondly describes a dance held three hundred feet down in a mine shaft, while Mrs. Blair rather impishly recalls decorating her home to resemble a casino when hosting a party with a gambling motif. The ladies also recount their travels; Death Valley seems to have been the favorite nearby vacation spot, while San Francisco beckoned to them from afar.

One description of a visit to that city, however, unwittingly exposes a limitation of retrospective writing: it is all too easy to remember the good and repress the bad. Mr. and Mrs. Brown were asleep in San Francisco's Palace Hotel when suddenly they were "awakened by a strange rumbling that grew louder and angrier" (Brown, 119). Glass shattered while "plaster and soot showered down," and the great 1906 earthquake had struck the city. Although Mrs. Brown narrates what happened next, she seems more concerned with saving her sewing machine and more upset by losing her layette than by witnessing the destruction of a city. Clearly, time had alleviated her horror. By comparison, she appears disproportionately unnerved by the Tonopah bank failure of 1907 when the Browns did lose a million dollars, but all on paper. Her lady friends laughed it off, her husband showed no regrets, and even she knew "the gambler's code is not to squeal when he loses" (Brown, 132). Still, she fell into a period of severe depression eased only by a rest cure at a distant ranch. So not only does the lady have a selective memory, but she indicates a remarkable ordering of her emotional priorities.

This is not the case, of course, with all pioneer women, as *The Life of an Ordinary Woman* so starkly reveals. Written, too, about twentieth-century mining camps, it describes what life was like on the other side of the tracks. Unlike Mrs. Brown, Mrs. Anne Ellis didn't marry the man of her dreams; instead, she married men who were available. When her first husband died in a mining accident, she regretted his death chiefly because she had learned "to manage him." After a second marriage she moved to Goldfield where, in quick succession, her husband lost his job, she had a miscarriage, and her daughter died from diphtheria. Her comment about the tragic series of events is both terse and stoic: "Fate was slapping me hard, trying to knock some sort of woman into shape" (Ellis, 268). A "woman" as defined by Mrs. Ellis and a "lady" as we have defined her, although of similar pioneer stock, are not synonymous. She demonstrates the real difference between the two after her husband left her in Nevada with sick, hungry, cold children while he looked for work elsewhere. She then explains how and why she stole, not firewood and not food, but a white stone step from the local school to make a tombstone for her daughter Joy's grave. No single episode so clearly marks the gap between what an ordinary woman might do and what would never occur to a lady to do. The ordinary woman gives a different emphasis to her writing, also. Neither Mrs. Brown nor Mrs. Blair share much about their children, while by contrast the reader knows Mrs. Ellis's son and daughter intimately. Children seemed the ordinary woman's unconscious means of dealing with her own mortality. The blows dealt by life could best be eased by dreaming for the future, for one's children, rather than by struggling against the present. This accounts for the importance placed upon the memorial to mark a child's grave, since only in that way could Mrs. Ellis be certain of achieving any kind of immortality, either for herself or for her family. By contrast, the ladies had many ways of making their marks—through their husband's careers, their own charitable works, their social successes—so they had no need to display their feelings or children to their readers.

The Brown, Blair, and Ellis accounts have more in common with each other, however, than they do with the Arthur, Croft, and Meadows books. The latter three were written by women who themselves experienced none of the events they narrate, but who wished to create memorials to certain men. Mrs. Lorena Meadows reconstructed her father's role as a Tonopah merchandiser in its pre-railroad days; Mrs. Zua Arthur wrote of her husband's adventures as a prospector, and Mrs. Helen Croft told of her husband's career as the chief assayer in Goldfield. Although these three books have women authors, they view southern Nevada through masculine eyes, and they analyze far different subjects than did the Tonopah ladies. From the men's pages the reader learns how to prospect, how to assay, how to run a business. Factual details of Nevada history are given, labor disputes are examined, the Gans-Nelson fight is described, and tall tales are narrated. With such different contents one would hardly know that these three books were written about the same boomtowns as the previous three under discussion; obviously, pioneer men and women thought about different things. It is not superfluous, however, to note that a woman's book displays a masculine aura when a man is the inspiration but retains a distinctly female air when the source is the woman herself. In other words, the male interests displace the female. As a corollary, there are few western accounts written by men in which the female interests displace the male.

Like most of the women's nonfiction, the Tonopah fiction is distinctly feminine in flavor. What makes it different is the manner in which the novelists blend imagined scenes and people with the real. Aileen Higgins, after seeing Tonopah firsthand on a 1906 visit, returned home to convert that reality into a fairy-tale milieu. In contrast, Zola Ross reconstructed the town from library research alone, and yet her account is far more realistic than Higgins's. Carl Glasscock's 1932 publication, *Gold in Them Hills,* apparently was Ross's primary source for *Tonopah Lady.* His record of the southern Nevada boom—like the Arthur, Croft, and Meadows books—reports only details attractive to male readers. Ross takes his information and then reworks it for a female audience, often with advantageous dramatic results. For example, in January, 1902, an epidemic hit the men of Tonopah. Glasscock cites a number of facts about the siege—the unseasonable heat, the black and spotted corpses, the need for more white shirts in which to clothe the dead, the end of the plague when fresh snow finally falls—and Ross repeats the identical grouping. However, she uses those facts, not solely for historicity, but also to further the characterization of the heroine. She establishes Judith's reputation by showing her nursing some men back to health, burying others, and inspiring still more when she shaves the corpses. Thus she shows how a character behaves when historical circumstances force her to adapt, while simultaneously revealing how a lady appears to the men around her.

A less successful borrowing from Glasscock occurs during and just after one of the novel's climactic scenes. First Ross adroitly mixes setting and plot so that, in the midst of a fierce electrical storm, Judith learns her husband is a bigamist. Then, in the scene's aftermath and for a transition on the next page, Ross tells how "the Key Pittmans had cashed in on their amateur photography" that night by taking "a picture of Mount Brougher and the worst lightning flash," and she further describes how "the Reynolds home had been struck . . . A bolt had melted the stove, burned a hole in the floor and blasted a hole in the earth" (Ross, 248). Glasscock had devoted three pages to the August 10, 1904, storm, to the photograph taken by the Pittmans, and to the bolt which had struck the Reynolds home and "passed into the kitchen where it melted part of an iron stove, burned a ragged hole in the floor and blasted a hole a foot deep in the earth below" (Glasscock, 131). Several sources—an oral history by Harry Atkinson in the UNR Library, for example—confirm both the storm and the Pittman photograph, but obviously Ross took her information from Glasscock, since her paragraph borders on plagiarism.

Such an offense, unfortunately only one of several, detracts from Ross's professionalism. On the positive side, she blends fact and fiction with little distortion or pedantry; but on the negative, she leans too heavily on a single source and then polishes off her story with a simplistic ending. The latter problem is characteristic of all three pieces of Tonopah fiction: since each was written primarily as an escape vehicle, each solves its dilemmas too glibly to be taken seriously. Furthermore, each moralizes so egregiously that any historical value is overshadowed. *The Parowan Bonanza,* written by B. M. Bower (the pen name of Mrs. Bertha "Muzzy" Sinclair) is the worst offender. It moves from a real landscape (Goldfield) to an imaginary one (somewhere near Death Valley), leads its protagonist through a series of misfortunes that appear and disappear miraculously, and then preaches that all woes will some day vanish (if one has faith). Any factual information about prospecting for gold or about developing a mining claim gets lost in its absurdly make-believe world.

Aileen Higgins's book is as one-dimensional as Bower's, but at least she designed it for children. For our purposes, The Rainbow Lady, an imaginative re-creation of Mrs. Hugh Brown, is *A Little Princess of Tonopah*'s most intriguing feature. The Rainbow Lady reminds the little princess "of ring-doves, and dew and a pink rosebud in the morning, and fringes of starlight on the water, and peacock feathers and soap bubbles in the sun—and the inside of seashells—and all those things" (Higgins, 82). Seen through rose-colored glasses, here is the same lady who refused to wash windows in front of the neighbors and who sent all her laundry to Reno. Mrs. Brown's own comment about the book reveals that she understood what her friend had done: "of course," she wrote, "Miss Higgins romanticized everything" (Brown, 92). What Mrs. Brown did not understand was that she had done exactly the same thing. In fact, the Tonopah fiction sounds no less flowery than Clara E. Douglas's *Sunset* magazine articles, Minnie Blair's recollection, or even Anne Ellis's reminiscences. On every dusty street corner and behind every clump of sage, these ladies found romance. Tonopah sits wedged between treeless, barren mountains. Yet Mrs. Brown remembers "the fascination of the pastel landscape," where "under the desert moonlight the hills looked as if they had been cut out of cardboard" (Brown, 19). This is no less idealistic than "the white stretches of incrusted alkali" that the little princess imagined "looked like silver shallows of water in ripple" (Higgins, 43). And not only did the ladies idealize, but they fantasized. Higgins, for example, extends sea imagery to the desert in her descriptions, while Brown stresses subtle and subdued tones. It is as if they were subconsciously depending upon inappropriate details to fill voids—that is, they were metaphorically bringing water to the desert.

Actually, the Tonopah ladies did that consistently. They romanticized their existence to make life seem not only tolerable but enjoyable. Mrs. Brown remarks, "you could almost tell by looking at the brides whether they would be able to stick it out"; those who did, "were successors to that wonderful race of pioneer women who have been scattered over the West since the Western trek began" (Brown, 51–52). Since the Tonopah ladies comprised the socially elite, we cannot quite call them typical; but we can view their writing as exemplary. They reveal exactly those abilities and concerns that all women must have had as they helped civilize the West. They transcended the mundane because they valued what they were doing, and they survived because they kept their dreams. Their most significant contribution was an ability to see beauty that others ignored while bringing culture to a society that had none. Indeed, this is the contribution made by most pioneer women. Read in this sense, not just the Tonopah ladies, but all women's writing from the westward movement opens a new dimension of the pioneer experience.

NOTES

1. To make life simpler for the reader, I include here a slightly annotated, complete bibliography of the Tonopah Ladies' writing. To make life simpler still, there will be no further footnotes; all citations are included in the text.

I. NONFICTION
   A. Firsthand experience, recounted in retrospect.
      Blair, Minnie P. "Days Remembered of Folsom and Placerville, California; Banking and Farming in Goldfield, Tonopah, and Fallon, Nevada." UNR Oral History Project, 1968.
      Brown, Mrs. Hugh. *Lady in Boomtown*. New York: Ballantine Books, 1968.
      Ellis, Anne. *The Life of an Ordinary Woman*. Boston: Houghton Mifflin, 1929.
   B. Firsthand experience, magazine articles.
      Douglas, Clara E. "What Tonopah's Gold has Wrought," *Sunset* 16 (February 1906), 350–54.
      Douglas, Clara E. "Those Nevada Bonanzas," *Sunset* 17 (September 1906), 262–65.
      Douglas, Clara E. "The Father of Tonopah," *Sunset* 27 (August 1911), 165–67.
   C. Heard from husband.
      Arthur, Zua. *Broken Hills* [The Story of Joe Arthur, Cowpuncher and Prospector, Who Struck It Rich in Nevada]. New York: Vantage Press, 1958.
      Croft, Helen Downer. *The Downs, The Rockies—and Desert Gold*. Caldwell, Idaho: Caxton, 1961.
   D. Heard from father.
      Meadows, Lorena Edwards. *A Sagebrush Heritage* [The Story of

Ben Edwards and his Family]. San Jose, Calif.: Harlan-Young Press, 1973.

E. Heard from women who lived in Tonopah or Goldfield during the boom.

Mitchell, Sharon. "A Pioneer Nevada Woman." Unpub. ms. Nevada Historical Society, n.d. [a number of these unpublished accounts are available; apparently classes have done interview projects and then deposited their findings in the historical society's archives].

II. FICTION

A. Children's story, based on author's visit to Tonopah.

Higgins, Aileen Cleveland. *A Little Princess of Tonopah.* Philadelphia: The Penn Publishing Co., 1909.

B. Novels for adults, based on author's research.

Bower, B. M. *The Parowan Bonanza.* Boston: Little, Brown, & Co., 1923.

Ross, Zola. *Tonopah Lady.* New York: Bobbs-Merrill, 1950.

CHAPTER THREE

Reno
Myth, Mystique, or Madness?

Walter Van Tilburg Clark, Nevada's best-known novelist, opens his *City of Trembling Leaves* with an evocation of the Reno he loved, the small but special Nevada community of the 1920s. First he describes it by orchestrating a symphony of its trees—"an air of antique melancholy," then "a brightening sound" of new growth, "the marching files of poplars," and finally "the twinkling aspen with their whispering and rushing leaves." He continues with a characterization of the city's sentinel mountains—Rose, "the white, exalted patron angel," and Peavine, "the great, humped child of the desert." For Clark, the essential Reno blends inseparably with its natural surroundings; what he calls the "moribund Reno," the treeless Reno, doesn't count. He dismisses the region behind the arch—"The Biggest Little City In The World"—as "the ersatz jungle, where the human animals, uneasy in the light, dart from cave to cave under steel and neon branches, where the voice of the croupier halloos in the secret glades, and high and far, like light among the top leaves, gleam the names of lawyers and hairdressers on upstairs windows."[1] His characters live and love in the other Reno, "the city of trembling leaves." Yet for most readers of fiction and for many non-Nevadans, Clark's Reno is the one that doesn't exist. Instead, it is "the biggest little city in the world" that is real,

33

the one that counts. Why? Because rumor, myth, and the power of the press have combined to create a sense of place unique in this country. For reasons simple and complex, writers have sold the public a Reno that, while it may dismay Renoites like Clark, fascinates most twentieth-century Americans.

A surprising amount of fiction—and I use that word in both a conventional and an ironic sense—has been written about "the biggest little city." Most of it was published in the days of Reno's fame as a haven for divorcées; little of it emphasizes gambling.[2] All the fiction apparently depicts individual authors' notions of the "real" Reno, notions as diverse as the books themselves. Certain common strains, however, do recur. Stock characters appear and reappear, as do stock situations and actions. A similarity in tone exists; even individual phrases and figures of speech are repeated. Some changes of scene can be found—Virginia City, Tahoe, Pyramid Lake, for example—but the stories always return to the banks of the Truckee River. Because downtown Reno most interests both authors and readers, we inevitably find the focus of the action there. The reasons for Reno's attraction are various, but I suggest they stem from people's ambivalent feelings about divorce. Certainly individual attitudes toward Reno's best-known business, and most of the novels themselves, tend to conclude in a wash of ambiguities. Yet I find it possible to make sense out of the apparent contradictory attitudes and interpretations. To understand the paradox that is Reno, we need initially to look at ways the city has been characterized, next at unwritten truths underlying its descriptions, and finally at discrepancies between the two. Only then will we be able to explain the magnetism of "the biggest little city in the world."

Since similar elements found in the fiction keynote the city's portrayal, we should examine these commonalities first. So repetitive are they, that nine times out of ten the main character is the same—a potential divorcée who has come to Reno to complete her residency requirement. She generally arrives by train and is taken to the Riverside Hotel. There she will remain, permanently (that is, for approximately six weeks) or she will relocate to a guest ranch or

boardinghouse. She never lives alone, because the author must create interaction between the heroine, other would-be divorcées, and
various local citizens. Occasionally the protagonist is a man, sometimes a Renoite, but most often the central figure is a young, attractive, introspective, misunderstood, Eastern woman who has come
west to end her marriage.

Her first few days in Reno are lonely. Initially she meets only
women—dowdy, middle-aged matrons whose husbands have
"sent them packing"; suave, sophisticated socialites trailed by un-
ending strings of gigolos; brokenhearted, often suicidal house-
wives from American suburbia. Few Nevada women cross her
path—only an occasional rancher's wife or housekeeper. However,
she gradually is allowed, then encouraged, to meet Nevada men.
Some are poor specimens—party-boys, gamblers, seducers. Others
include fatherly and understanding attorneys. But at least one man
per novel is handsome and competent, an outdoorsman with obvious duties to perform. He shows off the Nevada scenery, teaches
"the Western way of life," educates the heroine in an appreciation of
"true love." Sometimes an author allows an Easterner to fulfill this
function, but more often the privilege goes to a Nevada native.

Not only the characters but also the activities are repeated from
book to book. For example, we find a requisite number of auto
trips to mountains, lakes, and desert; we are taken on at least one
horseback ride and are offered at least one sunrise or sunset. We
usually are titillated, too, by the intimation of one afternoon of sex
in the great outdoors. Even more suggestive are the indoor and
evening pastimes. An almost unbelievable amount of liquor is con-
sumed, partying frequently lasts until dawn, and roadhouses are the
loci for much activity. What I characterize as "flapperish" behavior
continues for decades beyond the conventional 1920s boundaries.
The decadence of such action is emphasized by its juxtaposition
against desert scenery, clean mountain air, and pure outdoor life. A
majority of the protagonists, although first seduced by so-called
"Eastern" mores, eventually learn "Western" ways—clean out their
lungs, as it were—and then are allowed to live happily ever after.

"Happily ever after," however, may be achieved in a variety of ways—the heroine may be reunited with her husband, marry another divorcé, wed a cowboy, or simply arrive at some kind of self-realized maturity. No matter which course the action takes, the reader feels satisfied that the character's future success is assured.

In many ways this over-used plot recapitulates thousands of works written in America between the two world wars. For example, Zane Grey made a fortune from just such a formula of adversity and despair crowned with success and daydreams that come true. Grey's novels and others under consideration here, all published in the East, were directed towards Eastern readers who, presumably, read them for vicarious pleasure and not for veracity. Furthermore, many Reno novels were written by individuals like Cornelius Vanderbilt, Jr. who had come west for divorces of their own. Such writers, we must suppose, were inspired by a need for personal catharsis that inherently led to idealistic story lines. Some writers insisted that they portrayed reality, but most assuredly only Walter Clark among Nevada novelists remained uncaptivated by Virginia Street, the Riverside, the clubs and the divorce colony—in short, by the sensational side of Reno. One cannot fault these other writers, however, since for the most part their experiences isolated them from "the city of trembling leaves."

Their exaggerated perceptions of Reno are hardly surprising since even the local advertisements encouraged puffery. My favorite is a 1932 Chamber of Commerce brochure touting Reno as "A Land of Charm." The pamphleteer brags that

> the City—every foot of the way—looks the part! Finely paved streets and sidewalks, imposing business structures; most modern stores; substantial and attractive and, in many instances, imposing residences; a state university, comparing favorably with any like institution of its kind in the United States; a public school system that can probably be rated second to none, for its size, in the land; and progressive city, county, and state governments thoroughly appreciative of the value of leading the

way with public improvements. Epitomized, that is the story of the city!

The brochure then describes surrounding scenic wonders and convenient modes of transportation. Finally, just after "excellent hotels, with accommodations to meet every taste," are praised, the writer asserts that "Nevada has done much for the race, and her work has just begun."[3] So although divorce, per se, is not mentioned, the not-so-subtle attempt to justify its value indicates the intent of an apparently massive advertising campaign. *Reno, Land of Charm* is only one of the many pamphlets published in reply to a flood of inquiries from the East.

Much less restrained were the privately printed responses:

Reno . . . where the East and West meet, and greet, and kiss, and make up! Reno!—the ever boiling, seething, melting pot of grim Reality and alluring Illusion; where the multitude of Mistake Makers stage the mammoth battle of the world—The Battle of Human Hearts; where some win and some lose in their innermost struggle to become victors of the greatest asset to man—PEACE OF MIND![4]

And sometimes promoters even overrode the bounds of good taste.

Reno is situated on an island in the Sea of Matrimony. It is parted in the middle by the Truckee River, which flows from the Reef of Many Causes to the Harbor of Renewed Hope and More Trouble. The tide comes in regularly by the Southern Pacific and the untied depart the same way.[5]

I quote all these ostensibly nonfictional pieces because they demonstrate the kind of "truths" that people heard about Reno. In fact, from its earliest days Reno invited a reputation for fast living and greedy indifference. "There is no such thing as rest in Reno. People rush in Reno. The tavern keepers are bent on business, provide no rest and Reno cares nothing," wrote one journalist in 1868. "Busy

Reno . . . is bent on making her pile with what speed she can command."[6] As Reno moved into the twentieth century, her fame grew as a haven for loose morals, and a mecca for divorcées. Increasingly, writers chose to capitalize on this side of the biggest little city. For example, one lurid exposé, published in *Real Detective* and entitled "The City that Sex Built," opens with a step-by-step description of a girl disrobing in a downtown crib, then slickly continues with a discussion of divorce and current lax laws. The author concludes, "Reno's motto is: 'You can't do anything wrong—we'll legalize it!'"[7] Another magazine devotes itself solely to *The Reno Divorce Racket,* while contrasting "our mad race for sex freedom and return to paganism" with the "stabilizing force of a great church."[8] Yet the bulk of this 1931 issue is pure sensationalism, filled with pictures of celebrities in Reno and captioned with detailed explanations of divorce procedures. In short, it is a "how-to-do-it" handbook designed to attract, rather than repel, readers. One more journalist summarizes the prevailing tone of the sensationalists: "Curious little Reno! So pretty, so uneventful, so isolated—so very 'small town'—yet so manifestly linked to a brilliant and lawless past; bearing for all eyes in the broad light of day the light flotsam of divorcees, the heavy jetsam of shifty, broken men."[9]

These comments also suggest the general tenor of a small group of somewhat "sick" novels that stress the "flotsam and jetsam" of humanity, emphasizing morbid relationships with gruesome details. Of these, Latifa Johnson's *Sheila Goes to Reno* is perhaps the best known.[10] *Sheila's* plot is characteristic—she marries, has an abortion and thus alienates her husband, heads to Reno for a divorce, next marries a Nevada rancher, steps out on him, returns to New York, sleeps around, and finally loses her mind. The grotesque melodrama is a parody of any reasonable plot, but the physical setting is skillfully drawn. An undiscriminating reader, I suspect, might misinterpret Johnson's effort and believe such actions possible or even probable in the Western locale, although actually the story is too absurd to happen anywhere.

Reno's seamy reputation has attracted another kind of novelist, too, the detective story writer.[11] Several murder mysteries are set along the banks of the Truckee River. While some are better written than others, all feature divorcées, racketeering, and booze. Even the famous Charlie Chan comes to Tahoe and Reno, while the infamous Matt Helm also appears to aid his ex-wife, break up a drug ring, and kill a number of traitorous enemies in various unsightly ways.

No one who knows Reno could mistake the portrayals in these books for reality. Less clear cut, however, are the interpretations found in better writing, even though some readers were appalled by fictional descriptions of "their" city. Two authors in particular infuriated the natives. Cornelius Vanderbilt, Jr.'s *Reno,* published in 1929, sparked a heated protest from both the local Chamber of Commerce and the Reno 20-30 Club. The Chamber fired off a telegram to the author: "The exaggerated picture that you have drawn . . . could only have been seen, with all its uncleanliness, through glasses that were colored elsewhere or with eyes unfitted to the better things of life. . . . We must express our contempt for this departure in the realm of fiction."[12] The 20-30 Club echoed the Chamber's outrage: "His portrayal of the citizenry of the community is a contemptible lie . . . We believe the filthy situations pictured in Vanderbilt's book could be written by no one except one whose mind is filled with such degrading thoughts. Through his book defaming the name of this city Vanderbilt has shown Reno as a city of depravity, when as a matter of fact this is not true." Finally, the Club insinuated they would like to run him out of town because "his presence in our community is distasteful."[13]

Ironically, Vanderbilt's *Reno* seems mild compared to some of the lurid journalism available. Certainly the novel contains a fair amount of drinking, partying, and "flapperish" activities, but this outlay of decadence is carefully contrasted with the pure mountain air and vivid desert colors. Indeed, his characters are among those who "clean out their lungs" and adopt Western ways. Furthermore, in the midst of his book Vanderbilt heartily endorses the locale:

Reno isn't any worse than any other city. All the outside world sees is the sensational side of Reno, the mad antics of a small group of its divorce colony. It doesn't realize that what it sees is but a coarse, unnatural growth. The real city—the good, energetic, constructive city—lies beneath it, paying about as much attention to it as a cow does to a fly on her back. There's a world of honest goodness and beauty in that little city, and it's easy to see, if you're looking for the cleaner side of life.[14]

Apparently local businessmen lacked appreciation for his enthusiasm.

Two years later John Hamlin, author of *Whirlpool of Reno,* also came in for severe criticism. Less enamored of Nevada natives than Vanderbilt, Hamlin turned on them in an open letter to the editor of the University of Nevada *Sagebrush.* "Reno warrant[s] every line of notoriety circulated about it," he wrote. "This town is reaping precisely what it is sowing, and has no grounds to howl because others turn back upon it the fruits of its own planting." Hamlin argued that

> when your governor and your mayor broadcast invitations to the world to come to Nevada and Reno where there are so few laws to be broken, when the newspapers are filled with glaring headlines and feature stories about the gambling dives, the deluxe roadhouses, the weekly washday when the decrees are ground out by the scores, why shouldn't the world be curious to read about the "Biggest Little City in the World"?[15]

And so he "accepted the invitation and wrote *Whirlpool of Reno,*" a novel which anticipates the point of view stated in his letter. Its heroine, in particular, speaks for its author when she shouts at her aunt, a longtime Reno resident:

> "Listen, Aunt! If you and your pious friends are so terribly shocked by these loose divorcees, why blame us? You've made it perfectly legal for us to come here, haven't you? You shortened the time from six months to three, and not satisfied with

the results, you even cut that period in half as an added lure to unhappily married folk. And how about your wide open gambling, your glamorous roadhouses, swagger apartments and shops—the stand your mayor takes—broadcasting an invitation to the World and his wife to come to Reno where there are few laws to break! Your respectable voters and lawmakers are the ones to be condemned, not the divorce colony. You offer us every inducement to come here, then damn us because we do. Go after us hand over fist for all the money you can squeeze from us, then set up a howl of indignation because Reno is known far and wide for its divorce colony, its blatantly licensed gambling, and nothing else."[16]

John Hamlin knew that by expressing such sentiments he would be touching raw nerves of respectable Renoites, but he couldn't resist voicing his analysis of the ambiguous stance taken by the local citizenry.

Perhaps Hamlin intended to stir controversy, but Vanderbilt insisted he didn't mean to alienate his Reno readers. Vanderbilt dedicated his book to the Westerners he had met and appreciated. From the Sagebrush Ranch he penned the words that appear on his title page:

To my friends in Reno, who keep the hearthfires of gentleness, peace and beauty burning in the midst of the ugly wreckage that surrounds them; who take into their hearts and homes those world-weary pilgrims who are both heart-sick and homeless; to them—who have taught me to love the real Reno—I dedicate this, my first novel.[17]

Vanderbilt erred, I think, in trying to render verbatim the city around him, in attempting to copy exactly what he saw and in insisting that it was the truth. Those novelists who instead used Reno more creatively—as a jumping-off point, an inspiration, a metaphor or symbol for something they needed to say—more successfully and more meaningfully depicted "the biggest little city in the world," and, by the way, caused much less controversy. Jill Stern, author of *Not In Our Stars,* realized that Reno should be treated as more than just another Western community when she wrote, "Reno isn't a place [at all], it isn't real, it's just a symbol to America and the rest of the world, a symbol."[18] Instead, she defines Reno as "a state of mind, a general state of the collective American mind."[19]

I quite agree with Stern, but I further suggest that Reno represents a complicated web of contemporary concerns, some great and some small but all indicative of what troubles twentieth-century Americans. Dorothy Carman, writing in the 1930s, jumbles her metaphors while managing to convey the multiplicity of meanings carried by the city behind the arch. First she establishes its universality, generalizing that every family has somebody in Reno and affirming that "it's a cross section of our country."[20] Then Carman downgrades the seamier side of life in Reno, calling the city "a prostitute" while suggesting it is "losing its old identity but . . . making money."[21] Finally Carman reverses her point of view to one of optimistic idealism, comparing Reno to Oz, "set apart from the world,"[22] a land of enchantment where one takes "a vacation from life."[23] Assuming that Reno is indeed a universal symbol, and further, that its symbolism includes contradictory interpretations of the lax divorce and gaming laws, then Carman's other two observations generate some new perspectives. Divorce can be good or bad, gambling lucky or unlucky; Reno can symbolize either or both sides of life. The city can mean blight or blessing, last chance or first, nightmare or dream; that is, Reno can stand for what is wrong with America or for what is right. Most Reno authors agree that Reno is a paradox. Positive and negative depictions and interpretations alike can be found in their novels. Their opinions, advanced by the same stock characters and conventional plots already isolated, are then emphasized by some revealing figurative language.

Not In Our Stars serves as the best example. Stern's heroine, Sara Winston, joins a number of people at the Jolly-R Guest Ranch where each awaits a divorce. Their characters are all flawed—Sara's roommate Maggie is an alcoholic, as is her husband, who follows her to

Reno; Belle is an overweight, discarded Jewish mother; Lou, a homosexual designer who thought marriage would set him straight; Van, Sara's lover, is attractive, compelling, but, in the long run, weak. Sara, as insecure and maladjusted as the rest, initially finds Reno reflective of these diverse problems. Standing in Harolds Club, she muses:

> the last frontier, where everything goes. . . . Oh, America, erstwhile land of the free, what has become of thee? What have they done to thee, my beloved? The profound dream . . . land of the mighty . . . refuge, once, of the persecuted, where each might have his chance at life, liberty, and the pursuit of happiness. But what *was* happiness and *where* could you find it? Was this, in fact, America? Did all roads lead to Reno?[24]

Actually, Sara is questioning what has become of *her* and asking where *she* can find happiness. But like so many characters in these novels, she converts her own inadequacies into statements about the city. A man from the same book reveals even more about himself when he calls Reno "the boil on the cover-girl face of our decadent western culture, . . . the ulcer in the soft underbelly of our shining civilization, produced by our collective tension and greed and fear."[25] For this disagreeable character, Reno becomes emblematic of his own failure. In fact, those characters who see Reno as a "blight"[26] tend to be the malcontents, second-rate, the so-called "flotsam and jetsam," or, "The Women," as Clare Boothe called them collectively and ironically in her 1937 Broadway play by that name. To these outcasts, Reno symbolizes what's wrong with the nation and, more subtly, with themselves. "It isn't only Reno. Standards all over aren't as high as they were," laments one poor soul who is troubled by "the modern pace."[27] Conservative readers, finding their own beliefs confirmed, would agree. By using the breakup of the family unit as the cornerstone of their plots, exploitive authors have been able to turn Reno into a symbol of national decay, a "last frontier," as Stern writes in *Not In Our Stars,* of fast living and wasted lives.

However, those characters who succeed, and who achieve self-knowledge, view Reno quite differently by the time their stories end. Sara Winston, when she finally realizes that people's flaws arise "not in our stars" but in ourselves, is well on her way to maturity. No longer dismayed by Reno, "this tiny, tinseley, neon-lit metropolis, half circus, half resort,"[28] Sara sees the biggest little city in a different light. Stern explains the possibilities:

> a symbol of failure to some, of release to others, of despair to the unloved, of the promised land to the domestically trapped. It mean[s] quick marriage to impatient lovers, quick divorce to those who [have] found more desirable mates, the possibility of a quick killing for those with a lust for the wheel and the dice and the cards. *Could be, might be, maybe this time, maybe next time.* . . . Yes, Reno was a symbol of the second chance and the chance after that which every man always believed awaited him. . . . In America, everybody had a chance—and if they muffed it there was always the second chance. Reno . . . would give a second chance.[29]

So for people like Sara, Reno represents not the last frontier but a new one. Accordingly, Reno can be interpreted as a positive symbol of beginnings and possibilities, with the magic of Oz. Stern's characters acknowledge that "actually, all this is very peaceful. [They are] beginning to feel better already [after settling on the guest ranch]. Beginning to be able to face the future."[30] Faith Baldwin's collection of short stories, *Temporary Address: Reno,* stresses the same positive outlook, interpreting "Reno as a beginning and not an end,"[31] advocating ultimately successful adjustments and insisting upon using the word "beginning." Even a book which opens with a group of "misfits," Arthur Miller's screenplay by that title, turns the action around so that Reno becomes the jumping-off point for a meaningful relationship between the two main characters.

I already have indicated that most of the books under consideration here include both interpretations of Reno—blight and blessing, last frontier and first. *The Misfits* demonstrates exactly how that ambivalence works. The minor characters remain misfits; they succumb to the metaphorical "boil on the cover-girl face" of the nation. In contrast, the protagonists succeed, and, subsequently, view Reno in a different light. Able to take advantage of the opportunities offered by the new frontier, they reorient their attitudes and their lives in more positive directions. This pattern, which informs *The Misfits,* also recurs in *Not In Our Stars, Reno Fever, Reunion in Reno,* the stories in *Temporary Address: Reno,* even in Vanderbilt's *Reno* and Hamlin's *Whirlpool.* Apparently this mode of dual resolution—failure for secondary characters, success for major—is a convenient way of handling the paradox that is Reno. Each author can treat both sides of the city and include both philosophies at once, can create happy endings while describing depressing details, can project idealism while acknowledging decay. In effect, each author may have the reader eating spinach and dessert simultaneously, a feat which obviously attracts more patrons.

The audience must have been captivated, too, by a double set of extended metaphors used by most of these writers. Perhaps not surprisingly, the figures of speech grew from jargon used in the city by natives and divorcées alike. These metaphors are institutional in nature—that is, they universalize the city by tying it to familiar institutions, one medical, one educational. Thus both enable speakers to make abstractions concrete.

The first spreads from the notion of Reno as a malignancy, a symbol of decadent contemporary life. As one of Jill Stern's characters—the same man who earlier speaks of "cover-girl boils" and "ulcerated underbellies"—succinctly comments, "We're all marking time in our own self-created death house, we're all slowly dying of the same disease."[32] The disease? Loneliness, or, as one novelist called her book, *Reno Fever.* Paradoxically, marriage led to the loneliness of many would-be divorcées, so they headed to Reno to be cured. Indeed, in Reno of the '20s, '30s, and '40s, the euphemism for divorce was "the cure." Furthermore, Reno was known as "the clinic," or, "the national clinic for wrecked domestic nerves,"[33] as Max Miller describes it in his narrative. Stern attempts a comparison analogous to Miller's when she suggests similarities between the Jolly-R Guest Ranch and the sanitarium in Thomas Mann's *Magic Mountain*. Characters in both novels seek physical health, as well as emotional, spiritual, and intellectual well-being, by retiring to a self-contained retreat where their ills may be cured. Although I only with difficulty equate Sara Winston's stay with Hans Castorp's, the attempt remains interesting. Writers like Stern unknowingly show the pervasiveness in Nevada thinking of the metaphor of disease and the subsequent clinic and cure.

A somewhat different extended figure of speech was used to characterize Reno as an educational institution, where the interaction between would-be divorcées recaptures the atmosphere of college days. In *Reno Fever,* for example, four women take adjoining rooms at the Riverside and live like sorority sisters—flitting from room to room, forming intense friendships, swapping boy friends, and somehow managing to grow up. The title of Mary Warren's *Reunion in Reno* suggests a school theme, too, with old friends getting together again—and, in this instance, remarrying. However, the significant thrust of the metaphor comes with its conventional expression on the streets of Reno. The day one received a divorce was known as "graduation day"; a divorce decree, "the diploma"; the subsequent celebration, "a graduation party." Such language, reiterating the belief that Reno prepared people for the future and offered them a second chance, supplies another restatement of the frontier theme.

One could of course jumble both sets of institutional metaphors, and people often did, to express a continuous operation—illness, clinic, cure, graduation, diploma—so that all interpretations lead to a positive outcome. Certainly this would cohere with the "jackpot" mentality that has pervaded Reno's life from its earliest post-Comstock days to its latest twentieth-century casino boom. Despite Reno's tarnished reputation and the sensationalism foisted upon it by the press, the city, in the minds of most people, finally spells success—or at least it spells possibilities. The prevailing figurative language advances that optimistic point of view.

This is true, in part, because Reno tends to loom larger than life.

And Reno's reputation has been magnified because fiction and nonfiction alike have chosen to exaggerate it. For example, nearly every book or article mentions Reno's most famous myth—that each new divorcée, upon leaving the judge's chambers, first kisses the pillar on the courthouse porch and then tosses her old wedding ring into the Truckee River. Perpetrated by mocked-up photographs in slick magazines, this action took place mainly in the imagination. Yet advertising men favored the story in pamphlets, and fictional characters love to mention the supposed ceremony because it provides a moment of vicarious pleasure to the contemplator and to the reader: "Wouldn't it be fun to . . . ?" Even realizing that Reno novels exaggerate, the public reads them anyway because, quite simply, they stimulate the imagination. And by translating the city's symbolic potential into accessible terms, they also reinterpret contemporary life with its modern problems. So readers seeking escape and readers looking for answers can find what they want in novels written about Reno. In short, it's the old spinach/dessert conflation all over again.

For everybody, then, the city behind the arch serves a purpose. It emanates different ideas to diverse people, or, as one writer explains, "the theme of Reno is bigger than the little town itself."[34] That theme, I argue, is the theme of modern America, the curious paradox of the "decadent modern pace" juxtaposed against the perennial "pot of gold" mentality. The duality that is Reno thus is a projection of the ambivalent attitudes that make up the average twentieth-century mind. Hamlin said as much in *Whirlpool of Reno* when he portrayed the hypocrisy of the natives and the indolence of the divorcées as a microcosm of the country. Surely that contradicts Walter Clark's representation of the two "colonies" living separately, one in "the city of trembling leaves," the other in "the biggest little city in the world," but obviously Hamlin's portrayal is more attuned to that of the majority of Reno novelists. Symbolically, for the writers and for their readers, Reno reflects reality, ambiguous reality, and Reno *is* a big little city—indeed, "the biggest little city in the world."

NOTES

1. All quotations in the first paragraph are from the "Prelude," Walter Van Tilburg Clark, *The City of Trembling Leaves* (New York: Popular Library, 1945), pp. 5–13.

2. For casino novels, one must turn to the plethora of books set in Las Vegas.

3. Reno Chamber of Commerce, *Reno, Land of Charm* (Reno: A. Carlisle and Co., [1932]), [pp. 1–2].

4. Tom Gilbert, *Reno! "It Won't Be Long Now"* (Reno: Gilbert and Shapro, 1927), p. 25.

5. Leslie Curtis, *Reno Reveries* (Reno: Armanko Stationery Co., 1924), p. 42.

6. Annie Estelle Prouty, "The Development of Reno in Relation to its Topography," *Nevada Historical Society Papers,* 4 (1923–24), 101, quotes a San Francisco *Times* correspondent writing in the August 27, 1868, Carson *Daily Appeal.*

7. Con Ryan, "The City that Sex Built," *Real Detective,* 39 (1936), 15.

8. *The Reno Divorce Racket* (Minneapolis: Graphic Arts Corp., 1931), p. 3; significantly, this pamphlet was published in the same year that the Nevada State Legislature had enacted a six-week divorce law and had legalized open gambling.

9. Mrs. Katherine Fullerton Gerould, *The Aristocratic West* (New York: Harper & Brothers, 1925), p. 182.

10. Others include James Gunn's *Deadlier than the Male* and Gloria Hope's *Inside Reno* — actually a collection of repulsive little short stories.

11. See, for example, Helen Arre's *Corpse by the River,* Dean Evans' *No Slightest Whisper,* and Gay Greer's *The Case of the Well-Dressed Corpse.*

12. "Chamber Raps Novel On Reno," *Nevada State Journal,* March 6, 1929, p. 8, col. 8.

13. "Vanderbilt Told in Wire That He Disclosed Ingratitude," *Reno Evening Gazette,* March 5, 1929, p. 12, cols. 2–4.

14. Cornelius Vanderbilt, Jr., *Reno* (New York: Macaulay, 1929), p. 228.

15. "Letter to the Editor," *Sagebrush,* October 9, 1931, p. 4, cols. 3–6.

16. John Hamlin, *Whirlpool of Reno* (New York: The Dial Press, 1931), p. 164; again, the year of publication, 1931, is significant.

17. Vanderbilt, *Reno,* p. [3].

18. Jill Stern, *Not In Our Stars* (New York: David McKay Co., 1957), p. 28.

19. Ibid., p. 257.

20. Dorothy Wadsworth Carman, *Reno Fever* (New York: Ray Long & Richard R. Smith, Inc., 1932), p. 9.

21. Ibid., p. 37.

22. Ibid., p. 58.

23. Ibid., p. 208.

24. Stern, pp. 64–65.

25. Ibid., p. 148.

26. Earl Derr Biggers, *Keeper of the Keys* (Indianapolis: Bobbs-Merrill Co., 1932), p. 51.

27. Carman, p. 21.

28. Stern, p. 28.

29. Ibid., 256.

30. Ibid., 81.

31. Faith Baldwin, *Temporary Address: Reno* (New York: Farrar & Rinehart, Inc., 1941), p. 333.

32. Stern, p. 148.

33. Max Miller, *Reno* (New York: Dodd, Mead & Co., 1941), p. 1.

34. Ibid., p. ix.

CHAPTER FOUR

Idah Meacham Strobridge
The Second Mary Austin?

"What Mary Austin has done for the California desert, in 'The Land of Little Rain,' Mrs. Strobridge has done for the desert lands of Nevada," wrote a Los Angeles *Record* reviewer at the beginning of the twentieth century. The *Dial*, in Chicago, was even more enthusiastic about Idah Meacham Strobridge's comparative talents. "A study of the American desert that has quite as much atmosphere as Mrs. Austin's 'Land of Little Rain,' and that even seems to get closer to the strange heart of the matter," reported the *Dial*'s book editor.

Idah Meacham Strobridge? Closer to the strange heart of the desert than Mary Austin? Who was this Mrs. Strobridge whose prose, so enthusiastically read by her contemporaries, has been all but forgotten by later generations? What did she write? And was she really as accomplished as her reviewers insisted? "There is no author today," said someone at the old Kansas City *Post*, "who can write of the great stretch of cacti-studded, dull sand as Mrs. Strobridge" (*Trilogy* endpapers).

She was born in California in 1855, then moved with her family to Nevada a few years later. She grew up in Humboldt County, on a homestead located where the old Lassen-Applegate cutoff leaves the Overland Trail. She was well educated, graduating from Mills College in 1883, and could have made a life for herself in the city, but chose instead to return to rural Nevada the following year. She married and gave birth to three boys. The first son died the day after he was born, then her husband and other two sons died from pneumonia during the harsh winter of 1888–89.

Such tragedy, however, did not seem to dim Idah Strobridge's enthusiasm for an intellectual life in the desert. Not only did she continue ranching in semi-isolated northern Nevada but she taught herself the art of bookbinding, an activity that led to several medals in later years. Charles Fletcher Lummis, one-time city editor of the Los Angeles *Times,* early recognized her worth: "though this sagebrush artisan has been studying out this exigent trade by herself, off there in the wilderness, her work is emphatically worth while. A commercial-bound book looks cheap beside her staunch and honest and tasteful bindings; and when I have a book that merits to endure longer than the commercial binds can make it, off it goes to Humboldt, and never in vain" (*Trilogy* Intro. 9).

At the same time, Strobridge began to pursue another artistic interest. She began to write. She already had published a few pieces when she finally sold the family property in Nevada and, in 1901, moved permanently to southern California. There she and her book bindery ingratiated themselves into a circle of other writers that included Mary Austin, Eugene Manlove Rhodes and Maynard Dixon, and there she began to print her own creative efforts along with the work of others.

In just five years, her Artemesia Bindery published three books by Idah Meacham Strobridge—*In Miners' Mirage-Land* [1904], *The Loom of the Desert* [1907], and *The Land of Purple Shadows* [1909]. While she regularly told friends that she was working on more tales and sketches, she never actually put together any more collections after that. But she remained active in California literary circles until her death in 1932, even though most of her energies were devoted to genealogical research rather than creative writing.

The University of Nevada Press recently reprinted Strobridge's three books in a single volume, *Sagebrush Trilogy,* with introductory materials by Richard A. Dwyer and Richard E. Lingenfelter. A perusal of her *Sagebrush Trilogy* accomplishments invites this comparison with Mary Austin, for not only were the two members of the same group of friends but the two published somewhat similar books about the high desert east of the Sierra at about the same time. Since their contemporary reviewers were quick to point out their similarities and differences, it should be interesting for the modern reader to look more closely at the so-called second Mary Austin (even though no present-day critic would put the two writers in the same category).

Strobridge, in fact, had few literary pretensions. She saw herself more as a wordsmith and described her verbal sketches as very like what "the painter brings back to his studio after his working-vacation is over. Mere suggestions and rough outlines are they—the first impressions of what he saw." In her Foreword to *The Land of Purple Shadows* she went on to explain, "Not for the galleries did he make them, nor for the critics, nor for the careless. But the portfolio is opened to those who will understand." So, too, her word portraits brushstroke the outlines of character, plot, and scene, leaving the reader to fill in the flesh-and-blood details of conflict and color.

Although most of her pieces can be categorized as roughhewn, they do vary in design. Some are nonfiction, reportorial glances at the high desert landscape, painterly rather than scientific, preliminary sketches rather than drawings in depth. Others are half-told tales, stories that introduce slightly developed characters and set them in motion only to stop them. Each such anecdotal episode seems more like a short sequence of still frames from a movie, with no beginning and no compelling end.

One memorable interlude from *The Loom of the Desert* can serve as typical of Strobridge's craft. In less than ten pages Martha Scott marries young, lives a life that "has become but a gray reflection of its never-ending sameness," precipitously runs off to Hawaii for a year of romance (we are told she is "radiant with happiness"), then returns to "the old groove again" and "moves in the same apathetic way as before the stirring events of her life." But the sketchiness of Martha Scott's actions is not particularly offensive to the reader. The author tells us enough. She writes, for example, that Martha Scott's "limited intelligence only allowed her to perceive the dreariness of her own poor life, and when her longings touched no responsive chord in the man whom she had married, she deliberately took one year of her existence and hung its walls with all the gorgeous tapestries and rich paintings that could be wrought by the witchery of those magic days in the Pacific" (*Loom*, 21). Such an overview allows us to add our own details. We do not need the facts of her flight and her return because the author trusts us to properly embellish the tale.

While this technique may not be particularly fashionable in the nineteen-nineties, it was well-received by readers at the turn of the century. "The author has the power of drawing a character in a few strong strokes," wrote F. Marion Gallagher in the *Overland Monthly*, "and she has the real dramatic quality that is so rare in the ordinary short story." Her men and women invite the imagination to fill in all the missing details. As Elia W. Peattie of the Chicago *Tribune* so clearly understood, "There is material for a dozen novels in these pages."

It is easy to believe that Strobridge intended her tales to be read by easterners, that she, like Mary Halleck Foote, meant to depict a landscape seen by few who had actually set foot in the American West. After all, many of her reviewers lived east of the Rockies, and most of her romances echo popular formulas of the times. However the dedication of her third book, *The Land of Purple Shadows*, belies that assumption. It opens with the following words: "To YOU Who were born in the West—who live in the West—who love the West." So Idah Meacham Strobridge wanted to speak to the very reader who felt a personal affinity with her world.

Her descriptive passages, for example, seem designed for those who already know the landscape, who can "fill in the blanks" appropriately. "The mountains alter their outlines so rapidly that the eye can scarce note all their changes," she generalized in *Miner's Mirage-Land*,

> They change from great heights to a low chain of hills; and leap back again, to shoot in spires innumerable into the violet sky, or drop into a long, flat table-land with overhanging top . . . Then they disappear, and island pinnacles lift themselves from the mass of changing panorama, and the slender shafts reach far into the sky. Then—even as you are watching—one by one they dissolve, and the mountains have resumed their wonted shapes. (*Mirage*, 4)

Mary Austin looks at mountains somewhat differently. For one thing, she sees God there. For another, she sees a sublimity freshly wrought, a scene drawn boldly for the reader, a landscape portrayed with active voice and with neither trite phrase nor common word. A paragraph from *The Land of Little Rain* clearly differs from one in *Mirage-Land*.

> The shape of a new mountain is roughly pyramidal, running out into long shark-finned ridges that interfere and merge into other thunder-splintered sierras. You get the saw-tooth effect from a distance, but the near-by granite bulk glitters with the terrible keen polish of old glacial ages. I say terrible; so it seems. When those glossy domes swim into the alpenglow, wet after rain, you conceive how long and imperturbable are the purposes of God. (Austin, 116)

Strobridge's shapes are spires, flat table-land, pinnacles, shafts; Austin's are pyramidal, shark-finned, saw-tooth, bulk. Strobridge's verbs alter, change, disappear; Austin's run, merge, glitter, swim. Strobridge writes that "island pinnacles lift themselves from the mass of changing panorama"; Austin supposes that "the near-by granite bulk glitters with the terrible keen polish of old glacial ages." The difference is one of imaginative perception, of originality, of showing the reader a scene through eyes unencumbered by the expectations of tradition. Strobridge's readers see a hint of mountains on a printed page; Austin's see poetic recreation.

All of their readers, however, see an American West described with intimacy and with affection. With special fondness, both Strobridge and Austin looked sympathetically at the Indians who had been displaced from their lands and at the prospectors who roamed the remaining open spaces. These men and women emerge in Strobridge's writing as Old George, or Old Squaw, or Blue-Eyed Chief, or Little Savage. Or else they become types rather than individuals, exemplifying a species rather than a person. In any case, Strobridge tends to generalize about their lives, and makes them carry messages on their backs.

The Old George vignette relates a conversation between a well-dressed pair who, while waiting for a train, naively speculate about the life of a nearby Indian beggar. Next we are given an outline of the true story of Old George. Again Strobridge lets us fill in the fictional embellishments left out of the paragraphs, but then she tells us what conclusion we should reach. "It is a little story, but quite true," she explains. "It might very easily have been made a White man's story; but it isn't, it is only the true story of a Paiute."

> George is an Indian; but one in a whole tribe — each having his own story. And the tribe is but one of the race. And the race —
> Are we not brothers?
> For, the world over, under white skin or skin of bronze-brown, the human heart throb's the same; for we are brothers — ay! brothers all. (*Loom*, 106)

Mary Austin concluded her portrait of an aging Indian with a message, too, but hers is at once more subtle and more profound than Strobridge's. "So in her blanket Seyavi, sometime basket maker, sits by the unlit hearths of her tribe and digests her life, nourishing her spirit against the time of the spirit's need, for she knows in fact quite as much of these matters as you who have a larger hope, though she has none but the certainty that having borne her-self courageously to this end she will not be reborn a coyote" (Austin, 111). Austin's so-called message contains extended imagery ("the unlit hearths of her tribe"), metaphor ("digests her life, nour-ishing her spirit"), irony ("you who have a larger hope"), and even humor ("she will not be reborn a coyote"). Strobridge's does not, even though it is safe to say that Strobridge felt just as strongly about the comparative strengths of Indians and whites, just as deeply about their comparative fates.

If we turn to their prospectors, miners, and pocket hunters, however, we find Strobridge's depictions much closer to Austin's. Both writers well understood the peculiar character of those who search endlessly and both were well able to picture such souls. Strobridge introduces us to old man Berry—"gaunt, you would have called him; and you would have noticed at once how bowed he was. But not as other old men on whom age has rested a heavy hand. It was the head, not the back, that was bowed—as though he had walked long years, and far, with his eyes upon the ground" (*Mirage*, 28). Austin's pocket hunter is just as individualized in his own way, "a small bowed man, with a face and manner and speech of no character at all, as if he had that faculty of small hunted things of taking on the protective color of his surroundings" (Austin, 43).

A visual quirk or two brings these characters alive, sets them into motion on the printed page. And, indeed, Strobridge's vignettes of mining exploration tend to be more vibrant, more knowledgeable (after all, Strobridge grew up among such wandering men), and even more amusing than Austin's. Yet Strobridge cannot resist typ-ing a caption under her brushstrokes,

> And I wonder if he who follows the bell-wether is any wiser than that one who trails after the story of a will-o'-wisp mine that leads him across Desert valleys and rough mountain ridges where there is never a sign of gold? Which is the fool; and which is the wise man? And who has the right to judge? (*Mirage*, 53)

while Austin rests content with a punctuation mark. Her "Pocket Hunter" closes with one of her most famous lines—"No man can be stronger than his destiny" (Austin, 52)—and says no more.

Perhaps that is a fitting epithet for Idah Meacham Strobridge. Despite the accolades of her reviewers, she never was stronger than a destiny that placed her in Mary Austin's literary circle but not necessarily in that more famous writer's intellectual company. When a discerning reader now looks at essays by the two, that reader will find many similarities in point of view, in subject matter, and even in technique. It is safe to say, however, that the discerning reader will also find a dearth of ironic tension, an emptiness of philosophic inquiry, and a lack of intellectual discipline in Strobridge's work. She wrote for *Sunset Magazine*; Mary Austin did not.

Yet it may be unfair to wholly discredit Strobridge's achievements, especially if we allow her a starring role as "First Woman of Nevada Letters" (Amaral, 5). After all, not many men or women who grew up in the Silver State in the years before the turn of the century became writers. Even fewer could boast of the kind of attention Strobridge received. "The author knows what she is writing about," applauded Bailey Millard in the San Francisco *Examiner*, "and that in this day of cheap literary superficiality is something so rare, and rich, and strange, that one is bound to feel a keen sense of elation and keen appreciation as one turns the pages . . . If anyone . . . has more clearly laid bare the secrets of the desert, I do not know of it." So let's be fair to Idah Meacham Strobridge, and let's look at her prose apart from Mary Austin's.

Strobridge was at her best when she immersed herself in desert landscape, especially desert landscape that boasted a history. Thinking about the great pioneer migration west, she was able to conceive and articulate changes. "Cities have sprung up out of the once silent plains, and a hundred thousand homes of the living now line the great pathway which was marked out by the skeletons of the dead. Half a century ago it was the land of the dried-up alkali lakes; of the far-reaching sage; of the biting, white dust; of the ever-beckoning mirage" (*Mirage,* 121). Thinking about families like her own, she was able to explain a place that speaks most clearly through its silence and most deeply through its "utter desolation." The answer brings the reader back to Strobridge's reliance on a verbal brushstroke that requires the imagination to fill in the visual detail. "The sun rises each morning upon a scene which never alters, except when a change is wrought by the mirage in its illusive, elusive mystery" (*Mirage,* 12). Her prospectors wear colors from the same palette.

> Into the gray Desert (a land of gray sage, and gray sand; of lizards, and little horned-toads that are gray; a land where the coyote drifts by you, like a fragment from gray fog-banks blown by the wind), half a century ago, they came—the prospectors—seeking silver or gold. And some yet seek, in places where there is none. Some are following the mirage still. (*Mirage,* 13–14)

So a reader who is willing to follow Strobridge's own mirages— willing to let shapes materialize slowly, willing to paint in the spaces between the lines, and willing to ignore the fortuitous moralizing—can take pleasure in her words. For her words are like prospectors themselves: "Up and down the creek bed they move so noiselessly, working with pick and pan, that one can very easily fancy them but gray ghosts haunting the quiet canons, even as the shadowy wraiths of the dead years linger about the unroofed walls and weed-grown trails" (*Purple,* 27).

Idah Meacham Strobridge is no second Mary Austin, it is true. But she is the first lady of letters in the vastness of Nevada's desert, the first lady of letters to love that isolation, the first lady of letters to communicate that love. "Idah Meacham Strobridge has given to the world one of the best and most characteristic collections of Western desert sketches ever written," said a Pasadena *News* reviewer at the turn of the century. "She has shown us the great gray desert in an entirely new phase, a phase that attracts us and lures us on, enticed by the very magnetism of her sympathy and understanding."

WORKS CITED

Anthony Amaral. "Idah Meacham Strobridge: First Woman of Nevada Letters." *Nevada Historical Society Quarterly* 9 (Fall 1967): 5–12.

Mary Austin. *The Land of Little Rain.* 1903. Rpt. Albuquerque: University of New Mexico Press, 1974.

Idah Meacham Strobridge. *Sagebrush Trilogy: Idah Meacham Strobridge and Her Works.* Intro. by Richard A. Dwyer and Richard E. Lingenfelter. Reno: University of Nevada Press, 1990. (*Sagebrush Trilogy* reprints all three of Strobridge's published works—*In Miners' Mirage-Land, The Loom of the Desert,* and *The Land of Purple Shadows.* "The Second Mary Austin?," rather than referring only to *Sagebrush Trilogy* in the text above, more appropriately indicates the three titles separately, as *Mirage, Loom,* and *Purple.* All of the reviews have been taken from excerpts printed at the back of *Sagebrush Trilogy,* excerpts which originally were taken from the endpapers of Strobridge's three books.)

CHAPTER FIVE

Walter Van Tilburg Clark's
Brave Bird, "Hook"

A scan of the reconstituted membership of the *Studies in Short Fiction* Editorial Committee reveals a geographical slant little different from the past: almost everyone lives and works east of the Mississippi River. This suggests unfairly that the bulk of our journal's concerns focuses east of the Mississippi as well. But there is a world out here in the wilderness of the American West, too. It is the territory first staked by the Twains and the Hartes, unfortunately codified by the pulps, and now expanded and redefined by the imaginations of such recent writers as Norman Maclean, Elizabeth Tallent, William Kittredge, and Leslie Marmon Silko. At the risk of sounding provincial about these writers' goals and accomplishments, I plan to do just that—write regionally as my way of marking the twenty-fifth anniversary of *Studies in Short Fiction* and of reinforcing a more global perspective. I plan to do so by focusing on a single short story by a single Western writer, one that I believe signals the transition to contemporary Western creativity and one that contains several of the images and themes found there as well.

Walter Van Tilburg Clark didn't write many short stories—some early magazine pieces, a handful collected in *The Watchful Gods and Other Stories*, a few more in manuscript. Among them, critics agree,

"Hook" is superb. First published in the *Atlantic Monthly,* July 1940, and later a part of *The Watchful Gods and Other Stories* (1950), "Hook" has always received rave reviews. "A glittering tour de force,"[1] wrote one reviewer; "a perfect story,"[2] said another; "truly a masterpiece," rhapsodized a third, "one of the most fascinating [narratives] in modern literature."[3] Yet a fourth reviewer announced that "it far overshadows anything Steinbeck ever dreamed of,"[4] while a fifth termed the story "distinguished for possessing all the best elements of the short story and none of the usual shortcomings."[5] The almost unanimously heady praise was marred by only a lone dissenting voice, that of Bernard DeVoto, who did not care for "Hook" at all.

DeVoto's 1950 review, which begins by calling the story "an exercise in cloudily symbolic anthropomorphism," is worth examining in detail, for it raises major questions that suggest the way too many reviewers and critics callously dismiss Western American fiction. The gunslinging DeVoto objects to "Hook"'s lifeless characters; he shoots down the story's lifeless form. Then DeVoto fires point-blank: "The empty Western landscape sets two fatal traps for writers of fiction," he blasts, "and Mr. Clark falls into both of them, the pathetic fallacy which endows geology with emotions (and diminishes man . . .) and an inverted sentimentality that chases tragic significance through the cacti as such."[6] Since "Hook" takes place far from the nearest cactus, I cannot exactly chase Mr. DeVoto back east through his preordained route. But I can waylay him, and target the inadequacy of his perceptions.

First of all, DeVoto argues from a faulty premise when he insists that no story whose protagonist is an animal can be of consuming interest to an anthropocentric reader. He is mistaken, of course, as Herman Melville well proved. Creatures personified can make consuming reading indeed. Echoing John Ruskin, DeVoto faults use of the pathetic fallacy without distinguishing between pathetic use and effective use. While the former easily may cause a tale to degenerate into silliness and immaturity, the latter may add a dimension that reveals far more about ourselves than we recognized before. Besides, DeVoto states his case incorrectly. "Hook" certainly does not endow "geology with emotions." Rather, it tells us the story of a single bird.

Hook is a hawk, no more and no less.[7] The reader witnesses the course of the young raptor's life through the eyes of an omniscient narrator. If the narrative voice sometimes uses diction and syntax reminiscent of the pathetic fallacy, the author even more frequently selects language and style that distance both the bird and the reader from heavy-handed personification. The opening line sets the tone: "Hook, the hawks' child, was hatched in a dry spring among the oaks beside the seasonal river, and was struck from the nest early."[8] A phrase like "the hawks' child" may seem precious at first, but Clark, striking the fledgling from his nest, dashes such mawkishness almost immediately. The rest of the paragraph follows the same pattern. Sounding first like a Walt Disney portrayal, with the bird's "single-willed parents" flying nearby, it Peckinpah-ish-ly concludes that "they drove Hook down into the sand and brush" (82) and left him to die. Similar juxtapositions throughout the story first humanize the hawk and then underline the Darwinian nature of the narrative. This ability to control narrative voice[9] not only rescues "Hook" from any tendency toward sentimentality, but also contributes to the story's power. Although sympathizing with the creature as a champion and an embodiment of certain natural strengths, a reader never forgets the wildness of a "spirit wholly belligerent, swift and sharp, like his gaze" (86). Pathos has no part in this vocabulary.

Yet DeVoto's intimation of pathos reminds us of a dilemma regularly faced by Clark and his contemporaries. How does a Western writer convey the stark brutality of an unforgiving terrain without trapping himself in clichés—the so-called "rainbow trail" of Zane Grey, for example—or without making "nature red in tooth and claw" so distasteful that no one wants to read about it? Clark succeeds by disdaining a land of purple-clotted sunsets and drawing instead a realistic horizon that incorporates all facets of existence. And so the hawk "swept freely with the wind over the miles of coastal foothills, circling, and ever in sight of the sea, and used without struggle the warm currents lifting from the slopes, and no longer desired to scream at the range of his vision." (84) Just as freely, Clark soars above the confines suggested by DeVoto.

He is not the only Westerner to do so. Many others have endowed a part of the landscape with some kind of ironic or representational personification—Aldo Leopold's mountain, Willa Cather's plough, Edward Abbey's moon-eyed horse. One writer even found creative energy in birds like Clark's: for Robinson Jeffers, hawks were "totem birds, expressing what is noble, fierce, independent, and farsighted."[10] The poet himself actually spoke of the "symbolic values"[11] inherent in the predatory figure. He not only named his coastal refuge "Hawk House" and titled a book of his poems *"Give Your Heart to the Hawks" and Other Poems* (1933), but the image itself recurs in a number of his major works. The young Walter Clark, who wrote his M.A. thesis about the California author,[12] surely recognized this theme. Indeed, the first Jeffers book purchased by Clark contains the germ of "Hook" in the guise of a poem called "Hurt Hawks"; Jeffers's words there sound as forceful, as arrogant, as lacking in pathos as Clark's:

> *The broken pillar of the wing jags from the clotted shoulder,*
> *The wing trails like a banner in defeat,*
> *No more to use the sky forever but live with famine*
> *And pain a few days . . . .*[13]

So, too, we see Hook, as "his own blood throttled his breathing" (88).

Neither Jeffers's poem nor Clark's story is pleasant. Both examine the image of a noble bird brought down to earth. "He is strong and pain is worse to the strong, incapacity is worse," says the poetry (l.9); "often, at the choking thought of soaring and striking and the good, hot-blood kill, he strove to take off, but only one wing came up, winnowing with a hiss, and drove him over onto his side in the sand," says the prose (90). The former, however, ends in celebration, while the latter does not, exactly. Jeffers's hawk dies at the hand of a man who respects him and reveres his sacred energy.[14] Sympathizing with the "unable misery" (l.21) and the "implacable arrogance" (l.29) of a raptor that cannot fly, Jeffers's narrator gives him "freedom" (l.23), shoots and kills him with "the lead gift in the twilight" (l.29), then watches his spirit soar "unsheathed from reality" (l.32). Hook has no such esoteric denouement. Despite a crippling wound, he survives along the shore and grows increasingly frail as he scrabbles for food and dignity. When death finally comes, it comes in the confines of a chicken yard: "'Oh, kill the poor thing,' the woman begged. The man, though, encouraged the dog again, saying 'Sick him; sick him'" (98). The impotent hawk is no match. His "neck went limp, and between his gaping clappers came only a faint chittering, as from some small kill of his own in the grasses" (99).

The line which then concludes the story falls vapidly. "'Oh, the brave bird,' she said" (99). This fatuous remark surely led to DeVoto's assertion that sentimentality was chasing tragic significance in this kind of fiction. The woman's words compare badly with Jeffers's symbol of fierce, rushing nobility "unsheathed from reality." Nonetheless, by insisting upon Clark's control, I can defend "Hook"'s finale against DeVoto's claim. In "The Watchful Gods," the title story of Clark's 1950 collection, the poignant demise of a tiny rabbit coincides with the simultaneous lift of a hawk:

> In the moment it required to rise against the sea-wind that was beginning now, and then curve back on rigid wings and sink away inland to vanish against the dark brush of the hills, it seemed, so tiny, quick-rising and unexpected, to be ominously related to the rabbit, to have risen, indeed, directly out of it, and so to be the other, the enduring portion of the creature against whom the crime of murder, in a peculiarly lengthy, deliberate and despicable form, had been committed.[15]

Such a direct re-creation of the end of "Hurt Hawks" proves not only that Clark knew what Jeffers meant but that he also could replicate that meaning if he chose to do so. In "Hook," I believe this storyteller had something else in mind.

Hook is not a cloudy anthropomorphic symbol. As I indicated earlier, he is a flesh-and-blood raptor driven by an uncivilized Darwinian code. He behaves instinctively; he behaves violently. "In his rage, he struck . . . the urge to kill took him again . . . he was compelled to slaughter" (96). No barnyard pet, no stereotypical hero, "Hook revelled in mastery" (96) exactly like the wild, untamed creature that he is. That his death is so ignoble represents, for me at least, a careful working out of the Western writer's second major dilemma. What happens after the frontier spirit dies?

Most Western fiction is predicated on the viability of the American Dream. Whether a protagonist pursues justice or gold or a host of lesser treasures, his goal remains the same. He wants to tame the wilderness. Ironically, though, a tame wilderness is no longer a wilderness, and the most unlikely settler is often the one who craves settlement the least. Boone Caudill learned these lessons in A. B. Guthrie, Jr.'s *The Big Sky* (1947); the reader of "Hook" learns them as well. While I do not mean to imply that Hook plays any sort of civilizing role in Clark's story, the hawk does embody the wilderness spirit of the West. As such, he has nowhere to go. So Clark faces the problem of the closing of the frontier somewhat more abstractly than most writers, crippling it first with a shotgun, letting it spend a year "without flame, a snappish, dust-covered creature" (95), and then eliminating it. A domestic pet strikes the last blow.

Many analogies come to mind—strip-mining, clear-cutting, Lake Powell, the entire Colorado River. Each seems tragic in a sense unimagined by Bernard DeVoto, tragic, finally, in an inarticulate way. I would argue that Walter Clark understood this finality well, and that "Hook" represents his own rethinking of what extinguishing the spirit of the West really means. As the anonymous woman so foolishly reveals, not much can be said after all, although some Western writers have tried. Too often, the results of their analyses parallel their efforts to describe the land itself. Zane Grey and his followers let romantic clouds obscure the scene; others let human tragedy personalize the more global issues. Neither pattern allows readers to confront that crucial tenet of twentieth-century American life—the closing of the frontier.

Yet Clark created a structure that does just that. In the hands of a gifted writer, an everyday predatory hawk turns into an image not of animalistic extremes but of human balance. "If human beings, believing in their own supremacy, disturb the balance," says Herbert Wilner, writing of Clark's personal beliefs, "they only delude themselves with ideas of power and self-fulfillment."[16] Clark, disdaining that delusion, wrote "Hook" to prove his point. In the best Western tradition, it is a story that asks its readers to look at themselves in relation to their environment, asks them to reconsider how their lives may be impacted by the frontier spirit's death, asks them ultimately to remember the greater irony of that lesser "brave bird"'s fate. Quite unlike a simple fable, or a mindless animal tale for children, "Hook" ends in a complex irony that defies one-line explications. The hawk dies an imperious, yet provocative death. The ambiguity of his demise resonates far beyond the confines of his tale. So, too, the Western writer at the hands of an establishment reviewer like DeVoto.

No one from the East, however, was more critical of his own prose than Walter Clark himself. A decade after "Hook"'s 1940 appearance, his pen lay silent. He kept writing, to be sure, but he destroyed most manuscripts and, from 1950 until his death in 1971, published only a stiff edition of diaries kept by a forgotten Virginia City man. Nonetheless, he introduced the greater possibilities of Western fiction to a generation unfortunately nurtured on Zane Grey, Frank Norris, and Max Brand. A roll call of Clark's novels suggests his achievement. *The Ox-Bow Incident* (1940) remains the earliest, and arguably the finest, reworking of frontier justice as a tragic theme. *The City of Trembling Leaves* (1945), although in need of a stern blue pencil, does tackle head-on the problems of the young artist as a Western man. And *The Track of the Cat* (1949) brings Jung to a ranch house in Nevada. An intrepid explorer of unmapped lands himself, Clark wrote only fiction that would find new trails, too. Thus he pointed a way of intellectual, structural, and thematic rigor that such thoughtful Westerners as Wallace Stegner, Larry McMurty, and Ivan Doig could follow.

Meanwhile, "Hook" was one of the few pieces that came up to Clark's own high standards. A fine short story suggesting a host of Western concerns, it remains compelling in its simplicity and power. While I obviously cannot argue that "Hook" is the best short story ever written, or even the best to come out of the American West, an assessment of its strengths indeed seemed appropriate for this twenty-fifth anniversary issue of *Studies in Short Fiction*. An explanation of how easily a Western tale may be misinterpreted seemed appropriate, too, since a journal such as ours strives constantly to confute misreadings. Too often we let shortsighted critics and reviewers dim our vision, when instead we need to look freely at the images, themes, and ambiguities shown to us by a writer like Walter Van Tilburg Clark.

Why is it so easy, though, to make DeVoto's mistake? I answer finally by speculating not about what he said but about what he did not say. DeVoto never mentions the most salient feature of the story—its violence. Anyone reading "Hook" must necessarily be cognizant of the brutality, for Clark hammers at his audience with such phrases as "arena for killing" (83), "beat to death" (86), "fighter's pride and exultation" (87), "vengeful pleasure" (91), "cruel death" (97). No pacifist, no harbinger of civilization, the hawk not only epitomizes a way in which the Western environment can be described and a way in which the Western spirit can be captured, but he also represents something indomitable. That unbridled potency, strong even in defeat, defies literary analysis.

So critics and reviewers ignore it. DeVoto writes contrarily of "Hook"'s lifeless characters and structure, when he could be praising the hawk's many transformations and the cyclical design of the narrative line. DeVoto dismisses the "brave bird," when he could be acknowledging "the supreme fire" that effectively "burn[ed] off a year of shame" (99). DeVoto sees only what he wants to see. Looking through rose-colored glasses, he misses the subtle shades, the boldness, the complex power of "Hook." Tangentially, he misses the distinctive excellence of what will characterize so many later stories of the West, stories too often dismissed with epithets like "Oh, the brave bird" from critics who fail to see the irony of their words. The readers of *Studies in Short Fiction* need something different. We need brave critics—men and women who will take on the task of assessing more fully and re-evaluating more fairly the ranges of Western short fiction.

NOTES

1. Harvey Swados, "Hawks and Men," *The Nation,* 7 October 1950, p. 318.

2. Christopher Blake, in *The Old French Quarter News,* 22 September 1950, n. pag.

3. Naoma Warden, "Boy Acquires Gun but Ruins His Mystic World," *Los Angeles Times,* 24 September 1950, p. 8.

4. Chandler Brossard, "Noble Hawks and Neurotic Women," *The New American Mercury,* n.d., p. 232.

5. H.W.H., in *The New Haven Register,* n.d., n. pag.; this clipping, along with all the other reviews cited, is available in Special Collections Box # 527/2/9, University of Nevada, Reno.

6. Bernard DeVoto, "Tame Indian, Lone Sailor," *New York Times,* 24 July 1950, p. 18.

7. See Robert M. Gorrell, "Problems in 'The Watchful Gods' and Clark's Revisions," in *Walter Van Tilburg Clark: Critiques,* ed. Charlton Laird (Reno: University of Nevada Press, 1983), p. 192, where Gorrell argues persuasively that "the story is primarily about a real hawk."

8. Walter Van Tilburg Clark, "Hook," in *The Watchful Gods and Other Stories* (New York: New American Library, 1950), p. 82; all further citations from "Hook" will be included in the text.

9. See Robert M. Clark, "On the 'Voice' of Walter Clark," in *Critiques,* for a fuller treatment of the senior Clark's technique.

10. Robert Brophy, "Robinson Jeffers," in *Fifty Western Writers,* ed.

Fred Erisman and Richard W. Etulain (Westport, CT: Greenwood Press, 1982), p. 219.

11. Cited in William H. Nolte, *Rock and Hawk: Robinson Jeffers and the Romantic Agony* (Athens: University of Georgia Press, 1978), p. 25.

12. See Henry Nuwer, "Jeffers' Influence Upon Walter Van Tilburg Clark," *Robinson Jeffers Newsletter,* 44 (March 1976), 11–17, for an overview of the connections.

13. Robinson Jeffers, "Hurt Hawks," ll. 1–4, in *Cawdor* (London: Hogarth Press, 1929), p. 153. Subsequent references are cited in the text by line numbers only.

14. I borrow this term, and its attendant "sacrality," from Max Westbrook, *Walter Van Tilburg Clark* (New York: Twayne, 1969), and I use it ironically here. Of course Clark pays homage to that sacred unity, too.

15. Walter Van Tilburg Clark, "The Watchful Gods," in *The Watchful Gods and Other Stories,* p. 51.

16. Herbert Wilner, "Walter Clark: Complicated Simplicity," in *Critiques,* p. 31.

CHAPTER SIX

The Nevada Scene
Through Edward Abbey's Eyes

Any reader who enjoys literature of the contemporary American West should be familiar with the works of Edward Abbey. A talented and prolific author, Abbey has already written six novels and nine nonfiction books of natural and personal history.[1] Each of these, whether fiction or nonfiction, centers its attention on a crucial question: How is modern man to live harmoniously with his natural surroundings?

Because Abbey himself displays such respect for his environment, and because he writes such crisp persuasive prose, he is uniquely able to speak to this very significant issue of the twentieth century. He does so by focusing on a particular geographic corner of the land. While his explorations have ranged from Alaska to Mexico and from Pennsylvania to Australia, he returns time and again to his favorite place—the desert of the American Southwest. There he feels at home and there he writes most effectively. For Abbey, the red sandstone cliffs and the unbroken skylines of Utah and Arizona are concrete manifestations of a spiritual necessity. Looking at those surroundings, he can extrapolate philosophically about the wilderness, about the path of civilization, and about his own preservationist point of view.

Nevada, both civilized and wild, appears less frequently in his books than do her neighboring states. Nonetheless, an examination of Abbey's attitudes toward her boundaries reveals, in microcosm, his attitudes toward the past, the present, and the future of the modern world.

A chapter in *The Journey Home* called "Desert Places" contains his first printed acknowledgment of the Silver State. It begins inauspiciously,

Las Vegas: Fremont Street
HOWDY PARTNER . . .

but continues sarcastically, "These friendly words were addressed to me by a steel-and-neon cowboy fifty feet tall, with a six-foot-wide grin, and one moving arm. He towers above the street,"[2] dominating the Las Vegas scene. This artificial figure grows before the reader's eyes, quickly becoming a mechanical metaphor for the glitter, the tinsel, the superficiality, the emptiness that Abbey thinks he sees. "And the cowboy repeated his greeting, by rote and rheostat, and repeated it again and again, with mechanical persistence, at rigid one-minute intervals, all night long" [*JH,* 68].

HOWDY PARTNER . . .
HOWDY PARTNER . . .
HOWDY PARTNER . . .

To write about Edward Abbey's vision of Nevada is to start from a negative point of view or, even worse, to begin with a demoralizing look at modern life. Not only does the giant artificial cowboy symbolize the city he overlooks, but the city itself serves as a gaudy microcosm of an America that Abbey despises. Indeed, he metaphorically equates the Las Vegas setting with everything he hates about urbanism. Moreover, he associates that tinsel locale with a moment in contemporary history when the whole nation twisted awry: November 22, 1963. That evening, Abbey ruefully announces, was the first time he set foot in Nevada's largest city.

For an obvious reason, then, his impression of the nearby casinos becomes hopelessly tied to spiritual emptiness, the tragic void of modern life. To his right and his left he sees and hears "the California traffic and the clatter of dice, the rattle of chips, the jungle of silver dollars," surrounded by "the click and whirr of the roulette, the flutter of cards, the chant of the keno callers, the shuffle of the crowd, the slap of leather, the tramp of guards, the creaking pelvises of the change girls, the twinkling buttocks of the bar maids, . . . and the clash, roll, jangle, rumble, and rock of 10,000 concentrating mothers of America jerking in unison on the heavy members of 10,000 glittering slot machines" [*JH*, 68]. Building from simple observation to ironic extrapolation, Abbey compounds the superficiality of the gamblers' milieu. Switching from direct statement to more sexually suggestive imagery, he emasculates any virility that milieu might possess, adding, ironically, a faintly militaristic overlay of leather and guards. To expose the hollow facade of gambling is, for Abbey, to reveal the paucity of all urban existence. With a satiric slash of his pen, he perforates the guise of tinsel and luck and pleasure.

But one need not suppose Las Vegas is a single target; Abbey sees little virility in any plasticized version of twentieth-century America. Whether writing fiction or nonfiction, fantasy or personal history, he takes every available opportunity to jab at the edifices of modern life. Duke City, *The Brave Cowboy*'s barely disguised Albuquerque of the late 1950s, already boasts an urban sprawl of dust and dirt, while the fictional Phoenix foreshadowed by *Good News* is pictured in even harsher and more revolting terms. These two novels, along with *Fire on the Mountain* and *The Monkey-Wrench Gang*, attack the invasion that Abbey believes is upon us, the one which too rapidly is changing his beloved open desert country into artificial and impotent cities and towns.

His nonfiction, as directly and perhaps more critically, continues his onslaught. *Desert Solitaire* fires an opening salvo, although its core argument centers more on untouched desert than on encroaching cities. Abbey's later personal histories—*The Journey Home, Abbey's Road,* and *Down the River*—carry the battle forward with vituperative descriptions, "a thin chill greasy patina of poisonous dew. The fly ash everywhere, falling softly and perpetually from the pregnant sky" [*JH*, 90].

If this is true of the country from coast to coast, why should Las Vegas remain unscathed? A city like all other cities, unique only because of its special economic focus, Las Vegas is a convenient whipping boy for Abbey's annoyance at the generic urban milieu. Repeating trite aphorisms and cruel platitudes, Abbey isolates and interprets distinctive features of the southern Nevada locale. "Not a wide-open town at all. The police—public, private, plain, and secret—are everywhere, watching you with stony eyes, marking every move. It's a tight, clean, prim, bright, business-like town, run not by hoods but by sober-sided middle-class gangsters—Mormons from Utah, Baptists from Oklahoma, Presbyterians from Pennsylvania, Roman Catholics from New Jersey, Jews from Texas" [*JH*, 69]. Such generalizations, reminiscent of a thousand newspaper clippings, a hundred magazine exposés, add little to an understanding of the Silver State. Nonetheless, Abbey continues to slash at every credo and creed because he wishes to underscore the corruption of middle America and its hollow dreams. Everyone is guilty, he thinks, so no one should escape the collective responsibility.

Even peripheral participants receive his barbs. "The girls of Nevada are skillful and efficient," he observes. "For $100 a trip half-way around the world and back. By jetstream. A good buy at twice the price, more therapeutic by far than any osteopathic massage, psychoanalysis, colonic irrigation, or Gestalt group encounter known to man—the only honest game in the state" [*JH*, 70].

The only honest game? Perhaps a Nevada reader, or any open-minded reader, might querulously ask, "Is Edward Abbey's an honest game?" Can we trust his assessment of the state's latest and greatest boomtown? Circumstance, a bleak November day, of course dictated the response he felt when he first saw Fremont Street. Moreover, any writer's imagination must be influenced by the prejudices of more than a quarter century of popular denigrations. As we all know, the very name "Las Vegas" brings a host of associations—right or wrong—to mind. So Abbey's response, an honest one, differs little from what one might expect. Because he arrived with a preconceived distaste for the casino scene, he envisions a nightmare. "HOWDY PARTNER . . ." The sugary epithet speaks only to harried denizens of Los Angeles, bidding no welcome to a desert rat who prefers solitude to human company, distant stars to neon lights, a lonely mountain lookout to the phallic towers of any megatropolis. Edward Abbey has little interest in shaking hands—with the giant blinking cowboy, the pink polyester tourists, the 10,000 flashing slot machines. Rather, he prefers his desert undefiled.

"Goodbye to Las Vegas." He tries to escape its magnetic pull. "Very early next morning by the dawn's early light we lit out north by west," he reports, "passing en route a portion of the Las Vegas Bombing and Gunnery Range where the Pentagon plays furtively with its secret toys. Among the several lifeless hills in the area are two named by the poetry of pure coincidence Skull Mountain and Specter Mountain. Check your map if you don't believe it" [*JH*, 70]. Picturing Abbey's delight as he unfetters the city's chains, the reader knows the air smelled cleaner immediately, the sky looked bluer, the straight highway appeared a lifeline into the desert. Not "lifeless hills" but "interludes of illusion"[3] must lie ahead. Out there, in the open desert, waits the Nevada landscape Abbey admires.

Unfortunately, he now fears that it too may be savaged by powerful alien forces. Only the technique differs. Las Vegas grew from a sleepy railroad oasis into a twenty-four-hour adult playground filled with neon toys, but the Nevada desert has, until recently, remained relatively untouched. In 1977 Abbey could smile ironically about "the poetry of pure coincidence" and chuckle as he passed Skull and Specter mountains. The lonesome sterility of a distant firing range seemed self-contained, and was unlikely to swallow more sagebrush and sand. But in the 1980s its isolated landscape has been rediscovered. The military stands ready to extend its territory both north and east; the nation seems eager to base its defense in a distant West. As a result, Abbey is driven to write about the potential devastation. Otherwise, unless his audience is warned in time, he fears another part of Nevada may well become a nightmare.

He calls Chapter 6 in *Down the River* quite simply, "MX," and argues forthrightly about the issue. "The MX—Missile Experimental—casts a long shadow over the American West, and across most of Western civilization, for that matter. A shadow that extends from Tonopah, Nevada, to Vladivostok, Kamchatka, Siberia" [*DR,* 83]. He goes on, then, to equate his alarm for the Nevada desert with his alarm for desert everywhere, to measure his dismay at its possible destruction against his horror at the destructiveness of all mankind. His pattern is similar to the one used to describe Las Vegas. That is, Nevada scenery becomes a microcosm, a mini-version of the larger country and its twentieth-century ills.

What is different about the chapter called "MX," however, is its obvious appreciation for the land itself. While Abbey's prejudices against any plasticized urban conglomerate preclude any appreciation for Las Vegas and its environs, his love of this desert, all deserts, adds a welcome dimension to his prose. "Behind the dust," he writes in *Desert Solitaire,* "under the vulture-haunted sky, the desert waits—mesa, butte, canyon, reef, sink, escarpment, pinnacle, maze, dry lake, sand dune and barren mountain—untouched by the human mind."[4] The Nevada desert waits, too. And Abbey's fear that it will indeed be touched by a military human mind compels him to write a powerful essay about its essence. "Here is one place, surely, where the human world's confusion and hatred will never reach" [*DR,* 96–97]. Perhaps these merely are words cast into a bottomless desert wishing-well, for this thought that appears on the last page of the MX essay sounds an oddly naive note.

Otherwise, "MX" is a strongly argumentative, and logically argued, piece of prose. Abbey begins his attack subtly. First he quotes liberally from Pentagon brochures, and outlines the basic plan for what he calls a military "shell game." In so doing, he tacitly models his essay as propaganda—turning the Pentagon's polemics back in on themselves, stating his own case forthrightly, and cajoling the reader to agree with his point of view. "The effect of MX on the balance of terror appears vague, unpredictable," he summarizes. "As usual the experts disagree. What is neither vague nor unpredictable is the impact of the project on the farms, ranches, small towns, the water supply, the land and landscape and people, the life both animal and vegetable of the present inhabitants of Nevada and western Utah" [*DR*, 89]. In other words, the Pentagon position is untrustworthy—"vague," "The experts disagree"—while Abbey is to be listened to and respected, his position "neither vague nor unpredictable," his concern focused on the "impact" projected throughout the Great Basin.

Three years ago the Nevada Humanities Committee funded an eighty-page pamphlet entitled, *MX in Nevada: A Humanities Perspective*. A collection of ten short essays, the publication views the MX debate from a variety of perspectives, including the rhetorical. Thomas L. Clark's analysis of the linguistic techniques employed by both proponents and opponents of the MX system spotlights exactly what Edward Abbey means to do. "Part of an audience's response to any proposal," Clark explains, "is determined by the perceived self-interest on the part of the writer or speaker."[5] Surely Abbey's love for the desert fits into this category. In addition, responses may be influenced by such rhetorical techniques as playing on the emotions, intensifying certain arguments, downplaying others, and making a series of collective suggestions that build up an argument over a period of time. Finally, Clark summarizes, "The rhetorical stances taken by proponents and opponents of the MX proposal, whether by accident or design, appear to have three effects: the arguments sometimes convince one through clear and rational thinking; sometimes convince one through creating emotional response; and sometimes confuse one through apparently conflicting statements and figures."[6] Abbey, a determined propagandist, achieves the first two goals while eschewing the trap of the latter. He cogently presents his case by combining the most effective modes of persuasion.

The first six pages of "MX" exemplify the kind of clear thinking that characterizes this author's best prose. Systematically, he takes the Pentagon's own statements and dismembers them, sometimes dissecting them rationally, sometimes pricking them with sarcasm. When a handy brochure insists that the "MX will present new business opportunities for companies during construction and operation," Abbey responds: "The labor, brains, materials, and money required to build the thing must be subtracted from resources that might otherwise be expended upon food, clothing, shelter (human shelter), and, who knows, even love" [DR, 85–86]. "Frills," he adds sardonically.

It is the humorous undercutting of every governmental statement that adds life to Abbey's essay and attracts the reader to his point of view. Two further examples show off the technique. "For real lunacy on the grand scale you need a committee (better yet, an institution), staffed with hundreds and thousands of well-trained technicians, economists, intellectuals, engineers, and administrators" [DR, 84]. Both the Kremlin and the Pentagon fit this description, he decides. But after reading the handiwork of the American "committee," he can come to only one conclusion. "The functional drive-force behind the MX project is not so much military defense as intellectual inertia—the natural institutional tendency to continue along familiar grooves" [DR, 88–89]. Again, no reader can deny the truth of this observation. Even those who embrace the entire MX project must tacitly acknowledge the massive lethargy that blocks almost any governmental movement or change. Abbey merely points out the obvious, then gently twists it until it becomes effective propaganda.

After completing this satiric volley with the Pentagon's prose, he then turns away from the mechanics of argumentation and outlines a personal exploration into the desert country of western Utah and eastern Nevada. "I wanted to see for myself, smell, taste, touch, and divine for myself the sagebrush and juniper, the dry lakes and arid mountains, the color of the light, the feel of the place" [DR, 89]. In so doing, he obeys Clark's second condition for effective persuasion, and argues from the heart.

First he entices his readers by personally luring them into the landscape itself. "We drive on into the shimmering April afternoon. Grand, arid, primeval country opens before us, range after range of purple mountains, each separated from the next by a broad open basin" [DR, 91]. Then, as he does in his other personal histories, he catalogues a collection of desert treasures while rejecting any sort of technological intrusion:

> Contrary to the apparent belief of the military, this region is fully inhabited. It is not empty space. Wide, free, and open, yes, but not empty. The mountains and valleys are presently occupied to the limit of their economic carrying capacity by ranchers, farmers, miners, forest rangers and inspectors of sunsets, and by what remains of the original population of Indians, coyote, deer, black bear, mountain lion, eagles, hawks, buzzards, mice, lizards, snakes, antelope, and wild horses. To make room for MX, its thirty thousand construction workers, and its glacier of iron, steel, cement, and plastic, many of these creatures, both human and otherwise, would have to be displaced. [DR, 89]

No "inspector of sunsets" can read such a passage without feeling an emotional tug, so once again Abbey has met a criterion for convincing prose.

But he does not deal solely in generalizations. As his journey into the wilderness proceeds, he focuses his argument on the landscape's details. He stops, for example, at a desert spring where the stone walls of a Pony Express station still stand. Drinking from the cool seep, he considers the billions of gallons needed to maintain the proposed missile system and he speculates about a source. Down? Into the aquifers beneath the surface? The notion portends a fall of the current water table, a drying-up of the very spring from which he drinks. Without further comment, he allows the reader to reach his own conclusion. The next day he passes alkali flats and dry lake beds that extend from mountain range to mountain range. "What would happen to one of those 750-ton TEL missile transporters," he wonders, "if it had to be driven across or even near one of these lakebeds after a good rain? Might sink to the chassis frame in ole-aginous muck" [*DR*, 94]. Another small word-drawn picture is enough to suggest the larger futility of an entire MX project.

Edward Abbey's prose is at its best when he writes this way. As Clark explains, rhetorical devices sometimes can be confusing, while the proper tactics can be overwhelmingly effective. In "MX" Abbey avoids heavyhandedness, presenting his case cogently, com-bining logic with affection and laughter. The result is a persuasive assessment of what the proposed missile system would do to the Nevada scene.

It is instructive to compare this kind of propaganda with the techniques used by the same author to describe Las Vegas. In the essay discussed earlier, Abbey's sarcasm dominates. "HOWDY PARTNER . . ." Furthermore, the focus wavers between the city itself, the moment in history, and, unaccountably, a later bloody incident of guerrilla warfare. The chief connecting link is the pseudo-synthetic line, "HOWDY PARTNER . . . ," that exposes the superficiality of the environment Abbey perceives. But that con-nection is not enough, and the essay finally fails to convince the reader of much beyond the paucity of modern pleasure palaces. Las Vegas has been stripped bare, but in no freshly meaningful way.

The MX essay, on the other hand, makes an original contribu-tion to an already overly publicized point of view. For the past three years, readers in the western United States have been inundated by arguments opposing any installation of the proposed missile sys-tem, arguments every bit as thoughtful as Abbey's own. "It is al-most inconceivable that the people will have the privilege of con-tinuing the peaceful patterns of life that have become typical of their community," James W. Hulse writes of Pioche, Nevada. "It is highly unlikely that they will continue to have the free access to the millions of acres around them which they and their predecessors have always known. They wait, like the Utes and Shoshones whose culture was overwhelmed by the first white settlers slightly more than a century ago, for a surge of human development mandated by the new capabilities for warfare which are now the primary preoccupation of the government's."[7] Similarly, readers have been bombarded by sincere arguments from the opposite side, proponents of MX who are convinced it would add to the Great Basin economy and to the nation's defense. And the military can sound as emotional, too. "All of the solutions are ugly," one key Air Force general asserted. "But of all the uglies, the MX is the most attractive."[8]

Edward Abbey argues from a somewhat different perspective. What looks most ugly to his eyes is the defilement of a desert landscape, the intrusion of military might upon the sacred energy of the earth, the disappearance of a horizon at once both wild and free. And because he argues logically, because he appeals to one's love of the land, because he laces his prose with a humor that belies the seriousness of the situation, because he is an artist, his essay, "MX," is effective. To be sure, most MX arguments—both pro and con— are written by authors who care in one way or another. But the communication of that personal concern enhances the better pieces of propaganda (see Hulse's essay, for example), while the recital of cold statistics (see any governmental brochure) carries little persuasive power.

So we have come full circle. Just as Clark suggested, the finest propaganda asserts the self-interest of the author. In this case the desert interests Edward Abbey; Las Vegas does not. Or, rather, Las Vegas appeals to him only in a metaphorical sense, as a figurative image of the superficiality in modern existence. Conversely, the Great Basin speaks to him in a much more personal way. To defile its landscape is to damage Abbey himself; to take away its wildness is to subtract a crucial portion of Abbey's soul.

Quite possibly these generalizations hold true for all of his prose. When he writes about industrialization and urban crowding, he slashes aggressively at the "incredible *shit* . . . , the foul diseased and *hideous* cities and towns we live in" [*DS*, 177; italics Abbey's]. When he writes about the landscape, his deep-seated affection for the desert mutes his tone. "Even after years of intimate contact and search this quality of strangeness in the desert remains undimin-

ished. Transparent and intangible as sunlight, yet always and everywhere present, it lures a man on and on, from the red-walled canyons to the smoke-blue ranges beyond, in a futile but fascinating
quest for the great, unimaginable treasure which the desert seems
to promise" [*DS*, 272]. Nevada's Great Basin, undefiled, holds that
promise; Las Vegas does not. Abbey's perception of the Silver State
is but an echo of his interpretation of every portion of the American
West. Cities are to be rejected, and deserts respected. For him,
nothing less will satisfy the human spirit.

So a reader of Abbey's two Nevada essays is instructed in two
ways. First, "HOWDY PARTNER . . ." and "MX" well demonstrate the nature of his propaganda. The former repeats trite aphorisms and observations, while the latter shows his regard for a wilderness worthy of his homage. Each carries its own appeal,
although "MX" would seem to reach a wider audience in a more
profound way. Both, however, are microcosms of their author's
mental outlook. To read "HOWDY PARTNER . . ." and "MX" is
to whet one's appetite for other Abbey prose, to share his vision, to
see with him a western landscape that stretches from Nevada far
into the imagination and beyond. "The land tilts upward, stony
and harsh. The long shadows of the yucca, the cliff rose, the
squawbush, the scrubby juniper stretch across basins of sand, the
hump and hollows of monolithic sandstone—golden in the evening sun. I sense an emptiness ahead. I come to the edge. . . . The
silent desert makes no reply."[9]

NOTES

Nearly two decades have passed since "The Nevada Scene Through
Edward Abbey's Eyes" was written. More Abbey books, both novels and nonfiction, have been published; more governmental en-
croachments have taken place in Nevada. While the MX project is
but a distant memory, the Nuclear Waste Dump currently looms
large. So even though many details of this essay are dated, its analy-

sis of the difficulties created when easterners treat Nevada impru-
dently is all too current.

1. Edward Abbey's novels include: *The Brave Cowboy* (1956); *Fire on the
Mountain* (1962); *Good News* (1980); *The Monkey-Wrench Gang* (1976).
His works of nonfiction include: *Abbey's Road* (1979); *Cactus Country*
(1973); *Desert Solitaire* (1968); *Down the River* (1982); *The Journey Home*
(1977); *Slickrock* (1971). All are available in paperback.

2. Edward Abbey, *The Journey Home* (New York: E. P. Dutton, 1977),
p. 67; further references to this work will be included in the text, with the
letters *JH* followed by the appropriate page number.

3. Edward Abbey, *Down the River* (New York: E. P. Dutton, 1982),
p. 91; further references to this work will be included in the text, with the
letters *DR* followed by the appropriate page number.

4. Edward Abbey, *Desert Solitaire* (New York: Ballantine Books, 1968),
p. 272; further references to this work will be included in the text, with
the letters *DS* followed by the appropriate page number.

5. Thomas L. Clark, "The Rhetoric of MX," in *MX in Nevada: A Humanistic Perspective,* ed. Francis X. Hartigan (Reno: Nevada Humanities
Committee and the Center for Religion and Life, 1980), pp. 16–17.

6. Clark, "The Rhetoric of MX," p. 16.

7. James W. Hulse, "A View from Pioche," in *MX in Nevada: A Humanistic Perspective,* p. 73.

8. Quoted in Joseph A. Fry, "The History of Defense Spending in
Nevada: Preview of the MX?" in *MX in Nevada: A Humanistic Perspective,* p. 42.

9. Edward Abbey, *Abbey's Road* (New York: E. P. Dutton, 1979),
pp. 194, 196.

PART II

Other Western Writers of the Purple Sage

J ust as American nonfiction has developed since Henry David Thoreau made Walden Pond famous, just as environmental literature has changed since Edward Abbey first drafted *Desert Solitaire,* so the genre of the Western has evolved from the days of Owen Wister and Zane Grey. Walter Van Tilburg Clark, in *The Ox-Bow Incident,* showed us that good and evil are not always clearly delineated, and that the white hats may not always prevail. Subsequent writers took the formula several steps further, interposing the complications of gender and race and culture and vicissitudes. As a result, new western literature is flourishing. I often tell my students that some of the best writing in America is currently being published in western places about western spaces. This section of *Reader of the Purple Sage* not only introduces some noteworthy examples but also indicates ways in which the old categorical patterns have been thoroughly dispersed.

British-born Isabella Bird trekked alone from California to Colorado. The introduction to the Comstock edition of her book, *A Lady's Life in the Rocky Mountains,* sets the scene for this inquisitive woman's adventures. Traveling alone, or sometimes in the company of a notorious desperado, Isabella Bird rode horseback, scaled mountains, braved fierce winter storms, and learned to take care of herself in the wild. She was the prototype for today's women in the wilderness. Equally ahead of its time, Mildred Walker's *Winter Wheat* is perhaps the first American novel with a heroine who happily resolves her own personal destiny on her own terms. The book has always been a favorite with my Women and Literature students. I'm convinced it's a classic unfortunately forgotten, so I'm eager to attract new readers to its pages. Even though I've never been known as a feminist critic, I've always had a keen appreciation for women writers, especially western women writers, who are breaking new ground. These two, Bird and Walker, set the stage for our talented contemporaries—essayists and novelists like Teresa Jordan and Molly Gloss, for example, or Linda Hasselstrom and Linda Hogan, or Terry Tempest Williams and Leslie Marmon Silko, or the Zwingers, Ann and Susan.

At the other end of the spectrum is Archie Binns, who imagined the typical wagon train that proceeded along the Oregon Trail. His historical novel, though conventional, exemplifies western American literature as our childhood storybooks imagined it to be. Indeed, *This Land Is Bright* mythologizes Western settlement in very satisfactory ways. New historicism tells us, however, that the reality of the Old West differed significantly from the old pulp and Hollywood versions. Most contemporary Western novelists—and most contemporary films—reinterpret and transform the once-popular, male-dominated western myth. *Shane,* for example, has been reshaped from generation to generation. Its movie versions demonstrate how viewers respond to the same story reproduced in different decades. Alan Ladd becomes Clint Eastwood, a reincarnation that author Jack Schaefer surely didn't foresee when he visualized *Shane* in 1952. Larry McMurtry, however, purposely manipulated his readers' expectations, turning an ordinary cattle drive into *Lonesome Dove* by inverting his story lines completely. I personally think *Lonesome Dove* is one of the best of recent westerns, though many other critics have disagreed. Certainly, it's an insightful retelling of history reconceived.

Then there's Wallace Stegner, my William Faulkner of the West until a more farsighted visionary comes along. If *Lonesome Dove* is a three-star western novel, *Angle of Repose* is even better, a four-star narration of western settlement and cyclical history and human aspirations. Despite the fact that I admire Stegner's writing enormously, however, I acknowledge that he wasn't always consistent. In "Stegner and Stewardship," I take the master to task. Again, not everyone agrees with my assessment. But I am convinced that my interpretation of Stegner's environmental stance—his sometimes quirky insistence on our responsibility to the land—accurately reflects the balance and the complexity of his beliefs.

A list of talented contemporary western writers lengthens day by day. If I had time to write a dozen more essays about a dozen more authors of the purple sage, I'd start with James Galvin's *The Meadow,* which I nominated for the Western Literature Association tally of the best fiction published in the 1990s. I'm almost as fond of Molly Gloss's *The Jump-Off Creek.* Both novels touched my heart; both novels get to the heart of how humans interact with the land. Most critics, in fact, say that the defining characteristic of western American literature today is its profound affinity for scenery and setting. I agree. Talented western writers such as Galvin and Gloss—like Abbey and Stegner before them—are constantly questioning, probing, and interpreting what it means to live in a world surrounded by the purple sage.

CHAPTER SEVEN

Introduction to
A Lady's Life in the Rocky Mountains

Isabella Bird first set foot on American soil in 1854. After taking a Cunard steamer across the Atlantic to Halifax, the young English-woman then took a smaller "something post-diluvian"—as she described it—down the coast to Maine. Her arrival there, at the age of twenty-two, marked the beginning of a remarkable career. "As I stepped upon those shores on which the sanguine suppose that the Anglo-Saxon race is to renew the vigour of its youth," she wrote later, "I felt that a new era of my existence had begun." Indeed it had.

A twentieth-century imagination may well have trouble conceptualizing the kind of nineteenth-century existence Isabella Bird pursued. At a time when most women went nowhere unescorted, she travelled thousands of miles by herself. At a time when most women endured travel hardships to help settle new lands, she vacationed for pure pleasure. At a time when most women focused on hearth and home, she pioneered her way not only across America but through the Far East as well. At a time when most women kept their letters and journals private, she published hers. At a time when most women led sheltered lives, Isabella Bird filled her existence with a series of astonishing adventures.

Those adventures began because she was in ill-health. When a physician recommended ocean air, she made immediate plans to visit America. She spent 1854, then, meandering from Canada to Boston, from Boston to Cincinnati, from there to the end of the line at Rock Island, on to Chicago and Detroit, up the St. Lawrence to Quebec, back to Boston, to Halifax, and home. She covered several thousand miles, her illness almost forgotten in her enthusiasm for new scenes.

Two years after she returned to England, she published her first travel book, *The Englishwoman in America* (1856). A reworking of notes taken, journal entries transcribed, and letters sent, *The Englishwoman in America* pictures a self-willed, inquisitive young lady enjoying somewhat conventional tourism in a rather unconventional way. Many American travellers found ocean liners, railroads, and stagecoach adventures delightful, but few single women did so with such verve. "I have often heard it stated," remarks this independent soul, "that a lady, no matter what her youth or attractions might be, could travel alone through every State in the Union, and never meet with anything but attention and respect." Testing that supposition both in populated areas and far from the amenities of civilization, she most frequently travelled alone. A five-year marriage, quickly terminated by the death of her husband in 1886, provided the only exception.

Despite her independence and her preference for solitary travel, however, Isabella Bird was a gregarious woman who often enjoyed other people. Carrying letters of introduction and sometimes just announcing herself, she frequently spent her nights in strangers' houses and paid special attention to the patterns of their lives. Her books are filled with descriptions of and observations about the people she met. While she wrote cuttingly of those she disliked, she was exceedingly generous to those she admired. Nonetheless, her prose is sprinkled with such testy one-liners as: "Solitude is infinitely preferable to uncongeniality, and is bliss when compared with repulsiveness, so I was thoroughly glad when I got rid of my escort and set out upon the prairie alone."

The range of her solitary adventures is nothing short of phenomenal. Still suffering from the chronic spinal disorder that would bother her for the rest of her life, she returned to Canada and the eastern United States several more times. She also travelled to the Mediterranean, made a Hawaiian trip that resulted in *Six Months in the Sandwich Islands* (1875), and spent a season in the western part of the North American continent. *A Lady's Life in the Rocky Mountains* (1879) tells of that 1873 trip. It does not, however, mark the end of her travels.

A list of her subsequent books only begins to suggest the distances journeyed. *Unbeaten Tracks in Japan* (1880), *The Golden Chersonese* (1883), *Journeys in Persia and Kurdistan* (1891), *Among the Tibetans* (1894), *Korea and Her Neighbors* (1898), *The Yangtze Valley and Beyond* (1899), and *Chinese Pictures* (1900) all sign the directions she went. Propelled by an interest in missionary work and an eagerness to establish hospitals in out-of-the-way places, this staunch, well-to-do Anglican returned to the Far East again and again. Conventional tourist spots held no interest for her, so she trudged off to mountains and valleys where few visitors had walked before. With only coolies in attendance, she managed to see more of eastern Asia than any woman—and perhaps any man—of her generation.

The Royal Geographic Society, recognizing her accomplishments, elected her a Fellow in 1892. The first woman to be so named, she also became the first woman to address that august body when she spoke to them in 1897 about her trip to Szechwan. She was also a best-selling author, for her travel books were among the most popular written in the latter part of the nineteenth century. Seven editions of *A Lady's Life in the Rocky Mountains*, for example, were printed in the first three years after its initial publication.

Book reviewers as well as book buyers found her work impressive. The *Athenaeum* called her "a model tourist"; the *Spectator,* "an ideal traveller." One nineteenth-century enthusiast praised her by saying, "She has regard to the essentials of a scene or episode, and describes them with a simplicity that is as effective as it is artless.

Humour is here of a quality precisely suited to a traveller; never obtrusive, but never deficient when the time comes,—oiling the wheels of action just in time to counteract friction." Writing of *The Golden Chersonese,* that reviewer might well be characterizing *A Lady's Life in the Rocky Mountains.* "Not the least noteworthy among Miss Bird's gifts is a heaven-sent faculty for having adventures . . . Things turn out as if by special inspiration. She trusts to fortune, to what ought to happen, and it does happen . . . Her whole experience is a singular combination of the natural and the dramatic." Such is Isabella Bird's experience in Colorado, too.

Her Rocky Mountain adventures actually begin on the train from San Francisco, when she pauses briefly at Truckee, California, because she wants to see Lake Tahoe. The description of her stopover captures in miniature the flavor of all her adventures. She's alone. The train, drawing into a rough masculine setting, deposits her near a hotel with meager facilities. She spends the remainder of the night in a squalid windowless room, her sleep broken only by gunshots somewhere outside.

The next day, "slipping on my Hawaiian riding dress over a silk shirt, and a dust cloak over all," she locates a livery stable and arranges for a horse. The solo ride to Tahoe takes her through a tangled forest, alongside a tumbling river, and on to a series of picturesque views. One sight—a glimpse of snowcapped peaks—"was one of those glorious surprises in scenery which make one feel as if one must bow down and worship."

She has little time for scenic adoration, however, for this jaunt is taking place in what still was relatively unpredictable territory. When a bear rears out of the underbrush and her startled horse plunges out of control, panorama turns to panic. Isabella Bird suddenly finds herself on foot with a long, lonely walk ahead. But without hesitation and without complaint, she proceeds toward her goal.

The pattern of this first chapter of *A Lady's Life in the Rocky Mountains* repeats itself throughout the book. Alone in an unfamiliar setting, the traveller determinedly sets out to do exactly what she wants to do. She plans her own route, makes her own arrangements, and goes unattended. When difficulties arise, she copes. An intrepid spirit, she never fusses about situations she cannot control. Whether the problem is a bear, a snowstorm, an impassable trail, hunger, or an unexpected bank failure—all hardships that disrupt *A Lady's Life*—Isabella Bird not only copes successfully but does so with alacrity. Even the inability to recapture her mount in the midst of bear country leaves her unperturbed. The horse, "throwing up his heels as an act of final defiance, went off at full speed in the direction of Truckee, with the saddle over his shoulders and the great wooden stirrups thumping his side, while I trudged ignominiously along in the dust, laboriously carrying the bag and saddle-blanket." Undaunted, she carries on.

Her tone characterizes her point of view. No danger is too formidable; no vicissitude too difficult to solve. No matter what happens, she remains cheerfully prepared to go another mile. For example, when another horse dumps her unceremoniously and then, rolling, knocks her over a shelf, she calls the descent "fatuous." Several falls later, she observes: "I was cut and bruised, scratched and torn. A spine of cactus penetrated my foot, and some vicious thing cut the back of my neck. Poor Mrs. C. (her guide's wife) was much bruised, and I pitied her, for she got no fun out of it as I did."

Equally fun was her climb a few weeks later of Colorado's Long's Peak. Its fourteen thousand–foot summit had first been scaled only five years earlier, so Isabella Bird hardly had a beaten trail to follow. In fact, Mountain Jim had to haul her up "like a bale of goods," while she laughs about her "fatigue, giddiness, and pain from bruised ankles, and arms half pulled out of their sockets." On top at last and suffering from dehydration, she gasps for breath and rapturously surveys an unrivaled view.

The way down was no easier. "I had various falls, and once hung by my frock, which caught on a rock, and Jim severed it with his hunting knife, upon which I fell into a crevice full of snow." Half carried after that, she is finally laid to rest in what she calls "a humiliating termination of a great exploit." Yet she is up and about only a few hours later, her ordeal forgotten in the memory of some truly spectacular scenery.

It is interesting to compare this adventure with another Colorado climb made just a few years later by another intrepid Englishwoman. Mrs. Rose Pender, accompanying her husband to view his ranching investments, describes her travels in *A Lady's Experiences in the Wild West in 1883*. Since she was neither an unescorted lady nor an inveterate explorer, her adventures are comparatively unexceptional. Nonetheless, she does climb Pike's Peak. Shod in old patent leather boots wrapped in burlap, clutching her umbrella while nipping on brandy and cheese, she, too, carries on. "The snow was very deep and not hard, and often I slipped through up to my waist, struggling out as best I could. . . . My breath came in sobs—my feet felt like iron, and a terrible pain at my chest warned me" to proceed carefully. But the view was "wonderful," the coloring "splendid," and she "enjoyed the whole thing thoroughly."

Mrs. Pender's narrative is yet another example of popular nineteenth-century travel literature. The genre began as English men and women discovered an audience eager to read of American phenomena and frailties. Especially appealing at first were books like Mrs. Frances Trollope's *Domestic Manners of the Americana* (1832) and Charles Dickens's *American Notes* (1842) that denigrated certain social and political customs. Isabella Bird's *The Englishwoman in America,* while not so derogatory, followed the familiar pattern of incisive and comparative observation. Francis Parkman's *The Oregon Trail* (1849) took the travel narrative west. The latter part of the century, then, found other British travellers ranging further and further into the imagined wilderness. And just as women came to be the best-known recorders of journeys through the eastern United States, so women later achieved prominence as chroniclers of western scenes. Mrs. Pender's descriptions are first-rate; Isabella Bird's, even better.

Perhaps because she wrote so many travel narratives, the author of *A Lady's Life in the Rocky Mountains* learned to master her effusiveness and to characterize scenery without using clichés. Where her first book might contain "the rosy flush of a winter dawn," her last one—*The Yangtze Valley and Beyond*—designs "a red and gold sunset of crystalline clearness and beauty." In between these volumes are others with page after page of crisply developed observations that sound refreshingly specific when contrasted with Francis Parkman's "features of grandeur" or Mrs. Pender's "picturesque scenery."

A major reason, in fact, for the continued popularity of *A Lady's Life* is Isabella Bird's ability to write well. Not only does she view her surroundings evocatively, but she is able to retell adventures with clarity and vigor. Potential catastrophes turn into amusing anecdotes, while minor setbacks are optimistically recast. Equally intriguing are the people she meets—the ostensible desperado who "has pathos, poetry, and humor," or the teenager, "a sour, repellent-looking creature, with as much manners as a pig," or even real animals, "large and small, stinging, humming, buzzing, striking, rasping, devouring!"

In fresh, incisive prose, Isabella Bird reveals her courage, her resourcefulness, and her invincible good humor. She also shows her respect for the Rocky Mountain West and for all the distant lands she explored. While her first book closed by praising the glories of British soil, *A Lady's Life* sounds a much more universal note. There the inveterate explorer articulates her creed toward all the wonders around her. Writing of a specific view, she might well be explaining her entire philosophy of travel. "Estes Park is mine," she announces, "mine by right of love, appropriation, and appreciation; by the seizure of its peerless sunrises and sunsets, its glorious afterglow, its blazing noons, its hurricanes sharp and furious, its wild auroras, its glories of mountain and forest, of canyon, lake, and river, and the stereotyping them all in my memory." Such was her belief in the land, and in herself, wherever she roamed.

CHAPTER EIGHT

A Montana Maturity

The pattern for a cowboy novel of initiation has long been familiar to readers of pulp literature. An innocent or naive young man goes west, and there finds himself sucked into a maelstrom of angry Indians, malevolent gunslingers, assorted perpetrators of injustice, and an indifferent wilderness. Each of these external challenges poses an educational test which must be met and passed.

The young man learns his lessons well. Victorious at the end of his story, he reaches a plateau of maturity and self-knowledge by means of his own emerging physical competency. Even in those western novels that stretch beyond this Zane Grey/Louis L'Amour formula, experience develops from innocence when a naive youth bravely confronts the realities of a hostile milieu. But what if the hero is female? What if she is a young girl who naturally bears all the strengths and weaknesses of her sex, a young lady who finds herself in conflict with an unforgiving western world, a young woman who must survive?

Unfortunately there are too few samples from which to generalize. More often than not, those novels which feature a heroine— Grey's *Light of Western Stars,* for example—rely on a male hero rather than female competency to teach a girl the code of the West.

In western fiction, a young woman rarely manages an initiation into adulthood on her own. A happy exception, however, is Mildred Walker's little-known 1943 novel, *Winter Wheat*. Written by an author whose commitment to female individualism appears throughout the pages of her fiction, *Winter Wheat* attests to a girl's ability to learn from her own mistakes, from her own misperceptions, and from her native western environment. It is a western woman's novel of initiation.

The story begins and ends in the dry wheat farming country of northern Montana. Set at the start of World War II, it follows two years in the life of Ellen Webb, an attractive college freshman who must drop out of school after a lean crop season. She takes a job at a distant teacherage, hoping not only to earn enough money to send herself back to college but also to escape what she interprets as the insidious influence of her emotionally troubled parents. The long winter, dark and cold in northern Montana, initially stifles the growth of this inexperienced young woman. Nothing seems to go right.

Ellen's city-bred boyfriend, after one horrified look at her native surroundings, breaks their engagement. Then her work at the isolated one-room schoolhouse is cut short after the accidental death of one of her students and after her friendship with the father of another student leads to some unfortunate speculations. Finally she must return to the home of her parents, to the sphere of her Russian-born mother and her long-suffering father. But it is there that she puts the pieces of her life together—confronting her family, recognizing her own flawed reasoning, and solving at last the complicated puzzle that is Ellen Webb.

To trace how her initiation from innocence to experience differs from the process followed by a male counterpart, we first must define the pattern used by male authors long before anyone had imagined either "female" fiction or the "western" novel. Jerome Buckley, in his study *The Season of Youth*, abstracts the principle characteristics of the genre commonly called the *Bildungsroman*. Typically the pattern follows the path of a sensitive child who "grows up in the country or in a provincial town" and who must go elsewhere to find his mature self.

Before he departs, the prototypical boy "finds constraints, social and intellectual, placed upon the free imagination," and his family, "especially his father," seems hostile, antagonistic, and quite impervious. So the lad leaves the repressive atmosphere of home (and also the relative innocence), to make his way independently in the city (usually London, in English novels of this kind). There his real "education" begins. His experience "involves at least two love affairs or sexual encounters, one debasing, one exalting, and demands that in this respect and others the hero reappraise his values. By the time he has decided, after painful soul-searching, the sort of accommodation to the modern world he can honestly make, he has left his adolescence behind and entered upon his maturity" (17–18). Buckley softens the strictures of the pattern by acknowledging that very few novels follow the steps absolutely, but he insists nonetheless that no true *Bildungsroman* ignores more than two or three of the basic elements—"childhood, the conflict of generations, provinciality, the larger society, self-education, alienation, ordeal by love, the search for a vocation and a working philosophy" (18).

It appears that a formula western like Grey's *Heritage of the Desert* borrows such characteristics as the self-education (John Hare teaches himself to survive in a wicked sandstorm), the alienation (Hare feels isolated in the stand-offish Mormon community), the ordeal by love (Hare adores Mescal but is separated from her through much of the novel), and the search for a vocation (Hare, after learning to herd sheep and break wild horses, discovers his talents as a rancher), only to use them superficially. *Heritage of the Desert* is, after all, a piece of escape fiction rather than a piercing analytical portrait.

Winter Wheat, on the other hand, incorporates such qualities into a full-fledged and somewhat sophisticated American *Bildungsroman*. Where the formula western contracts the pattern into a repetitive lock-step story, *Winter Wheat* expands it into a provocative and intellectually satisfying narrative line. Certainly Mildred Walker's tale exemplifies a generic potential that all western writers, male and female, could achieve if only they would move from the formula to the principles behind it.

Keynoting *Winter Wheat* is the conflict between generations. Because she sorely misunderstands her parents' relationship, Ellen Webb misinterprets the quality of their life together. Because she knows her mother lied to her father and trapped him into marriage, she refuses to admit that the basis of that marriage is a deep, abiding love. The reader recognizes the depth of the Webbs' feelings, but for three-fourths of the novel the naive heroine sees only conflict. "Mom was standing in front of the stove. She was tired too, but it was Dad she thought of. Maybe, all these years she had been trying to make up to him for . . . tricking him" (*WW* 140–1). Ellen can empathize with neither her parents' emotions nor their intellects.

> I felt a kind of resentment. They were fools. The last war was to blame for Dad's ill-health ever since, it was to blame for his marrying Mom and all their bitterness and hatred and trouble. I couldn't understand them. They didn't even seem to notice that I was quiet. (*WW* 230)

Indeed, Ellen cannot perceive the wrongheadedness of her own diction—"bitterness and hatred and trouble." She thinks, instead, that she fully comprehends a deep-seated unhappiness and an apparent disillusionment at the core of each of her parents.

To escape, Ellen leaves her provincial environment for a Minnesota college. There, under the year-long tutelage of Gil Borden, she attains a measure of urban sophistication that, after her return to Gotham, Montana, makes her feel even more suffocated by her childhood surroundings. Gil's brief visit confirms her shallow perceptions. "For the first time in my life I noticed how thick the plates and cups were; that they didn't match" (*WW* 81). And at dinner that night, Ellen compares her mother's hands, "large and red and checked with black, . . . the broken nail," with Gil's, "their shapeliness, the wrists that were as slender as mine" (*WW* 82).

When Gil aborts his vacation after staying only three days, and pre-cipitously breaks their engagement—"I am afraid we are too sepa-rated in background and interests and ways of looking at things to be happy together" (*WW* 108), he writes—her poor judgment is corroborated. "'I should think people would go stark, raving crazy out here,' Gil had said. 'I should think they'd end by hating each other'" (*WW* 105). Tacitly, Ellen agrees.

More pressing now is her own need to escape "the unpainted box of a house and a barn and a shed [that] stood out ugly and bare" (*WW* 99). She cannot return to college because hail has de-stroyed much of the Webb wheat, so she escapes instead to a distant teacherage near Prairie Butte. For a while she relishes her misery there, enjoying her lonely isolation in a masochistic sort of way. Then, gradually, events force her to assess her own self-worth.

A retarded student, too slow to think for himself, gets lost in a blizzard and dies. The unfortunate accident challenges Ellen physi-cally—she braves the storm to search for the boy—and tests her psychologically. For the first time in her life, she looks squarely at her own inadequacies. "All day I had tried to keep my mind full of other things, but underneath I knew I could have saved Robert if I had only watched him more closely. Then I'd try to push that thought away. That night, lying wide-awake in bed, I stopped try-ing . . . I wouldn't be afraid of this; it was a time I had to remember; it was a part of my life" (*WW* 216). She recognizes, too, the kind of strength that comes from self-knowledge. "I found something out that night," she admits. "A thing doesn't hurt you so much if you take it to you as it does when you keep pushing it away" (*WW* 216).

A second trial at the remote schoolhouse comes after the young teacher makes a new friend, Warren Harper, a widower and the father of one of the pupils. Lonely and rather at loose ends himself, Warren offers strength and understanding during the ordeal of the blizzard and afterwards. Yet his presence itself leads to trouble, for late one night he shows up drunk at the teacherage and refuses to leave. When Ellen mistakenly lets him sleep off his binge in the schoolroom, the damage is done. Other parents find out, accuse her of immoral behavior, and dismiss her on the spot. Paradoxically, her isolation has led to greater alienation, and so drives her back to her family once more. "I almost wished I didn't have to go home, that I could be free of Mom and Dad and their hate and even their love for me. But I knew I couldn't. If I went away and got a job somewhere, in the city, I would feel I had run away" (*WW* 283). But Ellen has learned not to run away. Slowly emerging from her youthful pose into a more self-assured stature, the young woman returns to Gotham, faces her destiny, and completes her initiation.

Several events test her developing strengths. Secondhand, she learns of Gil's death in an Air Force training accident, a misadventure that forces her to take stock of her own emotional commitments once more. When Warren enlists in the service, she admits her affection and concern for him, but rejects his promise of love. Indeed, Ellen is unable to evaluate the nature of real love until she learns to respect the marriage of her parents. In two consecutive scenes, she immaturely confronts first her mother and then her father about the quality of their relationship. "Mom made a sound of disgust in her throat . . . '*Yolochka,* you don't know how love is yet'" (*WW* 317). Her father is equally bemused by his daughter's questions.

> I thought back over the things Dad had said. Even when I had made it easy for him he wouldn't say anything against Mom. He had acted almost as though he had not liked my criticizing her. And he had gone on to try to make me understand her as he did . . . My own thought startled me . . . I had to stop and look at it. AS HE DID! (*WW* 327; italics Walker's)

Mulling over this startling recognition, just as she introspectively considered the sense of Robert's death, Ellen climbs her final hurdle. Now she not only can evaluate the place of love in her own life but also can estimate fairly love's role in others'. "Why had I worried about them?" she concludes. "I had been as blind in this world as Mom had said. They had love that was deep-rooted and stronger than love that grows easily. It gave me faith for my own life" (*WW* 340–1). Thus she finally evolves a working philosophy, passes the last test in her *Bildungsroman* initiation, and becomes an adult. A comprehension of real love gives her faith for the future.

Interestingly enough, that comprehension does not propel her into Warren's arms. As a matter of fact, she is one of only a handful of mid-twentieth-century female heroes without a man at her novel's close. Instead of relying on a conventional happy ending, Walker trusts her protagonist with an undefined future. The reader doesn't know exactly what will happen to Ellen, but surely she will be happy. Not only can she take care of herself but, more important, she can judge herself (and others) honestly. Like so many *Bildungsroman* heroes—Stephen Dedalus and Dickens's original Pip come to mind—Ellen Webb is destined to move confidently beyond the pages of her tale.

In effect, this young woman from Montana has pursued most of the steps found in the *Bildungsroman* formulations of English fiction. Bound by her own sense of Great Plains provinciality, she struggles to move from a childlike immaturity to the adulthood she desires. In part, her pre-judgments make the move a difficult one; in part, conflict with her parents thwarts her course. Two "ordeals by love"—her infatuation with Gil and her later estrangement from Warren—produce further barriers that are difficult to surmount. Nonetheless, each of these relationships helps establish her growing self-awareness. The list of parallels to the *Bildungsroman* pattern continues with an increased alienation from her family and with her utter isolation at the teacherage. Only after Ellen develops a "working philosophy" does she embark on a course of maturity that leads to a realization of the potential that has been buried beneath her immature facade. Thus does she leave her adolescence behind.

Her character development is not wholly identical with Jerome Buckley's textbook conception, however, because both her female nature and her western heritage engender some basic differences. The fact that she is a young woman directs Ellen's story in certain ways. Her sex determines her fate—not only would no male teacher be fired under such innocent circumstances, but a man would have options other than a return to his parents. Despite her pretenses, Ellen has little choice. Furthermore, her close family ties parallel an inordinate interest in what might be called "feminine values." The assessment of love often is reinforced by a surplus of domestic details, like the mismatched dishes that suggest a mismatched relationship. And, where Buckley suggests that a young man more often comes into conflict with his father, Ellen's own relationship with her mother lies at the heart of her emotional stagnation. In several conventional ways, then, *Winter Wheat* can be labeled "women's fiction."

It cannot, however, be termed "trite." Both the dismissal from the teacherage and the decision to return to Gotham evolve naturally from 1940's beliefs. Walker imposes neither artificial barriers nor inappropriate conventions; Ellen's choices are restricted by the mores of her time. Her values are those of her time, too, since her interest in the niceties of homemaking befit the Great Plains heritage that surrounds her. The author describes the curtains, the couch, dish-washing, the egg- gathering simply because these items and activities are significant images in the lives of the Webbs. Unlike so many of today's romance fiction writers, Walker never drops domesticity into the narrative simply for the sake of attracting a female audience but only uses details of farm-life to echo her themes artistically.

Even more crucial to the novel's meaning is Ellen's communion with her mother. From the beginning, the two women seem at odds with each other—the daughter, withdrawn and judgmental, the mother, apparently incapable of understanding. In many ways, the plot is reminiscent of thousands of mother/daughter disjunctions. As it develops, however, some complex dimensions are added. Mrs. Webb demonstrates a sensitivity that belies her harsh peasant ancestry, while Ellen is initially slow to apprehend her mother's worth. Yet, when Ellen does transcend her own inadequate perceptions, she does so by learning from a maternal model. Quite different from sounding an echo to certain feminist theories, this pattern also has little in common with the conventional rejection of the father found in the *Bildungsromans* described in *The Season of Youth*. Together, not separately and not with insurmountable hostility, the Webb females work out a comfortable relationship that adds maturity to the behavior of both.

But the story of Ellen's maturation is also a western story. Her schooling, for example, takes place in the out-of-doors rather than from books. When she leaves the so-called "repressions" of home, no London waits on the horizon, just a hostile physical environment of failed crops and harsh snows to test her severely. Even so, she tames no wild horses, bests no rustlers, wins no fast-draw contest. In fact, she does not even live in surroundings conducive to that sort of activity, for dry wheat farming is not only a slow, unalluring process but it takes place long after the settlement of the frontier. So Ellen cannot possibly undergo the traditional tests of a frontier way of life. A product of the twentieth century, she must face the psychological trials of an altered western milieu.

Walter Van Tilburg Clark predicated this new mode when he imagined *The Ox-Bow Incident*. Even though he chose to set that novel in the Old West, he interlaced its environment with problems from the modern age. Innocence—Gerald Tetley's, Art Croft's—becomes experience when unalterable physical events spark profound psychological upheavals. A far cry from the muscular trials of pulp fiction, *The Ox-Bow Incident* projects mental duress and painful subjectivity into cowboy country. *Winter Wheat* does the same. Except that its author chooses a contemporary setting and a female hero, *Winter Wheat*'s narrative line follows a similar pattern. Physical events—the hail, the blizzard, the war, the death of Gil—precipitate psychological change. But like *The Ox-Bow Incident,* the real source of *Winter Wheat*'s energy comes from the forces within a human being rather than from a show of external bravado.

Here, then, is a crucial difference between the formula western and the intellectually provocative western. Where a *Heritage of the Desert* relies on a sandstorm or evil cattlemen for antagonists, an

READER OF THE PURPLE SAGE

Ox-Bow Incident or a *Winter Wheat* traces its elements back to the heads and hearts of the protagonists themselves. Ellen Webb, for example, is her own worst enemy.

> Slowly the thing I didn't want to know bore in on me like the awful rising heat at harvesttime. People made messes of their lives and then they had to live with them. Life didn't turn out right because you expected it to. There had never been any real love between Mom and Dad. (*WW* 106)

This confused, inadequate judgment is Ellen's own. Neither the result of a hostile environment nor the product of personal enmity, it arises from the main character's own faulty mental processes. Yet, in keeping with the novel's western tone, the consequent psychological revelations remain metaphorically, if not literally, tied to the land.

The final proof of Ellen's psychological change is a measure of that landscape—the winter wheat. A mature young woman harvests the mental crop necessary for her full development.

> But I thought often of Anna Petrovna and Ben Webb plowing this same dirt their first spring in Montana. I thought of them hardly speaking all day. I knew so well how Anna Petrovna's face could look when it closed all her feelings inside, and I knew how Ben Webb could look when he was discouraged and tired and sick. I thought of them going up to that unpainted house under the coulee and eating in silence and lying down beside each other at night. That they could plow under their hate and bitterness and grow any love for each other seemed a greater miracle than the spring. Sometimes it was hard to believe, I had believed in their hate so long, but I could look over and see the green of the winter wheat. . . . I took it as a kind of proof. (*WW* 334–5)

As Walker's controlling metaphor, the wheat grows along with Ellen throughout the novel. Buried, at first, under frozen snow-covered ground, winter wheat emerges when the sun finally warms the earth. Then, subject to late blizzards, hail, drought, and grass-hoppers, it battles to survive. Ellen equates its presence to love, heavy-handedly deciding that "It's been there all winter and it's had cold and snow on it and it hasn't been hurt any. See how green it is? How it's coming in spite of everything? That's the way love is" (*WW* 331). Walker, however, implies that winter wheat stands for more because it struggles against the harsh conditions just as all humans must strive against the inherent setbacks in life. So when Ellen and her parents celebrate their new crop on the novel's final page—"There's places where it winter-killed, but some of those spots were just wind-blown. It came through better than I thought it could," says Ellen's father. "It'll blaze now" (*WW* 340)—the reader knows that Ben Webb subconsciously is referring to his daughter, too.

Like all true westerns, this one reverts back to the land. Even though it imaginatively stretches the boundaries of the western novel almost beyond recognition, *Winter Wheat* finally relies on the earth itself to explain fully the germination and maturation of its female hero. Where a young Englishman goes to the city, a young westerner goes to the soil. Both, in the best fiction, develop through an inner strength, both incorporate external knowledge to expand an internal awareness, and both leave their stories to stride confidently into an unknown future. But Ellen's future, like her past and present, involves the land. Like winter wheat, she grows best under Montana's big sky; her western initiation and her female initiation are successful only when natural surroundings and cognitive maturity combine.

WORKS CITED

Buckley, Jerome. *The Season of Youth*. Cambridge, MA: Harvard UP, 1974.

Walker, Mildred. *Winter Wheat*. NY: Harcourt, Brace, Jovanovich, 1943.

CHAPTER NINE

Introduction to *The Land Is Bright*

The decade of the 1930s opened with America plunging into the depths of an economic depression and closed with a nation facing the specter of war. It was not a particularly happy time, as the country's leaders and workers struggled with bank failures, the Dust Bowl, unemployment, poverty and, across the ocean, increasing foreign aggression. With headlines suggesting the worst, readers turned from their newspapers to seek something better. Stories in the 1930s, then, were created for audiences who welcomed narrative escape. By the end of the decade, the inevitable result seemed clear. Among the most popular novels and films were those that conveyed dualities—despair laced with hope, failure transformed to success, nightmare tempered by dreams.

Two major 1939 works especially underscore such a dichotomy, exposing the dark side of the American landscape while simultaneously offering a ray of light. John Steinbeck's *The Grapes of Wrath* won the Pulitzer Prize that year. Even though many readers found Steinbeck's California novel relentlessly depressing, the final scene at least symbolically suggested a future more auspicious than the past. Likewise, *Gone with the Wind* projected an archetypal 1939 heroine onto the big screen, a Scarlett O'Hara who could face the worst and optimistically believe, "Tomorrow is another day." Into this mixed milieu of harsh reality and rosy promise came a lesser-known novel that followed the same pattern. Reissued here by the Oregon State University Press, Archie Binns's *The Land Is Bright* meshed perfectly with the other Darwinistic fiction of its age.

The Land Is Bright was published by Charles Scribner's Sons on February 27th, 1939, and sold in hardcover for $2.50 a copy. It recounts the misfortunes of one wagon train en route to the West along the Oregon Trail. In the spring of 1852, the Greenfields, the Blacks, the Lanes, the Trimbles, the Thomases, and their assorted companions crossed the Missouri River and set out across the plains. Before the survivors sighted the Columbia that fall, they had faced hardship, sickness, deprivation, and death. "All these emigrants," observes the schoolmaster when their wagon train leaves Kanesville for the prairies beyond, "all of us in this great, white caravan, starting out in the springtime, starting out in the morning—all of us are pilgrims to oblivion." Yet this so-called oblivion simultaneously became the Promised Land in the eyes of these beholders. Impelled by the same force that fired Steinbeck's Joads, the same spirit that brought Scarlett through the Civil War, the same instincts for survival, Binns's pioneers were carried westward by a vision of the possibilities that lay at the end of the Oregon Trail.

Nothing could stop them, and this explains why their story was so popular with readers whose contemporary world seemed dismal and bleak. As one reviewer wrote in the New Haven *Journal-Courier,* "We never grow tired of these accounts, we Americans; possibly because we are reminded by them of the rigors and the vigors of which we were capable when young, and for which we are, perhaps, less capable, now." That same reviewer went on to applaud *The Land Is Bright*'s protagonists, noting that "where they went there were no relief agencies to give them food if they could not find work. There were no government credit bureaus to buoy them up if they lost their own substance." His words were fairly typical of the initial responses to Binns's 1939 book; most reviewers sounded a common refrain. "In this day when so many are running to the government for help instead of trying to help themselves," proclaimed Max Miller in the San Diego *Union,* "this novel has a special timely meaning. It is a mirror to what we were once, and could be again." Working through some unpleasant details and depressing scenes of historic nightmare, Binns leads his readers along a trail that finally will culminate in victory. In so doing, he plots a formula for success.

Archie Binns was well equipped to write such a narrative, for he himself was a product of the American Dream. Born in western Washington in 1899, the son of a stump-farmer and part-time logger, Binns went on to graduate from Stanford with a degree in philosophy. He earned most of the money for his own education. After graduation, he moved to New York, where he worked for a small publishing firm and began to write his own books as well. The first, *The Maiden Voyage* (1931), was written in collaboration with Felix Riesenberg. The second, *Lightship* (1934), signaled the real start of a long productive career. Before his death in 1971, he had published seventeen more books — six works of nonfiction, four juvenile narratives, and nine novels in all.

Most of these books have connections with Binns's lifelong affinity for the Pacific Northwest. Even in exile in New York, his imagination never strayed far from his roots. *Lightship,* for example, anecdotally portrays key events in the lives of crewmen aboard a lightship anchored off the coast of Washington. The setting itself was drawn directly from the author's past, for at age seventeen he spent one hundred sixty days aboard such a vessel without coming ashore. That job provided some of the money for his Stanford education and most of the inspiration for what would always be Binns's own favorite of all the books he wrote.

His later novels moved inland, but not too far. *The Laurels Are Cut Down* (1937) considers historic exploitation by the Washington timber industry, as does *The Timber Beast* (1944) in more contemporary times. Neither novel was welcomed by Northwest loggers, but both books sold well and received a fair share of critical notice. Other Binns fictions, like *The Land Is Bright,* use explicit historical sources. One of the best known, *Mighty Mountain* (1940), recounts the travails of early Tacoma settlers, and is especially noteworthy for its sympathetic treatment of local Indians like Chief Leschi and his followers. *You Rolling River* (1947), another long-time Northwest favorite, takes its readers back to the Columbia River in the late nineteenth century during the romantic heyday of sea captains and river pilots. All these historical novels successfully invoke a sense of time and place that shies away from neither palpable hardship nor unabashed optimism.

Binns's juvenile books follow the same pattern, fusing steady growth to maturity with realistic setting and incident. The best take place on Hood Canal, near Puget Sound, and document the idyllic joys of growing up in that part of the country. It is safe to predict that children reading *Sea Pup* (1954) today will be just as charmed by its colloquial sense of place as those who read it some thirty years ago.

Binns's nonfiction focuses on Pacific Northwest scenery, too. Beginning with a history of Seattle, *Northwest Gateway* (1941), following with a history of Washington state, *The Roaring Land* (1942), including a long paean to Puget Sound, *Sea in the Forest* (1953), and culminating with *Peter Skene Ogden: Fur Trader* (1967), this Northwest author was extremely effective when researching and describing his native territory. Some critics have complained about Binns's occasional carelessness with facts, but the author would retort that he was a creative writer, not a historian. The ambience, to him, was more important than the accuracy. So the dust jacket of *Sea in the Forest* is correct when it describes such nonfiction as "a subtle blend of history, nostalgia, anecdote, and personal observation." This blend is the key to Archie Binns's success.

To read any of his books is not to lose oneself in pedantry, but rather to set foot on the land, to touch the earth, to breathe the smells, to feel the precipitation. "It was raining in the afternoon," he observed in one typical paragraph, "and the place seemed big and lonesome. But it was spring and the ground was tufted green with new bunch grass, and purple-dotted with violets; violets that were numberless, with heart-shaped leaves. They drifted away through the bunchgrass, and where they were too far away to be distinguished they gave the green prairie a tinge of purple. Away to the west the prairie ended against a wall of three-hundred-foot fir trees, gray-green and softly ragged against the damp gray of the sky." Thus he described Grand Mound Prairie in the 1860s, and thus he captured the wet beauty of Washington's undeveloped land.

Before too long, the writer realized the lure of home. When he left New York to do research on a commissioned biography of the actress, Minnie Fiske, he never looked back. Soon he moved to Seattle, where he continued to write books while working as a columnist for the *Argus* and teaching at the University of Washington as the Walker-Ames lecturer in creative writing. In his spare time, he became a craftsman of a different sort. He made furniture by hand, and even built a seaworthy boat of Alaskan yellow cedar, African mahogany, and oak. In 1964 he retired to Sequim on the Olympic Peninsula, but he never retired from writing. Even now, some unpublished manuscripts remain in his family's possession. The best of these, I'm told, is firmly grounded in the Pacific Northwest.

Contrarily, his best-known novel hardly takes place in the Pacific Northwest at all. Instead, *The Land Is Bright* propels people there. But that is the point. Before they reach their Promised Land, their lives are filled with routine horrors and dramatic confrontations. But once the survivors arrive in Oregon, once they embark down the Columbia toward Portland, once they are in touch with the landscape their author loves, these men and women are destined for success. Even though the final page is awash in precipitation— "On the mountainside, they could see the snow powdering over dark evergreens while they sat in falling rain"—a Northwest optimism prevails. The young folk "did not feel cold," because one appropriate Oregon marriage has already taken place and another may be impending. So despite the bad weather, the so-called Promised Land has been reached.

Such ability to shade emotion with landscape is typical of Binns's best writing. *Mighty Mountain*, in fact, utilizes Mount Rainier as a symbolic echo of failure and success. When things are not going well, the mountain is obscured; when the protagonist's life runs smoothly, the mountain appears from behind the clouds. "The logs of his new house caught the sunset light and shone as if they were really made of gold. The great trees behind it were green-gold, like some enchanted forest, and above them, a few points to the south, an incredible dome of snow floated in the sky, pink in the sunset and touched with blue shadows. Mount Rainier would be there forever, and his relationship to that eternal landmark had been defined in the land to which he had come home."

Because *The Land Is Bright* moves characters from place to place, no such overriding image appears. Nonetheless, scenery continues to define the pros and cons of life on the trail. The encampment at Kanesville looks "romantic," and Nancy Ann Greenfield sees it as "a bright blur of sound and color." Beyond, however, lies the unknown—"the wide Missouri, swift and muddy and pierced from underneath with sharp, black snags," an obvious foreshadowing of the tragedy that will take place on the next page. "Across the river was another country, or no country at all, but a wild territory." Into its mystery, the Greenfields and their friends will venture.

Binns tells their tale by means of anecdote. Rather than cataloguing a day-by-day account of life on the trail, he highlights certain scenes and settings. Some of those vignettes are dramatic; others, remarkably ordinary. All are seen through one or another traveler's point of view. Even though Nancy Ann is the ostensible heroine, and her development takes up the major portion of the novel, other characters share the spotlight, too.

Some of the most touching scenes, in fact, are viewed through the eyes of children. In Chapter 4, Binns imagines the trail as Nancy Ann's little brother saw it—"hotter than ever. There was sand in your shoes and dust in your mouth, and breathing didn't do you any good"—while in Chapter 9 he describes the trauma of Patience "Dollar-a-Pound" Trimble when she left her favorite doll behind.

In contrast with such everyday occurrences, the author skips over some key events. Crossing the Missouri, for example, takes place between chapters. Neither of the two major confrontations between Black and McBride is heard by the reader. And, except for one touching scene in the depths of Hell's Canyon, the Snake River disasters of Case and the Thomases are never directly observed. What Binns means to convey is clear. This is a wagon train comprised of ordinary people whose mishaps warrant no special or glamorous treatment. So the author builds the panoramic magnitude of their travels by pasting together a collage of lesser incidents and encounters. Some readers may be annoyed by the apparent avoidance of conflict but, as one reviewer concluded, "He does not need to invent dramatic happenings. The slow, painful trek across the plains is as dramatic as death."

Binns writes most effectively when he pursues this subtle collage technique. *You Rolling River* provides an excellent comparative model since it is an aggregate of anecdotal scenes that stun a reader's senses. One chapter, for example, exposes the emotions of a boy watching his father die. Safely on shore, Willard peers through a telescope at the sea-swept mast that holds Mr. Pearson. "The powerful glass brought him so close that when he turned the boy could see every feature. All expression seemed to have gone from his cold, haggard face and gathered in his eyes as he looked toward the land. 'Father!' He seemed almost close enough to touch, but when the boy stumbled from the telescope his father was suddenly a faraway figure on one of the black crosses above the boiling surf on Peacock Spit." A number of other vignettes in *You Rolling River*—like the wife burning her husband's treasured ledgers, one by one, or Mr. Fortune cruelly beating his sons—are just as compelling.

Such detail is worth noting because it proves to be a counterpoint to Binns's achievement in *The Land Is Bright*. *You Rolling River*, in sum, is a lesser book. A number of the individual scenes in the river novel are so strong that they overpower the underlying structure of the book. As a result, the collage that should inform the structure never comes together as a unified whole, and the pieces turn out to be more memorable than the sum of the parts. In contrast, the pieces of *The Land Is Bright* mesh into a panoramic whole that convincingly defines the trail experience. Like a string of beads, the trail novel hangs together. "Instead of painting in the heroic mood," said the Philadelphia *Record*, "the author prefers to etch and tells the tale through daily incidents of camp and trail. The result is even more effective, becomes in spots almost unforgettable. Dirt, dust and sheer animal fatigue were harder to endure than Indians."

Reviewers such as this were not the only fans of Archie Binns's books. The author's editor at Charles Scribner's Sons waxed just as enthusiastic about the northwesterner's achievements. "I am sending you now up to galley 66,—that is where the adventure with the Indians begins," wrote Maxwell E. Perkins on October 21, 1938. "I am really enjoying this book [*The Land Is Bright*] almost beyond belief." Unlike his more famous editorial work with such writers as Thomas Wolfe and F. Scott Fitzgerald, Perkins had very little to say to Binns about matters of content and style. Most of the correspondence, in fact, centers on royalties and advances, although Perkins adds comments now and then about characters, verb tenses, and future projects. But it is clear that the editor respected Binns, admired his writing, indeed sought him out.

A year and a half before the publication of *The Land Is Bright*, Perkins addressed a telling letter to Binns, whose previous fiction had been published by Reynal and Hitchcock: "I wish to say on behalf of this House, and emphatically, that if it is true that you are considering a change of publisher, we should be eager to cooperate with you in bringing out your future books. We have always stood,—against great temptation at times,—by the old principle, which has lately fallen into more or less disrepute, of not approaching authors who have satisfactory arrangements elsewhere. But we have heard in a way that makes us believe it, that you are not in this situation and it seemed to us, in view of our admiration of your writings, that we should be justified in telling you how we felt. If you should write us that we may consider ourselves in a position to make a proposal for your next novel, we feel certain that we can make one which will please you." The August 9, 1937, date of this letter suggests that an agreement was soon reached; the "next novel" was *The Land Is Bright*. So literature's finest twentieth-century editor, recognizing a genuine—and perhaps profitable—talent, took responsibility for the fictional heart of Archie Binns's career. In writing *The Land Is Bright,* Binns did not disappoint his New York publishing house.

As already noted, among the trail novel's strengths were setting, scene, and point of view. Just as proficient were the characterizations. Some, Binns accomplished with a flick of the pen. "'They must be Californians,' Grandma Parker said. She impressed the young people with the fact that there was all the difference in the world between godless Californians in search of gold and honest people going to Oregon for land and homes . . . Anything that went wrong could be blamed on the Californians, their influence. 'They must be Californians.'" In so pronouncing, the wagon train elder spokeswoman sets a tone for her fellow travelers.

Other figures Binns drew with less caricature and more depth. While Gideon Black enters the novel as a potential suitor for Nancy Ann, he soon develops into a man of mixed motives. Nancy Ann, herself unable to judge him clearly, nonetheless acknowledges both his weaknesses and strengths. For the reader, then, he immediately becomes multidimensional, a presence who adds intricate twists and turns to the vignettes where he appears. "She had just misunderstood Gideon. She thought he had come deliberately to spoil their good time. Now she knew he wanted to take part in it, but hadn't known just how to begin. He was lonesome from having to think about everyone, without being very close to any one. It was wrong to have supposed he wanted to be that way." Thus Nancy Ann's intuitive assessment invites further, more profound, speculation on the part of the reader.

Her other suitors, equally complex, invite sagacious judgment as well. Edwin, of course, is only a figment of her romantic imagination. McBride, on the other hand, changes from the romantic to the all too real. When he starts out from Kanesville, "his secret was this: he was a young man, or almost a young man, and he was growing younger." By the end of his particular trail, "he had changed greatly, and looked as if he had been sick. His face was white and sunken, and he was wearing a scrubby beard." En route to Oregon, McBride grows old psychologically. Case, still another competitor for the hand of Nancy Ann, develops psychologically, too. Binns easily could have molded him into a prototypical romantic hero, but Instead the author shows restraint. Case, long and gangly with an exaggerated Kentucky drawl, must slowly win the affections of the reader as well as the heart of Nancy Ann. That he does so under a variety of circumstances in a wide range of places proves his worth by the novel's end.

Nancy Ann herself provides the focus, since both romantic interest and narrative continuity center on her presence. If the Oregon Trail is the string on which the episodic beads are strung, she is its most fascinating pearl. To view large segments of the trek through her consciousness is to share the ordeal with a young woman who is following her own path to maturity. "Sometimes she thought it would be easier to go on travelling forever, and sometimes she did not think she could take another step." But her strengths—emotional as well as physical—prevail, leaving her in Oregon "more firmly rooted in the earth." She is not as memorable as Scarlett O'Hara or even Ma Joad, but she remains an affective and effective survivor, a heroine who causes readers to care about her life.

Actually, Nancy Ann Greenfield—or someone like her—was the original inspiration for *The Land Is Bright*. A Pacific Northwest book dealer found a dozen or so letters written by a young woman about her experiences along the Oregon Trail. When the book dealer shared the letters with Archie Binns, the author's imagination took off. Before long, he himself was following the old Oregon Trail by car and on foot. Many newspaper reviews remark on his thorough research, and several quote his discovery that "much of the scenery and some of the old wheel tracks [were] unchanged." Once he completed his explorations, he put together the book— *The Land Is Bright*—that would combine a personable young woman's adventures with his own eye for scenic detail.

Binns and Max Perkins had a hard time deciding what to call the finished product. On September 16, 1938, Perkins suggested *Don't You Cry Over Me*. "It may seem frivolous at first," he wrote "but everyone will know that it's from 'O Susanna' by Stephen Foster and when one has read the book they will realize the meaning. — That it expresses the unconquerable spirit of these pioneers who in spite of everything didn't feel that they ought to be cried over." Four days later, Perkins wrote again. He had misremembered the quote. Perhaps the new book could be called *Don't You Cry For Me*. Two weeks later, Perkins had second or third thoughts. "Yes," he responded to Binns's wife, Mollie. "I do think that is a very good title, — *The Wind Blows West*. I should be perfectly satisfied with that."

Of course none of these options turned out to be the final choice. Instead, the book was called *The Land Is Bright*. The words themselves come from the last line in a fairly well-known 1849 poem by Arthur Hugh Clough, "Say Not the Struggle Nought Availeth." Even more than the other potential titles, "the land is bright" in context expresses the indomitable pioneer spirit Maxwell Perkins wanted to invoke. Clough's poem opens somewhat antithetically, with two stanzas which suggest more hardships than heroics:

> *Say not the struggle nought availeth,*
> *The labour and the wounds are vain,*
> *The enemy faints not, nor faileth,*
> *And as things have been, things remain.*
>
> *If hopes were dupes, fears may be liars;*
> *It may be, in yon smoke concealed,*
> *Your comrades chase e'en now the fliers,*
> *And, but for you, possess the field.*

While the English poet intended to remind his readers of the 1848 revolutions in Europe, and the subsequent defeats by reactionary forces in France and Italy, Binns interpreted the lines analogously. He pictured, not liberal European freedom fighters, but a long line of American pioneers.

Clough's poetic voice suited him, especially as it swelled to an optimistic climax. The lines of the last two stanzas tangibly served to underscore a proud sense of pioneer fortitude:

For while the tired waves, vainly breaking,
  Seem here no painful inch to gain,
Far back through creeks and inlets making
  Came, silent, flooding in, the main,

And not by eastern windows only,
  When daylight comes, comes in the light,
In front the sun climbs slow, how slowly,
  But westward, look, the land is bright.

The image of eastern light propelling the forces of victory to the west, the brightening optimism of the western frontier, and the relentlessness of the Darwinistic progression all point poetically toward what the novelist meant to say in prose. Despite misfortune and pain, the struggle would lead to success. In the West, indeed, the land would be brighter.

It is interesting to note that, two years after *The Land Is Bright* was published, Winston Churchill quoted Clough's poem in one of his most famous oratory efforts. Made just months before the Americans entered World War II, the prime minister's speech carried a dual message. On the one hand, Churchill wanted to shore up the English spirits; on the other, he hoped to spur American involvement in the conflicts abroad. In a letter dated August 19, 1941, Perkins asks Binns if he "noticed how Churchill quoted the poem that ended with your title." Perkins also tells Binns that Scribner's "London Office, which has been bombed into pretty much nothing, bought for our store the original manuscript of Clough's poem." The editor explains further that Scribner's had decided to present the manuscript to the Prime Minister. Perkins reports, "Churchill received it graciously and it was told about in the papers."

A cynic might suspect Scribner's of trying to get some press attention for *The Land Is Bright,* but the point is probably more subtle than that. Most likely the coincidence only indicates the flavor of the times and the appropriateness of Clough's poem to a generation that once again was looking west. Such a coincidence reminds readers today not only of what was going on between 1939 and 1941, but of all those reviews which interpreted Binns's novel as a paradigm. *The Land Is Bright,* said Charles Lee in the Boston *Herald,* spoke to "an audience eager to relive the glory of the past, eager vicariously to trudge, in a day of foreign isms, in the footsteps that opened up and built the United States." In fact, Lee went so far as to suggest that, "should Uncle Sam, fearful of enemies abroad and tolerant of them at home, ever need a little moral·pick-me-up, let him go to such a novel as Archie Binns gives us in *The Land Is Bright.*" The Greensboro *News* wondered as well, "Is it the war scare, or have we just awakened to a national pride?"

Whatever the impetus, homespun novels became popular during those early war years, and *The Land Is Bright* was one of the best. Binns's novel quickly took its place with such other contemporary pioneer tales as H. L. Davis's *Honey in the Horn* (1935), Sophus Winther's *Take All to Nebraska* (1936), Conrad Richter's *Sea of Grass* (1937), Vardis Fisher's *Children of God* (1939), and Walter Van Tilburg Clark's *The Ox-Bow Incident* (1940). While none of these achieved overnight fame like *The Grapes of Wrath* or *Gone with the Wind,* all of them examined important dimensions of the Western myth that their readers cherished. Such tales as *The Land Is Bright* tell the "story of America and the American dream," boasted the San Francisco *Call-Bulletin,* "of goals won and romance fulfilled." Even though individual novelists challenged the myth in different ways—Davis, romantically; Fisher, darkly; Clark, ironically, for example—each one imagined the dream as a vital component of the American heritage.

Archie Binns's vision echoed his peers'. *The Land Is Bright's* narrative line—sometimes romantically, sometimes darkly, sometimes ironically—propels its characters toward the American Dream. Nancy Ann and her friends were "caught in the great tide of people and were being carried away somewhere." Where and why? "We're going because poor people like us are always hungry for a Promised Land," preaches Mr. Thomas. "There was no disagreement among them. Surely, a Promised Land is a need of the human heart when it appeals alike to Universalist and Mormon and infidel."

Binns uses several tangible images to communicate the breadth of this Utopian vision. Each seems romantic, dark, ironic, in turn. One is a book, *Utopia* in fact, which Mr. Thomas carries across the plains. In the beginning, *Utopia* signifies their goal; in the end, it augurs apparent defeat. When Sir Thomas More's narrative becomes the only combustible fuel and when its owner gently lays its pages on a small fire, the Promised Land seems very far away indeed. Some of Mr. Thomas's fruit trees are part of that fire, too, but one of them does survive the terrible journey down Hell's Canyon. Carried faithfully by Case, the "bit of brush" plays a prominent role in the scene that finally unites the young man with his friends. One romantic reviewer suggested that saving the single fruit tree was "equivalent to transplanting America to the shores of the Columbia." While this flowery interpretation may stretch the imagination, some acknowledgment of the literal fruit tree as figurative symbol is nonetheless appropriate. Certainly Binns meant to represent the ultimate survival of the dream.

Another extended metaphor, like the fruit trees and like the novel itself, turns out to be just as positive in a subtle kind of way. Along the Snake River, Case and Nancy Ann observe a salmon run. "It ain't natural," Case complains as the lovers eye a pool of dying fish. "They didn't have to leave the sea." Case's conversation makes his girl friend uneasy. Both Nancy Ann and her author are aware of the unspoken. "If Case talked too much about the migrating salmon, if she thought too much about them, it might develop there was some connection between that migration and their own; between themselves and those desperate, leaping things, battering themselves against rocks and braving the torchlight and the spears." Binns stretches the metaphor over several pages not only because a critical scene will take place near the falls but also because the salmon imperative so closely parallels that of the migrating pioneers. To reach their instinctive goals, salmon and emigrants alike must fight against seemingly insurmountable odds.

Below the falls, Indians by torchlight spear the weakest fish. Analogous to the Idaho trader, cholera, all the other ills along the way, the Indians and the falls themselves are inevitable instruments of death. The hellish scene forces Nancy Ann to articulate a connection. "She and Case were caught in that roaring machinery of the world. Two salmon hurtling through the light of torches. Beyond this moment was the dark. . . ." However Nancy Ann's intuition turns out to be false, for her destiny is bright, not dark. Like those salmon whose upstream momentum carries them to natural fulfillment, so the young woman will find satisfaction in Oregon. But her experience at the falls throws light on the historic destiny in which she found herself. With the potential for disaster on every side, only instinct, luck, and obstinate fortitude kept survivors like Case and Nancy Ann on track to their Promised Land.

Archie Binns would have called it social Darwinism, and his contemporaries would have taken some measure of comfort from his characters' success. Indeed a 1939 audience would have perceived that fictional characters were not the only fittest to survive. In spite of all their problems, a large percentage of flesh-and-blood pioneers finally reached the Promised Land, too. These were the men and women that Archie Binns and his generation—themselves hoping to survive their own unsettled times—admired most. To read a western success story in the novel *The Land Is Bright* is to share the typical aspirations of the late 1930s as well. It is to embrace, as Binns did, a cyclical theory of history, and to see, as he explained, "that the past and the present are the same, and time is only an illusion." In other words, to read *The Land Is Bright* is to take hold of a myth that has satisfied Americans for hundreds of years. It is to rediscover a past that Binns could well glorify not just for his own generation but for ours.

CHAPTER TEN

Shane's Pale Ghost

That "Pale Rider" imitates "Shane" is unquestionably true. If mov-
iegoers seemed unable to see the common patterns, reviewers were
quick to point them out. "Pure 'Shane,'" wrote David Ansen in
Newsweek;[1] "shameless plagiarism," carped John Simon in the *National Review*.[2] The two films' story lines, to be sure, sound almost
identical.

Each stars a mysterious protagonist who materializes unexpect-
edly and who, at that point, has opted for pacifism. He finds a collection of nesters/miners in need of his two-fisted services, is attracted to the wife/lover of their leader, and must confront that love
as well as the malevolence of the entrepreneurial antagonist and his
hired guns. Then, although psychologically battered, the hero
emerges victorious only to disappear as mysteriously as he arrived.
Details, as well as plot sequences, are equally reminiscent of each
other. Where Shane helps Joe Starrett remove a stump, for example, the pale rider works with Hull Barret to excise a boulder.
Similar names, similar relationships, and similar scenes repeat
themselves so often that the astute moviegoer cannot help but see
the connections.

But those connections seem more fortuitous than wise. Pauline
Kael pinpointed the difference when, after acknowledging that

"Pale Rider" lifts its general outlines from "Shane," she damned the Eastwood venture with metaphorical enthusiasm: "This may be an ecologically minded Western, but it's strip-mining "Shane.'"[3] It does so, I think, because "Pale Rider" is a product that was designed for a different generation.

"Shane" belongs to the decade following World War II. Jack Schaefer first wrote it in 1946 as a three-part *Argosy* serial called *Rider from Nowhere*. The story later was expanded slightly and is-sued in a 1949 hardcover edition. From its inception, Schaefer meant the piece to be a literary endeavor, "classical in form," he said, "stripped to the absolute essentials."[4] Indeed, he speaks freely of the conscious artistry he brought to the novel, designing its narrative technique and shaping its story line so that layers of meaning gradually are revealed. As one critic summarizes: "Through its use of illustrations and captions, *Argosy* clearly attempts to place *Rider from Nowhere* in the pulp Western tradition. The novel version of "Shane" attempts to refine the original structure so that the story's classic and timeless elements are presented in their most natural rhythms."[5] Most viewers would agree that the film version, pro-duced four years after the novel, aspires after similarly mythic goals.

"Pale Rider," on the other hand, metamorphosed in reverse. Clint Eastwood, with myth in mind, commissioned the movie script from Michael Butler and Dennis Shyrack. Then Alan Dean Foster wrote two hundred and eighteen pages based on the screen-play—a novelization, as *Pale Rider*'s title page boldly announces, not a novel. The book's execution may have been consciously liter-ary, though, for Foster tried superficially to infuse what was inher-ent organically in *Pale Rider*'s predecessor. By including historical allusions to John Sutter and literary allusions to John Muir's "Range of Light," he apparently thought he was elevating the text. Foster failed, of course, because allusions alone are not enough, but he also failed because the whole conception of *Pale Rider* is insuffi-cient. First, Eastwood, Butler, Shyrack, and Foster put archetype before humanity. Second, the plot, the characters, even the mythic foundations, so appropriate for a hungrily romantic generation, are out of place now. Thus, *Pale Rider* creaks on the hinges of out-moded conception and present-day execution.

To begin with, both versions of *Pale Rider* appear hastily imag-ined. Pauline Kael points out several structural lapses that detract from the movie: the bigamist implications of Hull Barret's frequent marriage proposals, the irregular patches of snow that appear and disappear from scene to scene, the mining claims clustered together, the utter absurdity of hardscrabblers working the same streambed for generations. *Shane* (the novel) is held together by no such oddi-ties. That film's major inconsistency—daylight and darkness dis-solving together—comes from a technical source, while "Pale Rider"'s more frequent incongruities stem from carelessness. Like-wise, the vernacular language of the Foster book sounds forced—"Women didn't settle in a mining camp unless they had thoughts of living there permanent"[6]—where *Shane*'s prose authentically repli-cates colloquial speech: "Can I call the turn for you, Shane?"[7] These are just details, however. Far more telling are the elemental ways in which these two westerns differ.

Part of *Shane*'s power comes through its point of view. Narrated by a man who was once the boy of the story, its action unfolds retro-spectively. Indeed, this is the major difference between Schaefer's novel and the film, for the book's "characters are not so much con-crete human beings as memories, subjectively conceived, which are summoned up only before the mind's eye," as James K. Folsom acutely observes.[8] He goes on to explain that because film must be visualized directly, no such retrospective point of view is possible. Young Joey and Shane, especially, are living figures on the screen, not nostalgic re-creations of someone's imagination. But George Stevens, the producer and director of "Shane," was able to work within this cinematographic constraint, while Clint Eastwood tried to exceed the limits.

The first production decision for "Pale Rider" was logical but in-appropriate. Perhaps because a 1980's audience expects sexual- rather than hero-worship and probably because Eastwood liked the idea, "Pale Rider"'s innocent is female. She's also older than Joey Starrett (or Bobby, as he's called in the novel), a nubile adolescent instead of a reverent boy. And just as the viewer sees the film's Joey more directly than the reader apprehends the fictional Bobby, so we watch Megan Wheeler functioning more actively than either *Shane* counterpart.

"Pale Rider" opens aggressively, with a pack of miscreants trampling through Carbon Canyon and killing Megan's dog. She is immediately a part of the action, then, rescuing the mongrel's body, cradling it to a secluded grave, praying for the appearance of a miracle. Later, as events unfold, she is personally responsible for getting entangled with Lahood's men. Where Joey only spies on violence, Megan precipitates it. "She was pounding very weakly at Josh Lahood's chest now, her tiny fists like gusts of wind on his shirt. He was using his weight to hold her in place while he worked on her with his hands" (163). Her subsequent rescue by the Preacher sends the movie on to its climactic scenes.

But the finales of both "Pale Rider" and "Shane" reveal that neither Megan or Joey is designed as subtly as their novelistic archetypes. "Shane," calls the boyish voice to one receding figure; "Preacher! I love you, Preacher," cries the girl. Two heroes ride off into Technicolor landscapes followed only by the voices of immaturity. *Shane* (the novel), however, sends Bobby back to his parents and offers two more chapters of retrospective analysis.

Those chapters get to the heart of *Shane*'s mystique. The first, taking place immediately after the final gunfight, voices a major premise about the hero's character. "No bullet can kill that man," Mr. Weir reports. "Sometimes I wonder whether anything ever could" (266). Such musing seems far more provocative than the blatant resurrection of Clint Eastwood's Preacher. Scarred by five bullet holes (or six—the book and the movie disagree), the pale rider pretends his immortality unconditionally. His initial appearance is vague, for it is "difficult to determine whether he was resting on the near ridge or the one behind it" (15). Later the marshal speculates, "Couldn't be him. The man I'm thinking about is dead," yet changes his mind when he meets the Preacher face-to-face

(170). "You," he gasps his last words. "*You!*" (215). Clearly the audience is supposed to believe the avenging spirit has risen from the dead. But that spirit isn't mythic, and Shane's is.

Five (or six) patterned bullet holes and Marshal Stockburn's recognition tell us that the Preacher is a ghost. Mr. Weir's remarks—"No bullet can kill that man"—tell us that Shane is something more. What can never die is not this particular man but the conception of the man, the invincible American hero who can regenerate peace and civilization through violence on the frontier.[9] Immediately after World War II, Americans still believed in regeneration through violence—the impetus for an American presence in Europe and Asia and the thrust of our mid-twentieth-century foreign policy. Shane images the pattern. A 1950's audience necessarily would admire him because a 1950's audience would recognize a role that embodies an important ingredient of the masculine spirit informing this country's past. Truly no bullet can kill him, for he is crucial to the American Dream.

The Preacher, on the other hand, comes from a different milieu, one where archetype quickly turns to stereotype. He, too, shares heroic stature, of course, but his heroism grows out of a post-Vietnam age that admires Rambo and Sylvester Stallone. The mysterious aura is forced, the immortality imposed, the omnipotence almost a caricature. Sarah, trying to penetrate "the veil of mystery," asks, "Who are you? Who are you, really?" (193). An inhuman howl answers from somewhere in the heavens; then the man answers sexually. Neither engages us in mythic proportions.

Yet Shane does, especially when Bobby's larger-than-life interpretation evolves naturally from flesh-and-blood knowledge. The boy eyes someone "tall and terrible there in the road, looming up gigantic in the mystic half-light. He was the man I saw that first day, a stranger, dark and forbidding, forging his lone way out of an unknown past in the utter loneliness of his own immovable and instinctive defiance. He was the symbol of all the dim, formless imaginings of danger and terror in the untested realm of human potentialities beyond my understanding" (249). In short, he was both human and something more than human, both a man and a mythic symbol.

The final chapter of *Shane,* ostensibly written years after the action of the story, codifies the figure's true immortality. "For mother was right," writes Schaefer in Bobby's voice, sounding a 1950's frame of reference. "Shane was there. He was there in our place and in us. Whenever I needed him, he was there" (272). Marian Starrett and Bobby both understand, as Sarah Wheeler and her daughter never could, that the hero's name and physical presence are immaterial. Real archetypes belong to a universal consciousness, ghosts, only to the particular. "He was the man who rode into our little valley out of the heart of the great glowing West," Schaefer's novel concludes philosophically, "and when his work was done rode back whence he had come and he was Shane" (274). When the pale rider's work was done, he could only ride off to the echo—"I love you, Preacher"—of Megan's voice insisting that she can conjure him up any time, "if I ever need him again" (218). A member of the me-generation, Megan has no conception of her Preacher's greater possibilities.

Apparently Eastwood didn't either. Indeed he suppresses greater possibilities in other "Pale Rider" characterizations, too. Sarah's attraction to the mysterious man, for example, displays little of the psychological ambivalence Marian feels for Shane. And while Marian turns to her husband for tacit understanding, Sarah succumbs to the pale rider's charms. One is tempted to extrapolate, here, about immediate sexual gratification in the 1980s. But the fact is that Marian's dilemma and painful resolution are far more compelling than Sarah's ready acceptance.

The same generalization can be made about the men in their lives. Joe Starrett's motivations are historically plausible as well as more psychologically keen. On the one hand a settler like so many others who pioneered the West and tamed the frontier and, on the other, a man sensitive to his wife's emotions, Schaefer's character plays a multidimensional role. Hull Barret, in contrast, is flat. Not only does he bear little resemblance to any real-life hardscrabbler, but he wears his heart on his sleeve. Lacking the dignity so inherent in his counterpart, Hull's personality remains superficial.

Pale Rider's villain also could have been developed further. Like *Shane*'s Fletcher, Coy Lahood represents a genuine historical force on a collision course with historical change. Fletcher was a Wyoming rancher whose cattle roamed freely; Lahood, an empire-builder whose hydraulic mining operation scoured California canyons. Both make impassioned speeches about their respective corporate rights versus the whims and wills of nesters and squatters. Both are interesting emblems of their respective eras.

"Shane"'s Fletcher straightforwardly represents a capitalist doomed to be replaced by individual entrepreneurs, the ranch giving way to farms. A product of the 1880's and yet reminiscent, perhaps, of 1940's warmongers, he was ripe for destruction in his time.[10] "Pale Rider"'s Lahood is a capitalist on somewhat different ground. Carrying more baggage of the 1980's than of the century before, his venture not only pits the corporation against the workers but does so at the expense of the environment. As cinematography makes clear, sluicing is the forerunner of ecological disaster, and Lahood's operation, in contrast to the claims to Carbon Canyon, rapes the land. Still, "Pale Rider" isn't capable of taking its special effects any further. Its filmmakers disregard the futility of a hardscrabble enterprise and the ironic fact that hydraulic mining is more profitable. Instead, they expect their 1980's audience to cheer against the techno-industrial model and to imagine that a single gunfighter can right environmental, as well as legal and moral, ills.

"Shane" makes fewer pretensions. Its hero simply battles against a single rancher, and prevails because he can draw a six-gun faster. Meanwhile, an overlay of meaning traps "Pale Rider"'s creators one more time. "I've built an empire here with my own two hands, and I never asked for anyone's help," Coy Lahood waxes comprehensively. "All I ever asked for was a fair chance to build" (99). But, because psychological motivations like his love for his son remain obscurely undeveloped, viewers understand little beyond his corporate mentality. Like his nemesis, he's a symbol before he's a man.

(On the plus side, Lahood's demise allows Hull Barret a singular moment of bravery, but that in itself is inexplicable in terms of the logistics of the film.)

If "Pale Rider"'s characters aren't interesting, though, perhaps their deaths are worthwhile. In this respect, "Pale Rider" proves itself timely if not profound. Where "Shane" is content with fist fights, a quick murder, and a climactic shoot-out, its imitator must fill the screen with eruptive violence and blood. From the opening death of Megan's dog to the final dispersal of Marshal Stockburn and his men, killing abounds. Since Clint Eastwood is no Sam Peckinpah, the mayhem isn't necessarily gruesome—but gratuitous violence is there nonetheless.

Two scenes near the film's end are noteworthy. The first has no counterpart in "Shane." It sends Hull and the hero into Lahood's camp, where the two boyishly toss dynamite sticks into the operation. Wonderful explosions occur while miners, unable to ferret out the source of the confusion, run in all directions. The scene is pure spectacle. "The platform exploded in a geyser of splinters. The monitor teetered drunkenly atop it for a moment before tumbling heavily to the ground. Metal bent and rivets popped free as the water cannon smashed against the boulders below" (196). An audience attuned to television and movie brutality expects such detonations, even if no one is killed. By contrast, Shane's relatively quiet battles are fought along much less sensational lines.

However, the explosions in "Pale Rider" are just skirmishes before the war. Leaving Hull afoot to protect him from danger (Shane, in a far more provocative gesture, taps Joe gently with his gun), the solitary hero turns toward town. There, he faces an imported armada. Where Shane confronted the lone Stark Wilson, the pale rider must face seven deputies along with a corrupt marshal. Where Shane fast-draws a known opponent, the pale rider impersonally mows his foes down with stoic precision. And where Shane is badly wounded in the fray, the pale rider's immortality stands him in good stead. He leaves majestically; Rambo (or Clint Eastwood), superimposed on a western setting, has done his job.

It was a job neither "Shane" nor his audience would have chosen. Several "Shane" scenes indicate his reluctance to don his gunslinger guise. The man appears to Schaefer and Bobby as "strange and stricken in his own secret bitterness" (135). Fearless and skillful, Shane is every bit as competent as the pale rider, but the former—as Marian well understands—agonizes when he has to take up his guns. The latter may have preferred pacifism too, but he exchanges his collar for his firearms and transforms himself into a killer without a word. "Right or wrong, the brand sticks and there's no going back," Shane explains (263). His counterpart says nothing. "Slipping smoothly into the saddle, the Preacher flicked the reins" (216). Ours, an age that expects no remorse, is given none.

But we do expect certain things from Clint Eastwood—the taciturn presence, the sardonic omnipotence, the capacity for violence, the ultimate victory. Perhaps we should compare the pale rider with his high plains drifter instead of with Shane. Certainly the denouements of those two Eastwood films are the same (although I prefer the drifter's red aura to the Preacher's dark clouds). *High Plains Drifter*, however, with characterizations like the Mayor's and the minister's, with controlled irony, and with a properly hellish ending, is a much more satisfying film than "Pale Rider." *Drifter*'s cynical exaggeration finally turns serious, and the result is the most complex and provocative western that Eastwood has made. "Pale Rider," on the other hand, takes itself and its remake of "Shane" far too seriously from the start. The result is almost a caricature of the Eastwood power. And I think the problems stem primarily from its reliance on someone else's plot.

Although Eastwood adjusts certain layers of the romanticism of the *Shane* story line, he does so mistakenly. By bringing corporate villainy up to date, he destroys the credibility of the plot's motivation. By flattening the characters, he loses the grace of subtlety and innuendo. By replacing a whole complex of pleasures with mere sex appeal, he dismisses too much. By adding impersonal violence, he actually eases the impact of the blows. And finally, by eliminating innocent interaction between youth and adulthood, he destroys the mystic possibilities of the tale. In short, *Shane*'s myth is neither Eastwood's nor ours, although he tries to make it so.

"He's not gone," Marian rightly said of Jack Schaefer's hero. Shane is "all around us and in us, and he always will be" (270). Unfortunately, Clint Eastwood believed her. Thus the larger picture of "Pale Rider" was doomed from its inception.

NOTES

1. David Ansen, "Shane," *Newsweek* 106 (1 July 1985): 55.

2. John Simon, "Cowboyless Indians, Indianless Cowboys," *National Review* 37 (9 Aug. 1985): 50.

3. Pauline Kael, "Pop Mystics," *New Yorker* 61 (12 Aug. 1985): 64–5.

4. Gerald Haslam, "Jack Schaefer," in *Shane, The Critical Edition,* ed. James C. Work (Lincoln: Univ. of Nebraska Press, 1984) 22.

5. Michael T. Marsden, "A Story for All Media," in *Shane, The Critical Edition* 342.

6. Alan Dean Foster, *Pale Rider* (New York: Warner Books 1985) 4.

7. Jack Schaefer, *Shane, The Critical Edition* 231.

8. James Folsom, "*Shane* and *Hud:* Two Stories in Search of Medium," in *Shane, The Critical Edition* 378.

9. See Richard Slotkin, *Regeneration Through Violence* (Middletown, Conn.: Wesleyan University Press, 1973), for an extended treatment of this important American phenomenon.

10. Ironically, the pattern has reversed itself in the 1980s; now family farms are giving way to agribusiness corporations.

CHAPTER ELEVEN

Company for a *Lonesome Dove*

The dust jacket proclaims that Larry McMurtry's *Lonesome Dove* "is his long-awaited masterpiece, the major novel at last of the American West as it really was." A second paragraph sounds almost as sweeping in its pronouncement. "A love story, an adventure, an American epic, *Lonesome Dove* embraces *all* the West—legend and fact, heroes and outlaws, whores and ladies, Indians and settlers—in a novel that recreates the central American experience, the most enduring of our national myths."

Such purple prose ought to stir the curiosity of all of us who read and love western American literature. Can it be that someone finally has written the definitive western novel? Has a Faulkner finally emerged beyond the hundredth meridian? Do we at last have a book against which we can measure *Angle of Repose, The Big Sky, The Ox-Bow Incident, Shane, The Virginian* (to name a few of my particular candidates for greatness), a writer against whom we can project Zane Grey or Louis L'Amour, Vardis Fisher or Frank Waters, William Eastlake or Edward Abbey? Is *Lonesome Dove* indeed "the major novel" of the American West?

The Pulitzer Prize people were willing to give it a lot of credit. My local public library says its waiting list of readers is a long one, while its paperback edition highlights supermarket shelves across the country. And quite frankly, I liked it so well that I haven't been able to shake it loose from my imagination. If it isn't "the major novel" of the American West, it's certainly among the top ten.

That generalization leads directly to a second (and even more debatable) issue. Just what *is* a "major novel" of the American West? What kind of story line, characters, and thematic complexities appear? What kind of ambience pervades? And how are we to judge? That is, even as we contemplate measuring a variety of novels against *Lonesome Dove,* we must also discern those touchstones alongside which *Lonesome Dove* must stand.

The problem is compounded by the fact that our touchstones for the great western novel have been generated inappropriately. Whereas William Faulkner defined a literature of the South by writing a series of superior novels, a formula defines the literature of the West. We measure greatness not by analyzing the achievements of a master but by examining the intelligence with which a given author treats a list of expected ingredients. Focusing on such elements as the chronological and geographical settings, a somewhat specialized group of human beings, and the essential themes of the frontier experience, we simply decide whether or not a novelist treats them seriously enough. Until the West generates an author who transcends the genre, we have no other option. Witness my assessment of *Lonesome Dove.*

Many readers insist first on a historical perspective, with action set a hundred years ago and characters involved in events that conceivably might have taken place. Although most aficionados accept tales of mountain men, of explorers, of forty-niners, or of pioneers as appropriate to the genre, some purists even go so far as to require the presence of cowboys. *Lonesome Dove* would satisfy them. Set in the latter part of the nineteenth century—after the Civil War and before the closing of the frontier—*Lonesome Dove* not only exudes history but also takes place in the Great Plains West. A dimension of history shapes every page, as cowboys who once were Texas Rangers embark on a cattle drive typical of—though longer than—a thousand other such ventures in the 1870s.

Andy Adams's *Log of a Cowboy,* a 1903 narrative that compresses one such cowhand's experiences, reveals that those real-life adventures were not as romantic as Zane Grey would have us believe. Trail driving actually was dusty, lonely, unpleasant work. Storms, stampedes, dry treks, and river crossings provided dangers to make any man uneasy, while the distances involved made a long drive feel interminable. Even the infrequent pockets of civilization—Abilene, Dodge, Ogallala—were anything but glamorous. In a word, the trail was a harsh one, testing character, ingenuity, and endurance at every bend.

Adams's and McMurtry's cowboys faced strikingly similar obstacles. Some were relatively benign irritants ("swarms of mosquitoes, which attacked horses and men alike, settling on them so thickly that they could be wiped off like stains" [*LD,* 273]); others were fatal ("a scream cut the air, so terrible it almost made him faint . . . Sean was barely clinging to his horse . . . a lot of brown things were wiggling around him and over him . . . they seemed like giant worms . . . the giant worms were snakes—water moccasins" [*LD,* 277]). When Sean's companions finally dragged the victim from the river and cut his shirt off, they found "eight sets of fang marks, including one on his neck. 'That don't count the legs,' Augustus said. 'There ain't no point in counting the legs'" (*LD,* 278). The horror of that crossing is only one such instance of pain in *Lonesome Dove.* Like Sam Peckinpah's, McMurtry's West is a place where romantic possibilities too often are destroyed by violence and degradation.

In his 1902 novel *The Virginian,* Owen Wister outlined the formula of romanticized adventures and pseudoviolence that Zane Grey was content to borrow and that early twentieth-century readers soon came to expect. In most cases, the harsh realities of the frontier were tinted by the colors of the rainbow, Grey's so-called rainbow trail. After the 1950s, however, Technicolor no longer beautified the path. Where Shane and the Virginian once had ridden, the Wild Bunch and Clint Eastwood's gunslingers followed, and now the men of the Hat Creek Cattle Company find the brutal track.

When a renegade Indian kidnaps a *Lonesome Dove* heroine, "it wasn't death she got—just the four men" (*LD,* 385). Later she is forced to witness scenes perhaps gratuitously savage.

> One Kiowa cut his belt and two more pulled his pants off. Before Lorena could even turn her head, they castrated him. Another slashed a knife across his forehead and began to rip off his hair. Dog Face screamed again, but it was soon muffled as the Kiowas held his head and stuffed his own bloody organs into his mouth, shoving them down his throat with the handle of a knife. His hair was soon ripped off and the Kiowa took the scalp and tied it to his lance. Dog Face struggled for breath, a pool of blood beneath his legs. Yet he wasn't dead. Lorena had her face in her arms, but she could still hear him moan and gurgle for breath. She wished he would die—it shouldn't take so long just to die. (*LD,* 450)

If that episode isn't grotesque enough, even her rescue turns bitter when her kidnapper methodically axes three innocent people while escaping unhurt. So *Lonesome Dove* differs significantly from earlier predecessors in that its genuine atrocities upset a reader's formulaic expectations. Just when one least expects it, the romance of the Old West gives way to an onslaught of naturalistic detail.

The characters, as well as the scenes in this novel, are disarmingly different. Content to enjoy an afternoon jug and gabble away his remaining years, Augustus McCrae at first seems wholly unheroic. Yet when heroics become necessary, when the renegade Blue Duck needs tracking or when a swarm of Indians needs dispersing ("He then proceeded to shoot six times, rapidly. Five of the Indians [*sic*] horses dropped, and a sixth ran squealing over the prairie—it fell several hundred yards away" [*LD,* 753]), Gus McCrae's verbosity gives way to amazingly competent action. Reminiscent of John Wayne's Rooster Cogburn, Gus oscillates between antihero and hero, idling away page after page with "pokes" and poker, then executing courageous deeds without hesitation. In either guise he is likable. Thoughtful, reasonably considerate of women and other men, sensitive, he belies the stereotype of the macho western male even as he functions just as potently.

His partner, Capt. Woodrow F. Call, is equally valorous, as effective in a tense situation and just as unique. A superb commander of men, he displays his leadership without aggression. He would rather give his orders and then ride alone, rally his cowhands by day and simply disappear at night. Provocation, however, may make him explode. "Call had destruction in him and would go on killing when there was no need. Once his blood heated, it was slow to cool" (*LD,* 440). More like a bad guy than good, he may charge beyond the bounds of conventional civilized behavior. His strong, silent reluctance to express his feelings overstates a stereotype, too. Both Call and Gus, then, are viewed somewhat askew, conventional western heroes portrayed finally as genuinely multifaceted human beings. "As a team, the two of them were perfectly balanced" (*LD,* 167). A study in contrasts (one taciturn, the other loquacious), the two leaders counterpoint each other in ways that confound our formulaic expectations.

Their troops are presented stereotypically and then behave in unusual ways, too. The most surprising is the handsome but balding cowboy Jake Spoon. "There was no more likable man in the west, and no better rider, either; but riding wasn't everything, and neither was likableness. Something in Jake didn't quite stick," McMurtry explains when the man first rides into the novel. "Something wasn't quite consistent" (*LD,* 65). That inconsistency drives Jake to abandon Lorena and finally to follow the unsavory Suggs brothers. By then, "life had slipped out of line. It was unfair, it was too bad, but he couldn't find the energy to fight it any longer" (*LD,* 574). Blessed by so many of the characteristics that comprise a cowboy hero, Jake fails instead.

Jake's admirer, young Newt, is another character who initially reminds the reader of someone from a Zane Grey western. A boy becoming a man, he watches the action around him, develops his own skills, and grows to maturity in the process. Yet his behavior—

whether riding in the heart of a stampede, discovering the suddenness of death, or learning about sex for the first time—isn't trite. "He trotted the last two hundred yards to where he had tied Mouse. But the horse wasn't there! He had used a boulder as a landmark, and the boulder was where it should be—but not the horse. Newt knew the stampede might have scared him and caused him to break the rein, but there was no broken rein hanging from the tree where Mouse had been tied. Before he could stop himself, Newt began to cry" (*LD*, 364). In the western novels that preceded *Lonesome Dove*, few young protagonists were seen in tears. But Newt unabashedly sobs at least ten different times during the course of his maturation. Learning of Gus's death, "He cried all afternoon, riding as far back on the drags as he could get. For once he was grateful for the dust the herd raised" (*LD*, 792).

On the distaff side, the characterizations are just as surprising. Clara, the earth mother, and her opposite, Elmira Johnson, exemplify a real polarity of female behavior. Where the one sacrifices self for family, the other sacrifices family for self. More interesting, though, is the woman whom the dust jacket calls "the whore with the proverbial heart of gold." Damaged first by her life-style and then by her kidnapping, Lorena retreats into a childlike state from which she never quite emerges. The subtleties of her personality—her responses to the individual men, her reactions to episodes on the trail, her inscrutable silence at the novel's end—take her well beyond the confines of caricature or even formula.

One of my friends complains that the people in *Lonesome Dove* are somewhat hastily drawn and too quickly discarded. He sees Lorena, for example, as a character with enormous possibilities, arguing that to deposit her with Clara is to give up on her potential. While I agree that a lot of men and women come and go rather precipitously, I dispute my colleague's conclusion because I view *Lonesome Dove* as a panorama of types. Its artistic goal is the creation of a broad-swept canvas rather than the portraiture of psychological cameos.

Certainly Lorena could have been developed further. McMurtry emotionally drops her just as, when the catalytic result suits him, he more permanently disposes of other people, too. Sean, Deets, Jake, Elmira, and even Gus are expendable in time. "Though he had seen hundreds of surprising things in battle, this was the most shocking. An Indian boy who probably hadn't been fifteen years old had run up to Deets and killed him" (*LD,* 718). Ignominiously eliminating Deets, the seasoned fighter and the leaders' right-hand man, McMurtry makes his point clear. *Lonesome Dove* is not the story of any one cliché.

Rather, *Lonesome Dove* is all the stories of the Old West, 843 pages of neophytes and heroes, horses and longhorns, mothers and whores, good guys and bad. The book judges those people and their lives from a perspective designed to elicit surprise.

McMurtry sets the pattern at the beginning. Unlike an adventure yarn, not much happens at first. The first quarter of this novel occurs before the cattle drive even begins, with slow delicious moments on the Hat Creek Cattle Company and Livery Emporium property and at the nearby Dry Bean Saloon. The leisurely pace—perhaps more typical of the rural West than most novelists care to admit—belies the conventional rhythm of formula fiction. "As was his custom, Augustus drank a fair amount of whiskey as he sat and watched the sun ease out of the day" (*LD,* 16). His partner, on the other hand, just looks busier. "Call walked the river for an hour, though he knew there was no real need. It was just an old habit he had, left over from wilder times" (*LD,* 26). So the days—and two hundred pages—pass, without incident.

Highlighting the two men's lives are infrequent forays into Mexico when, reversing their earlier Texas Ranger roles, the cowboys rustle available horses and cattle. Even that turns out to be a joke, though. Pedro Flores, their nemesis, is dead. "We might as well go on to Montana," Call says quietly. "The fun's over around here" (*LD,* 170). The fun isn't over in McMurtry's imagination, however, as he delimits life off the range. "The piano was the pride of the saloon, and, for that matter, of the town. The church folks even borrowed it on Sundays. Luckily the church house was right next to the saloon and the piano had wheels. Some of the deacons had built a ramp out at the back of the saloon, and a board track across to the church, so that all they had to do was push the piano right across to the church. Even so, the arrangement was a threat to the sobriety of the deacons, some of whom considered it their duty to spend their evenings in the saloon, safeguarding the piano" (*LD*, 30–31).

Trailing away from *Lonesome Dove* leads to more sobering experiences, but a lightheartedness makes the tension easier to bear. Like *Little Big Man* and *The Monkey-Wrench Gang* before it, this novel disguises serious themes in comic dress. Not surprisingly, those themes are appropriate to the frontier.

The first of these I call the "jackpot mentality"—the idealistic notion that the grass will be greener on the other side. What should be the energy of the American Dream but instead is the impetus of boredom sends Call north to Montana. Once there, he turns back to Texas again, a cyclical movement that highlights the futility of the quest in the first place. Macabre, hollow, even silly, his final adventure ends almost pathetically. One might say that Augustus McCrae's last moments are just as counterproductive.

In fact, most of *Lonesome Dove*'s adventures are ultimately counterproductive. Elmira runs away from her husband because she wants to go back to her ex-lover and live free again. She finds Dee Boot in jail. "He seemed scared, and his hair had little pieces of cotton ticking in it from a tear in the thin mattress he slept on. The scruffy growth of whiskers made him seem a lot older than she had remembered him" (*LD*, 606). Running away one more time, she finds a cruel death at the hands of a band of marauding Indians—another dream dashed.

Another theme is dashed, too. Experience regularly replaces innocence in many western novels. Sometimes that innocence is painfully apparent, as we see in the narrator of *The Virginian* or of *Shane;* sometimes it's trite, as we discover in a Zane Grey formulaic rendition of learning the "Code of the West"; sometimes it's less obtrusive but no less significant. Neither Elmira nor her husband, July Johnson, knows anything about survival in the West, yet they're decisively educated McMurtry-style. July, for example, joins Gus in a bloody confrontation with the Kiowas. "I didn't shoot a one," he moans after the last man falls. "You shot the whole bunch" (*LD*, 451). The lesson he learns an hour later is even more painful. "For a long time, July did not go into the camp. He couldn't. He stood and listened to the flies buzz over them. He didn't want to see what had been done" (*LD*, 456). Education, in this case, embraces violence and pain. It isn't the least bit romantic or Technicolorful.

Newt's learning process takes painful form, too. Dusty trail rides, lonely nights with the herd, violent weather, and blind stampedes shape his physical development. Deaths like Sean's and Deet's and Jake's age him psychologically. "'Have we got to hang Jake too?' he asked. 'He was my ma's friend'" (*LD*, 572). Newt's question elicits no comment from the men of the Hat Creek Cattle Company.

Good and evil are as clear-cut in *Lonesome Dove* as they are in most western novels, but they well may be mixed in a single human being. That is to say, a strong ethical code informs the novel, though not everyone wears a white hat or a black hat and not every character receives his just deserts. Jake, of course, deserves punishment because he silently allowed the Suggs brothers to perpetrate mayhem. That he spurs his horse from under the noose—"He died fine," says Gus (*LD*, 576)—reminds us of his good qualities; that he must be hung iterates the bad. So, too, do we see other mixed indications of frontier justice. Innocents like Roscoe, Joe, and Janey, for example, are brutally dismembered, while their murderer, Blue Duck, escapes. About to be hung a year later, the renegade dies instead by leaping, in chains, through a third-story courthouse window. Once again McMurtry raises expectations and then dashes them to the prairie sod.

This, then, is *Lonesome Dove*'s pattern. Not a theme exists that hasn't, in one form or another, appeared in another western novel, just as no character or setting occurs that the reader hasn't seen before. But McMurtry, rather than simply revisiting the past, turns it topsy-turvy. Familiar river crossings, familiar faces, familiar formulas emerge and fade in twisted fashion.

For readers who take their cowboys seriously, the reversals and dispersals may prove unsettling; the black humor and the inhuman violence unpleasant. For the iconoclast who finds George Washington Hayduke a welcome antidote, however, the one who would like to see the high plains drifter ride into Dallas, *Lonesome Dove*'s heroes are perfectly fine. As a matter of fact, the iconoclast would approve of the entire ambience of the book. While not taking the formulas too seriously, it takes the Old West very seriously indeed.

On a level we haven't touched yet, *Lonesome Dove* is profound. A penetrating examination of historical forces and the passage of time, it explores what happens when generations permute and dreams fail to materialize. This particular theme I believe dominates the best of western fiction. *The Big Sky* and *Angle of Repose,* to choose two outstanding examples, both turn on fulcrums of change—Boone Caudill's West disappears in the irony of his own actions, Susan and Oliver Ward's is transmuted through the years. In both cases, and in *Lonesome Dove,* change and perpetuity weave together as one generation gives way to the next and as the ever-present American Dream reasserts itself in different guise.

In a scene reminiscent of Shane's final heroic departure, Woodrow Call leaves his horse, his rifle, and his father's pocket watch to Newt, newly dubbed range boss of the Montana spread. Much could be made, I suppose, of the symbolism, but in actuality the entire scene takes place in almost utter silence. The painfully inarticulate Call can transfer the artifacts, not the wisdom, the strength, the heart. Later Call defends himself by saying, "'I gave him my horse.'" Clara counters, "'Your horse but not your name? . . . You haven't even given him your name?' 'I put more value on the horse,'" Call rightly replies (*LD,* 831). Penetrating the stereotypes with an almost painful irony, McMurtry successfully warps the formula one more time.

When I finished *Lonesome Dove,* I was struck not only by how thoroughly the old formulas had been dispersed but also by how completely the Hat Creek Cattle Company and Livery Emporium had disappeared. Call hears a dinner bell that "made him feel that he rode through a land of ghosts. He felt lost in his mind and wondered if all the boys would be there when he got home" (*LD*, 841). They aren't, of course. The novel ends two pages after that, but not before exposing one more instance of fraudulent idealism—the Dry Bean Saloon, burned to the ground because its owner "missed that whore" (*LD*, 843). So the reader closes the book with inadvertent thoughts of Dish Boggett, another cowboy pursuing the same futility into an unknown future.

In scenes like the preceding, *Lonesome Dove* addresses what Wallace Stegner calls the crucial issue of western fiction. Time passes, generations come and go, the same mistakes are made again—variations on a theme. Like the author of *Angle of Repose*, McMurtry discerns the sweep of history as cyclical, then points to its transitory ironies.

> "Imagine getting killed by an arrow in this day and age," Augustus said. "It's ridiculous, especially since they shot at us fifty times with modern weapons and did no harm."
> "You always was careless," Call said. "Pea said you rode over a hill and right into them. I've warned you about that very thing a thousand times. There's better ways to approach a hill."
> "Yes, but I like being free on the earth," Augustus said. "I'll cross the hills where I please." (*LD*, 784–85)

So will the author of *Lonesome Dove*.

McMurtry rides in the company of the Stegners and the Abbeys and the Clarks and all the first-rate western novelists who ever described a cowboy without quite keeping to the trail. The characters are all there in his book, the setting, the themes, the social and psychological milieus—all combined in a panoramic vista of the Old West. But just when the reader thinks a cliché will materialize, McMurtry stands the formula on its head. Just when the expected turns up, the unexpected turns it upside down. Sometimes comically, sometimes violently, often with emotions mixed, the world of

Lonesome Dove moves south to north and back again via a route signed by reversals of what should be familiar. "'Why in the hell would anybody think they wanted to take cattle to Montana?'" someone asks. "'We thought it would be a good place to sit back and watch 'em shit,'" comes the irreverent answer (*LD*, 649).

That McMurtry's imagination sees a landscape beyond the rainbow trail is what makes *Lonesome Dove* first-rate. That he crafts a panorama which makes all the old expectations seem fresh and new is a measure of his talent. That he addresses significant themes in a fresh way is obviously a mark of excellence. *A* major novel of the American West? Absolutely. *The* major novel? No.

The very characteristic that makes this book great is also the one that keeps it from being the greatest. Rather than challenging the formulas and clichés from the past, the greatest literature makes its own. McMurtry, content to warp the pattern, finally has done nothing more. *Lonesome Dove* is the best epic western of the last ten years, but it wasn't made by a man imagining a masterpiece. Its author isn't the Faulkner of the West; its dust jacket is wrong. On the other hand, I like the book enormously. So maybe that dust jacket, when it labels *Lonesome Dove* "the novel about the West that [we have] long been waiting for," isn't out of line after all. I was indeed waiting for *Lonesome Dove,* though I continue to fancy a Faulkner wearing spurs.

NOTE

All citations included in the text are from Larry McMurtry, *Lonesome Dove* (New York: Simon and Schuster, 1985). During the 1990s, Larry McMurtry published three more novels engaging the same cast of characters in different adventures. An interested reader can consider the cowboys' and their friends' actions and developing characterizations in a broader context now. *Streets of Laredo* (1993) is a sequel to *Lonesome Dove*; *Dead Man's Walk* (1995) and *Comanche Moon* (1997) are prequels.

CHAPTER TWELVE

Stegner and Stewardship

Even though Wallace Stegner has never been specifically labeled as a nature writer or an author of natural history, his prose has always revealed his respect for and his affinity toward the environment. Readers find in his books and essays not only verbal photographs of the West but special feelings for the landscapes of his youth. Nowhere does this fusion of the pictorial and the romantic come together more successfully than in the "Overture" to *The Sound of Mountain Water.* "I gave my heart to the mountains," Stegner wrote many years ago, "the minute I stood beside this river with its spray in my face and watched it thunder into foam, smooth to green glass over sunken rocks, shatter to foam again."[1] Such a line is typical of his heartfelt response to a natural scene undefiled by man.

Susan J. Tyburski published an article about the "Overture" in a 1983 issue of *Western American Literature.* There she generalized about Stegner's vision of the land and argued that "wilderness was a source of religious inspiration and renewal for Stegner."[2] Drawing upon such diverse resources as Max Westbrook and Mircea Eliade,[3] Tyburski determined a geography of "holy places" for Stegner, a geography developed almost entirely from descriptions in *The Sound of Mountain Water* essays and an earlier Stegner chapter of *This Is Dinosaur.* With reference primarily to the most subjective of pictorial passages, she was able to conclude that, "for Stegner, the invasion of commercial elements into a wilderness area constitutes the profanation of sacred ground."

While Tyburski may have been correct in her interpretation of Stegner's "essential source of emotional, aesthetic, psychological, and spiritual regeneration,"[4] her discussion was necessarily selective. She unfortunately focused only on those sentences and paragraphs which supported her thesis, and ignored those words which might confound it. I say this, however, not to point my finger at a particular critic. Rather, I want to point at what is problematic in any generalization about Stegner's environmental point of view.

On the surface, Wallace Stegner's attitude reflects that of any contemporary author who has an emotional attachment and philosophical commitment to the land. Somewhat deeper, though, is a point of view that appears inconsistent at best and downright contradictory at worst. Somewhere deeper still, lies another stratum both organic and rational, both flexible and systematic. Here is the place that I believe constitutes the core of Stegner's sense of the land. Here also is a level no critic has yet explored. So "Stegner and Stewardship"—my name for the heart of his environmental point of view—proposes to sink a shaft through layers and mine some new terrain.

On the surface, Stegner behaves and writes predictably. His role in the twentieth-century American conservation movement is both wide-ranging and exemplary. It includes not only the production of a number of essays written for *The Reporter, The New Republic, The Atlantic, Harper's, The Saturday Review of Literature, Blair & Ketchum's Country Journal, Esquire, American Heritage,* the Sierra Club *Bulletin,* and *The Living Wilderness,* but the editing of a book that helped thwart a proposed Echo Canyon dam.[5] It also embraces such divergent activities as a stint working for Interior Secretary Stewart Udall, two years on the Board of Directors of the Sierra Club, a role as founder and Honorary President of the Committee for Green Foothills in California, and a willingness to give speeches about what Americans are doing to the land.[6] "I can toss my pebbles," he remarked of his quiet activism in 1983, "onto what I wish were an avalanche of protest."[7]

Stegner's most definitive—and best-known—comment on the subject of the environment is his 1960 "Wilderness Letter," the "Coda" of *The Sound of Mountain Water.* Originally written to David Pesonen of the Wildland Research Center at the University of California, Berkeley, the "Wilderness Letter" has been anthologized and reprinted dozens of times. It argues forcefully for the abstract notion of wilderness—"The idea alone can sustain me"[8]— as well as for the tangible desirability of unscarred land. Of the Robbers' Roost country in Utah, he extrapolates: "Save a piece of country like that intact, and it does not matter in the slightest that only a few people every year will go into it. That is precisely its value. . . . We simply need that wild country available to us, even if we never do more than drive to its edge and look in."[9] Such a statement presages/echoes Edward Abbey and a host of other wilderness advocates, and such a statement is often quoted by those who see Wallace Stegner as a spokesman.

T. H. Watkins, in fact, calls Stegner "one of the central figures in the modern conservation movement." Even though Watkins acknowledges Stegner's discomfort at such a label, he insists upon its appropriateness. "For forty years [Stegner] has borne witness for the land that has enriched his life and art, and the measured cadence of his splendid prose has played a significant role in the shaping of the sensibility we now call environmentalism."[10] Certainly Stegner's ostensible wilderness position was—and still is—highly regarded for its articulation of a consistent pattern of ecological awareness. And "conservationist" assuredly is the best word to characterize the most obvious pattern of Stegner's ideas.

His conservationism seems to grow from two deep roots, one physical and tangible, the other intellectual and more abstract. The former had its beginnings in boyhood, especially in the early years spent on the Saskatchewan/Montana border; the latter, in the author's study of John Wesley Powell.

Between 1914 and 1920, Stegner's parents homesteaded in the

Cypress Hills country of southern Saskatchewan. So the young boy's days and nights were spent in close intimacy with a pristine and relatively inhospitable land. From this experience—the homesteading venture was a failure—Stegner learned exactly what could and could not be done with arid land. *Wolf Willow,* his memoir of the time spent as an erstwhile Canadian, recounts both beauty and despair. He recalls "the mystery of nights when the stars were scoured clean and the prairie was full of breathings from a long way off, and the strange, friendly barking of night- hunting owls,"[11] but he also ponders the futility of such toil.

> How does one know in his bones what this continent has meant to Western man unless he has, though briefly and in the midst of failure, belatedly and in the wrong place, made trails and paths on an untouched country and built human living places, however transitory, at the edge of a field that he helped break from prairie sod? How does one know what wilderness has meant to Americans unless he has shared the guilt of wastefully and ignorantly tampering with it in the name of Progress?

He answers for himself. "One who has lived the dream, the temporary fulfillment, and the disappointment has had the full course."[12]

The boy who lived both the dream and the disappointment never forgot the lessons of his youth. So when he went on to become the man who studied John Wesley Powell, Stegner was ready to espouse the truths spoken by a historical figure whose ideas coincided with his own. In 1954, Wallace Stegner published *Beyond the Hundredth Meridian,*[13] a narration of Powell's exploration of the Grand Canyon and the second opening of the West. Yet *Beyond the Hundredth Meridian* covers far more philosophical territory than its title or subtitle would have the reader believe.

The visionary nature of Powell's conclusions appealed to Stegner, particularly as examined from the perspectives of time and space and history. For Powell said to nineteenth-century deaf ears what a twentieth-century Stegner knew to be true—"the West is defined . . . by inadequate rainfall."[14] Powell suggested a radical but rational solution, "proposing to close, apparently forever, a great part of the remaining public domain, and to bring to a close, except within the irrigable lands, the agricultural expansion which had been part of the national expectation for almost a century." When powerful congressional forces combined to suppress Powell's point of view, the suggestion was defeated and his career was destroyed. Stegner compares his fate with that of "all leaders who go too far ahead, and of all thinkers who think straighter than their contemporaries."[15]

John Wesley Powell's straight thinking about the finite nature of water in the West has come to haunt more recent generations. The West is indeed a dry place. "Aridity, and aridity alone, makes the various Wests one," repeats Stegner in a recent chapter appropriately called "Living Dry." No plan for settlement, for agriculture, for mineral extraction, for industrialization, he argues, can prudently ignore this fact. "And what do you do about aridity, if you are a nation inured to plenty and impatient of restrictions . . . ? You may deny it for a while. Then you must either adapt to it or try to engineer it out of existence."[16]

One would expect any good conservationist, I think, to embrace adaptation while disdaining engineering. Certainly that is the intuitive message of an Aldo Leopold or the battle cry of an Edward Abbey. Certainly that is the gist of Stegner's words much of the time. A fairly predictable sentiment of his can be found, for example, in a chapter called "The Gift of Wilderness" in *One Way to Spell Man*. There Stegner wrote, "We need to learn to listen to the land, hear what it says, understand what it can and can't do over the long haul; what, especially in the West, it should not be asked to do."[17] This passage directly follows a page that implicitly harks back to Leopold and explicitly calls for "a land ethic that unites science, religion, and human feeling."[18]

While such phrases underscore Stegner's prevailing commitment to the ethics of conservation, the latter quotation includes a curious anomaly. The word "science" sounds strangely out of place—naming something closely akin to technology, something many conservationists would blame rather than embrace. Here is the first indication of that layer of environmental viscosity which critics to date have ignored.

Its most blatant manifestation is a full-length book called *Discovery!*, a nonfiction product from 1971 whose focus is engineering. Stegner's *Discovery!* describes the Arabian American Oil Company's corporate implementation of a plan that ultimately sent Arabian oil out to the western world and brought the western world to Saudi Arabia.[19] It is a book apparently commissioned by Aramco itself—at least its title page pronounces it "As Abridged for *Aramco World Magazine*." It does not appear to be a book about which Stegner brags, and few of his readers are aware of its existence.

Whether a curious aberration, however, or an integral part of Stegner's thought pattern, *Discovery!* does exist, and needs to be assessed in the context of his conservationist point of view. At least he took measures to distance himself from the task. Of all Stegner's prose, *Discovery!* is the one text that keeps the point of view at arm's length, so the author must have consciously removed himself from the material in question. The omniscient narrator remains as impartial as possible, making no real value judgments, neither cheerleading nor castigating. Even so, the subject matter itself leads him into paradox.

The introduction, for example, guides the reader into unfamiliar territory while setting a tone for the book as a whole. "Whatever the uncertainties of the future," Stegner wrote before the days of OPEC, "Aramco can congratulate itself on a record that is a long way from being grossly exploitative or 'imperialist.' Its record probably contains both mistakes and inconsistencies, and it has indeed earned impressive profits, but in general its role and its intention have been to provide an alternative between willful foreign exploitation of the 19th-century kind, and willful nationalization such as has happened more recently." Such a description of the company that changed the course of a nation and of an entire segment of the world sounds very odd indeed. But it does reveal the author's apparent intent—to glamorize Aramco's accomplishments. The whole point of the book is to boast of the changes one powerful corporation brought to the land.

Stegner goes on, then, to recount the course of negotiations, explorations, and discoveries that accompanied Aramco's first decade in Saudi Arabia. Essentially his narration focuses on those who brought Aramco into being, and their energy and zeal. "Predominantly from the western United States," he wrote of their commitment, "the Hundred Men [those who stayed on in Saudi Arabia during the Second World War] responded to a reclamation dream as kindling responds to fire." While such a simile makes no directly evaluative statement, it does imply tacit approval of the Hundred Men's task. So do the incidents selected to tell the tale.

The back cover of the book itemizes the contents: "an oil-well fire out of control, a tragic mid-gulf explosion, bombs falling out of a moonlit sky. Above all, it is the story of men—the men who came to Saudi Arabia in 1933, bringing the skills and strengths of another world, and the proud men of the desert awaiting with grave concern the impact that this vital discovery would have on their time-honored ways." Little evidence exists, however, that Stegner has any concomitant grave concern. His narrative voice neither probes the impact nor ponders the results. He simply describes the processes of dealing with the bedouins, of sinking dry wells, of protecting the company's property, of striking it very rich in a foreign desert. Even the wildlife, uniquely precious in that part of the world, is treated from a distance.

Shooting three rare oryx for dinner, or lassoing them for sport, ought to be cause for complaint, I think. Yet the reader learns only that "for the next day or two they ate the best meat that Arabia provided, and they kept the calf, Butch, force-fed with a medicine dropper." Butch's demise is equally unfortunate—both for the oryx and for the conservationist mind-set.

He was everybody's baby. But he was symbolic of the losses that accompanied the gains of the industrial invasion. Butch's parents had been unable to escape hunters chasing them in a

car, the kind of hunting that was to virtually wipe out both
oryx and gazelle before conservation laws were put into effect.
And Butch himself, treated more kindly by the newcomers,
died of their kindness; born to subsist on an occasional wisp of
grass, he fell so greedily upon the alfalfa they brought him in
the supply truck from Hofuf that he bloated up and perished in
convulsions.[20]

The next paragraph immediately deploys the men against five
more of the rare species. While not exactly applauding such behavior, Stegner nonetheless treats the incidents lightheartedly and
withholds the judgment a reader might expect. That the baby oryx
"was symbolic of the losses that accompanied the gains of the industrial invasion" is the only directly evaluative statement in the
book, but even it minimizes the impact of killing endangered species and ignores the more general environmental disruption that
must have swept across the Saudi Arabian desert after the Americans arrived.

Stegner's seeming indifference to mineral exploitation counters
sharply with his pronouncements of a decade earlier. "For mining I
cannot say much good except that its operations are generally
short-lived,"[21] he wrote in *The Sound of Mountain Water*. This statement is difficult to correlate with the one hundred ninety pages of
engineering enthusiasm that mark *Discovery!,* and even harder to
conjoin with the apparent long-term effects of oil production in the
Middle East, pipelines in Alaska, open pits or offshore drills.

But perhaps we can guess how he justified *Discovery!* to himself.
In one conversation with Richard Etulain, Stegner defines a theme
that is relevant here. "Discovery, raid, settlement," he says, referring
to a major American triumvirate, "those make an obvious solid
topic; the Westward Movement essentially. I suppose most historians like that because it's romantic, because it's encompassable, and
because it makes a nice unified sort of theme."[22] "Discovery" makes
a nice romantic title, too, and I find it an appropriate choice for this
particular book. First, it distances itself from its companions, "raid"

and "settlement." Then it glamorizes a process while dismissing its effects, and allows Stegner the same latitude. At the same time, however, *Discovery!* implies the presence of an author whose themes are not as simple as our conservationists would insist.

Let's go back to that critical essay by Susan Tyburski. At the beginning of this piece I accused her of selecting only a Stegner whose paragraphs led naturally to her conclusions and of ignoring a Stegner whose words might suggest an alternative attitude toward nature. Specifically, I was thinking about page fifteen in *This Is Dinosaur,* the page immediately following one from which Tyburski quoted and the page that is at the heart of another puzzling Stegner conundrum. There, in the book that was to put the first chink in the armor of the Army Corps of Engineers, Stegner positioned an extraordinarily anthropocentric paragraph. "A place is nothing in itself," he declared back in 1955. "It has no meaning, it can hardly be said to exist, except in terms of human perception, use, and response. The wealth and resources and usefulness of any region are only inert potential until man's hands and brain have gone to work; and natural beauty is nothing until it comes to the eye of the beholder."

Observations like "a place is nothing in itself," or "it has no meaning . . . except in terms of human perception, use, and response" sound contradictory when judged against the "Wilderness Letter" or the many other Stegner allusions to the "idea" of wilderness as an abstract necessity. Yet in *Dinosaur* he is insistent about this man-centeredness. "We cannot even describe a place except in terms of its human uses," he contends. "It would be idiotic to preach conservation of such a wilderness in perpetuity, just to keep it safe from all human use. It is only for human use that it has any meaning, or is worth preserving."[23] A lot of environmentalists would disagree.

Sometimes Stegner himself sounds like he disagrees. Just recently, in a lecture series given at the University of Michigan, he quoted the Mormon hierarch, John Widstoe, who said: "The destiny of man is to possess the whole earth; the destiny of the earth is to be subject to man. There can be no full conquest of the earth, and no real satisfaction to humanity, if large portions of the earth remain beyond his highest control." Stegner's immediate response could not be more forthright—"That doctrine offends me."[24] On the other hand, this is the same Stegner who said of the Grand Canyon, "Incorrigibly anthropocentric as we are, we can only respond humanly."[25] And the same Stegner who said of Capitol Reef, "The land is not complete without its human history and associations. Scenery by itself is pretty sterile."[26]

To fabricate a Stegner of utter contradictions might be possible now, but that would be as critically irresponsible as to contrive one stamped from a single mold. The responsible task is to pull the apparent contradictions together in a way that spells out the deep-seated consistency in his environmental point of view without violating his artistic license. For despite the problematic *Discovery!* and despite the anthropocentricity that would alienate many an ardent preservationist, Wallace Stegner does hold a fairly uniform vision of the environment and of man's relationship to it. What he believes—which resembles the thinking of a man like Aldo Leopold but is absolutely contrary to the notions of an Edward Abbey[27]—he calls "stewardship."

The dictionary, tracing "steward" back to two Old English words for "hall" and "keeper," defines the modern term in a number of complementary ways. "A person put in charge of the affairs of a large household or estate." Or, "one who acts as a supervisor or administrator . . . for another or others." Or, "a person variously responsible." Or, "a person . . . in charge of arrangements, . . . an attendant, . . . an officer."[28] Those dictionary definitions impact significantly upon Stegner's environmental sense of the word. To him, a "steward" is someone in charge of the land around him, someone who consciously takes responsibility for its well-being, someone who acts upon it in ecologically sound ways.[29]

One becomes especially aware of Stegner's use of the word when reading the chapters he wrote for *American Places*. Co-authored with his son and published in 1983, this book focuses on observed interactions between the American people and their surroundings. Stegner's contributions meander across the countryside from New England's Long Pond to a series of small towns along the Mississippi and from the Great Salt Lake to Montana's Crow Country. The word "stewardship" appears with surprising regularity.

The first occurrence echoes a solemnity that pervades Stegner's recent prose. "These are soberer times," he observes of the present-day United States. "What a young American just coming of age confronts now is not a limitless potential, but developed power attended by destruction and depletion. Though we should have recognized the land as a living organism demanding care and stewardship, we have treated it as a warehouse." Here he distantly alludes to stewardship as something we have completely missed in our ongoing transactions with the land.

Then his tone changes to a more matter-of-fact one—"land is a heritage as well as a resource, and ownership suggests stewardship, not exploitation." At this point he implies that, if Americans can learn to recognize the integrity of the land, perhaps stewardship is a concept well within our grasp. Finally, when looking at some Montana property where the owners have cared well for their land, Stegner voices genuine optimism. "Work to be done, the chores of an unremitting but satisfying stewardship." These ranchers apparently understand how to function effectively in their natural surroundings, and their children, especially, suggest to Stegner a kind of interactive continuity. "Ten or fifteen years from now, . . . one or more of them will perhaps be running this ranch, exercising the same stewardship,"[30] which their parents have been able to display.

That Stegner uses the same word so many times in succession cannot be accidental. He repeats it because it so appropriately defines his sense of man's relationship to the land. Here lies what I earlier projected as the core of Stegner's environmental point of view. Stewardship is the keystone—the concept both organic and rational, both flexible and systematic. It is the tenet that can embrace such diverse things as Stegner's abstract "idea" of wilderness, a book like *Discovery!,* his studied anthropocentrism, some crotchetiness, and an abiding concern that has stayed with him for nearly four score years.

In a literary context Stegner once pinpointed "the human response to a set of environmental and temporal circumstances."[31] That phrase appropriately fits an environmental context, too. I believe he has embraced stewardship today because our twentieth-century environmental and temporal circumstances have dictated such an alliance. As a nation of entrepreneurs, we have changed the face of the land. Now we have a responsibility to see that those changes do not damage the world irrevocably; we are in charge.

Stegner likes to refer to George Perkins Marsh, the author of *Man and Nature* who, in 1864, first warned Americans about the consequences of tampering with the environment. Marsh's book outlined the extent of changes already wrought by human actions to plants, animals, water, and topography, pointed out the dangers of imprudence, and suggested the importance of restored harmony between man and his natural surroundings. Like Powell, his ideas were dismissed in his own time but have been adopted and advocated by subsequent generations. His ideas are particularly relevant to Stegner, for they lead inherently to stewardship. Once man has altered the environment, he cannot stop doing so. Each diversion of a waterway, each destruction of plant or animal life, each transaction with nature inevitably leads to further transactions. Unless these are the result of stewardship, man will unleash destruction in his world.

Aldo Leopold understood Marsh's concept, too, most ironically when he defined a conservationist as "one who is humbly aware that with each stroke [of an axe] he is writing his signature on the face of his land."[32] Leopold, in fact, made this apparent incongruity the basis for his proposals regarding deer hunting in Wisconsin. When potential predators have been eliminated from an environment hospitable to deer, the deer naturally increase out of proportion to the land's ability to sustain them. After this happens, man must take over the role formerly played by natural forces, must accept responsibility for culling the herd and managing the deer population. As Leopold explained in the 1940s, "man-made changes are of a different order than evolutionary changes, and have effects more comprehensive than is intended or foreseen." Therefore, it is man's place to do what is "right . . . to preserve the integrity, stability, and beauty of the biotic community."[33] Consequently it becomes man's place to use hunting as a means of regulating an animal population, or logging as a means of patterning the forests.

Stegner would describe the permutation less indirectly and perhaps more emphatically. In *One Way to Spell Man* he zeroes in on the unhappy consequences of the American Dream. "We have been fruitful, and multiplied . . . but in doing so we have plundered our living space. If we have loved the land fate gave us—and most of us did—we went on destroying it even while we loved it, until now we can point to many places we once pointed to in pride, and say with an appalled sense of complicity and guilt, 'Look what we've done!'"[34]

If he complains about plundering our living space in *One Way to Spell Man,* however, he turns the term around in *The American West as Living Space.* This, his most recent commentary on the subject, proposes new ways in which Americans might further their relationship with the land. The answer does not involve the bulldozer. In the past, "we have tried to make the country and climate over to fit our existing habits and desires," he observes. "Instead of listening to the silence, we have shouted into the void."[35] Without shouting, Leopold made the same point. His best-known book ended quietly, "We shall hardly relinquish the shovel, which after all has many good points, but we are in need of gentler and more objective criteria for its successful use."[36] A generation later, Wallace Stegner more explicitly suggests a solution that lies in adaptation and stewardship.

Part of the burden rests with the individual. From the heritage of his boyhood, Stegner still holds the dream of the yeoman farmer, and from the heritage of his study, he still sings the praises of Thomas Jefferson and St. Jean de Crèvecoeur. He even titles the last chapter of *The American West as Living Space* "Variations on a

Theme by Crèvecoeur," referring the reader to Crèvecoeur's *Letters* of two hundred years ago and speculating why the Frenchman's idealized yeoman American farmer has either disappeared or been transformed. So in good faith Stegner can romantically applaud Montana ranching, even though he knows how difficult such a life of yeomanry and stewardship can be.

"They do not kid themselves. Theirs is a holding action, perhaps a rearguard action, and it could easily lose. Many forces, economic and social, work against the subsistence ranch."[37] Yet the steward-ship there is satisfying, Stegner thinks, because the men and women themselves cherish the land. And this notion meshes with that puz-zling Stegner anthropocentrism from the past. When he wrote, "the wealth and resources and usefulness of any region are only in-ert potential until man's hands and brain have gone to work . . . the natural world, actually, is the test by which each man proves him-self: I see, I feel, I love, I use, I alter, I appropriate, therefore I am,"[38] he could have been talking about the Bench Ranch in the West Rosebud. There, day after day, Jack and Susan Heyneman prove themselves in relationship with, and thus provide steward-ship to, the land. I think Oliver Ward, the protagonist of Stegner's novel, *Angle of Repose,* was trying to do the same.[39]

Not all of us can live in a Bench Ranch world, however, so our stewardship must be exercised in a somewhat different way. Stegner suggests a partial reliance on the federal government. In this respect he differs quite radically from a number of his fellow conservation-ists, since he genuinely believes that proper governmental interven-tion is a viable course of action. History may have proved other-wise, but Stegner retains a measure of confidence that sounds almost uncharacteristically optimistic. He rejects what he regards as the bad agencies—the Bureau of Reclamation, for example—and embraces the good. The good, in this context, are those land-man-aging bureaus that "have as at least part of their purpose the preser-vation of the West in a relatively natural, healthy, and sustainable condition." Indeed, Stegner thinks Westerners especially should re-think their relationship to the government in Washington, D.C.

"The federal presence should be recognized as what it is," he explains, "a reaction against our former profligacy and wastefulness, an effort at adaptation and *stewardship* [emphasis mine] in the interest of the environment and the future."[40] While his faith in federal control sets Stegner apart from many other environmentalists, it does fit the context of Stegner's career. After all, he has for years admired the John Wesley Powell who advocated governmental oversight of Western lands, as long as the parameters were scientifically sound. And he worked for Stewart Udall once, supported the Secretary of the Interior's efforts, and applauded the results. "As a *steward* [emphasis mine] of the land," Stegner once said, "I would rate [Udall] very high indeed."[41]

Perhaps this is the place to fit *Discovery!* into Stegner's career, too. Despite my own reservations, the book does boast a sympathy with the bureaucratic potential to weld a corporate entity with a native population, to marry happily a power with the less powerful. "Not inconceivably," Stegner admits, "the thing they all thought of as 'progress' and 'development' would blow them all up, and their world with it. But that is another story. This one is purely and simply the story of a frontier."[42] I read that final disclaimer not only as the author's attempt to place his book in the context of the pioneering spirit that permeates his fiction and nonfiction alike, but also as an effort to set this particular story apart. *Discovery!* deals with potential, nothing more.

And potential lies at the heart of stewardship's promise. Perhaps that is the beauty of Stegner's organic concept for future generations. Occasionally a curmudgeon and often a grouch, he nonetheless keeps his eyes on the heritage we might leave our children. With the proper restraint, he can envision that heritage as better than what we ourselves received. "America is the world's greatest undeveloped nation," he says ironically, "and by its very premises, nobody can develop it except its citizens." But we have a chance, he conjoins, "to assert the long-range public interest against short-term economic interests—in effect to promote civilized responsibility, both public and private, over frontier carelessness and greed."[43]

This is a rational view of stewardship, of—to return to those dictionary definitions—persons "variously responsible . . . in charge of arrangements." From the beginning of his career, Stegner has hoped not only that man can accept the appropriate responsibility for his relationship with the earth, but can make adequate provisions for its future. He has persuasively repeated:

> We need an environmental ethic that will reach all the way
> from the preservation of untouched wilderness to the beautifi-
> cation of industrial cities, that will concern itself with saving
> the still-savable and healing the half-ruined and cleansing the
> polluted, that will touch not only land but air and water, that
> will have as its purpose the creation of a better environment for
> men, as well as the creation or preservation of viable habitats
> for the species that our expansion threatens.[44]

Unlike the ardent preservationists, or even the most studied conservationists, Stegner assumes an ongoing need for man's participation in things environmental because, as he well knows, whole ecological systems no longer remain intact. For what the anthropocentric has already manipulated, the anthropocentric must accept responsibility for managing further. In so doing, Stegner insists, we must "apply to ourselves and our habitat the intelligence that has endangered both. That means drastically and voluntarily reducing our numbers, decontaminating our earth, and thereafter husbanding, building, and nourishing, instead of squandering and poisoning."[45] And while our actions must be judicious and respectful, they must also be strong enough to keep the unacceptable alternative at bay.

Stegner looks forward to the challenge. Gone are the negative overtones when he talks about stewardship. "Angry as one may be at what careless people have done and still do to a noble habitat," he summarizes, "it is hard to be pessimistic about the West. This is the native home of hope. When it fully learns that cooperation, not rugged individualism, is the pattern that most characterizes and preserves it, then it will have achieved itself and outlived its origins.

Then it has a chance to create a society to match its scenery."[46] In stewardship, he firmly believes, we and the land together have a chance.

NOTES

1. Wallace Stegner, *The Sound of Mountain Water* 1980 (Lincoln: University of Nebraska Press, 1985), 42.

2. Susan J. Tyburski, "Wallace Stegner's Vision of Wilderness," *Western American Literature,* 18 (August 1983): 135.

3. See Max Westbrook, "Conservative, Liberal, and Western: Three Modes of American Realism," in *The Literature of the American West,* ed. J. Golden Taylor, Boston: Houghton Mifflin, 1971; and Mircea Eliade, *The Sacred and the Profane,* New York: Harcourt, Brace & World, Inc., 1957.

4. Tyburski, "Wallace Stegner's Vision of Wilderness," 141.

5. See Wallace Stegner, ed., *This Is Dinosaur: Echo Park and Its Magic Rivers,* New York: Alfred A. Knopf, 1955.

6. I am indebted to T. H. Watkins, "Bearing Witness for the Land: The Conservation Career of Wallace Stegner," *South Dakota Review,* 23 (Winter 1985): 42–57, for specific details of Stegner's contributions.

7. Wallace Stegner and Richard W. Etulain, *Conversations with Wallace Stegner on Western History and Literature* (Salt Lake City: University of Utah Press, 1983), 183.

8. Wallace Stegner, "Coda: Wilderness Letter," in *The Sound of Mountain Water,* 150.

9. Ibid., 153.

10. Watkins, "Bearing Witness for the Land," 42, 43.

11. Wallace Stegner, *Wolf Willow* 1955 (Lincoln: University of Nebraska Press, 1980), 281.

12. Ibid., 281–82.

13. See Wallace Stegner, *Beyond the Hundredth Meridian,* Boston: Houghton Mifflin, 1954.

14. Wallace Stegner, *The American West as Living Space* (Ann Arbor: University of Michigan Press, 1987), 6.

15. *Beyond the Hundredth Meridian,* 307, 366–67.

16. *The American West as Living Space,* 8, 27.

17. Wallace Stegner, *One Way to Spell Man* (Garden City, New York: Doubleday and Company, 1982), 177.

18. Ibid., 176.

19. Wallace Stegner, *Discovery!* (Beirut: Middle East Export Press, Inc., 1971), 13.

20. Ibid., vi, 170, 139, 140.

21. *The Sound of Mountain Water,* 151.

22. *Conversations,* 145

23. *This Is Dinosaur,* 15.

24. *The American West as Living Space,* 45. Stegner himself quotes from Widstoe's *Success on Irrigation Projects* (1928), 138.

25. Wallace Stegner, "Foreword" to *The Grand Colorado,* by T. H. Watkins and Contributors (USA: American West Publishing Company, 1969), 10.

26. Wallace Stegner and Page Stegner, *American Places* (Moscow, Idaho: University of Idaho Press, 1983) 143. Citations from *American Places* will be taken only from chapters written by Wallace Stegner.

27. Shortly after drafting this Stegner essay, I read Edward Abbey's last novel. In its pages, I found Abbey's definition of "what the Forest Service calls stewardship," a counterpoint to Stegner's point of view. "Managing the land for the best interests of industrial society and fuck anything else like deer or elk or black bear or red squirrels or people who like to get out in the woods. . . . To make the forests neat and orderly and easy to cut. Like a cornfield, that's what they want. They want the whole West to look like an Illinois cornfield. Like a farm. We are stewards of the earth, they say, appointed by God to manage the earth (every bit of it) in whatever way seems best (to us stewards). That's our holy mission, to be good little stewards and keep that old raw cranky smelly unpredictable Mother Nature where she belongs." Edward Abbey, *Hayduke Lives!* (Boston: Little, Brown and Company, 1990), 127.

28. *Webster's New World Dictionary,* 2nd ed. (New York: World Publishing Company, 1970), 1397–98.

29. To Edward Abbey, the word's etymology can be interpreted in a slightly different way. "A steward is a sty-warden," he clarifies. "Look it up. It's from the Anglo-Saxon *stigeweard,* meaning guardian of the pigpen. That's what our noble stewards are—people who guard pigs" [*Hayduke Lives!,* 127].

30. *American Places,* 27, 49, 123.

31. *Conversations,* 196.

32. Aldo Leopold, *A Sand County Almanac and Sketches Here and There* (1949; New York: Oxford University Press, 1981), 68.

33. Ibid., 218, 224–25.

34. *One Way to Spell Man,* 163.

35. *Living Space,* 33.

36. Leopold, *A Sand County Almanac,* 226.

37. *American Places,* 113.

38. *This Is Dinosaur,* 15; see endnote 23.

39. "They were the makers and doers," wrote Stegner of his fictional protagonists, "they wanted to take a piece of the wilderness and turn it into a home for a civilization." *Angle of Repose,* New York: Fawcett Crest Books, 1971, 344.

40. *Living Space,* 38.

41. Quoted in Watkins, "Bearing Witness for the Land," 53.

42. *Discovery!,* 190.

43. *American Places,* 259, 255.

44. Wallace Stegner, "What Ever Happened to the Great Outdoors?," *Saturday Review* 48 (22 May 1965): 36. On the same page Stegner uses the word "stewardship."

45. Wallace Stegner, "Conservation Equals Survival," in *Crossroads,* ed. Tom E. Kakonis and James C. Wilcox (Lexington, Mass.: D. C. Heath and Co., 1972) 128; rpt. from an article in *American Heritage Magazine,* December 1969.

46. *The Sound of Mountain Water,* 38.

PART III

The Purple Sage

ecause my career goes hand in hand with the modern proliferation of environmental books, essays, and articles, my own work reflects the uneasy outlines of an embryonic genre. When I began my doctoral dissertation in 1969, I couldn't find a single book that contemplated the importance of sense of place in fiction. Art historians, not literary critics, were most interested in the framing of scenes. I had to make up my own terminology, borrowing words like "sublime" and "pictorial" from the eighteenth century, speculating about how "atmosphere" was transmuted into "symbol." When I published *Words for the Wild* in 1987, a collection of excerpts a reader might enjoy while sitting beside a campfire, I was treading in relatively new territory, too. I relied on Emerson and Thoreau for the genre's lineage, and I chose essays that were readily available—a few women writers, no authors of color, a preponderance of white males.

If *Words for the Wild* ended up being less than inclusive, my early literary criticism enshrines an equally narrow point of view. "Environmental Journalism" is now a field of inquiry with its own specific descriptors and its own set of texts. In 1986, however, "environmental journalism" was but a gleam in many writers' eyes. So, too, "Western Literature and Natural Resources" sounds rather naive today, though in 1989 we literary critics were just beginning to explore the connections between the ways we live on the land and the ways we write about it. I include these two somewhat repetitive essays in *Reader of the Purple Sage* because they image the tentative birth of the specialty we now so confidently call "environmental literature." They also iterate my personal touchstones—Edward Abbey, Wallace Stegner, Bob Marshall, the MX debate, Glen Canyon, and the Colorado River.

Two recent essays suggest my sense of environmental literature's current strengths and weaknesses. "Kingdom, Phylum, Class, Order" discusses inherent biases and attendant rhetorical strategies used by contemporary nature writers. Training and temperament alike influence our interpretations of the physical world. Cattlemen and sheepherders see money on the hoof; John Muir calls sheep "hooved locusts." Naturalist Gary Nabhan describes edible plants; art historian Ann Zwinger draws their pictures. I even categorize myself in this essay. Since I know the Nevada desert more intimately than before, I think I describe it more accurately now, understand it more perceptively, see it from the inside in, rather from the outside out. What might other essayists be contemplating about their favorite corners of the West?

"Raising the Bar," a review essay written for *Western American Literature,* considers twenty authors whose books appeared just at the close of the twentieth century. In another twenty years, I suppose, these explications will sound dated, too. For now, however, they spell out what I think is currently happening in the field of literature and the environment, and why, and what I hope will occur in the future. Fewer personal tangents; more dissemination of intellectual content. Less idealization; more discussion of environmental issues. Fewer effusions; more analysis. Better stories; better insights. New characters; new directions. The West is a literary garden these days. Its authors are articulate, passionate, strongly pictorial, fiercely determined to portray what the Western landscape means to us individually, culturally, communally.

And I'm part of the deluge. *Reader of the Purple Sage* ends with some of my own creative writing about the natural world. While I was researching *Words for the Wild,* I began thinking that I could write this stuff. The afterword is my first foray into the field. Soon I collaborated to produce *Earthtones: A Nevada Album,* with my own essays about Nevada distances and with photographs by Stephen Trimble. Our goal was to show the reader how to see this incredible landscape, how to appreciate a land few people love, how—as Wallace Stegner put it—to get over the color green. One of my favorite *Earthtones* chapters is titled "Ghosts." Even as I finished that particular piece, I knew I had more to say. Another book followed, *GhostWest: Reflections Past and Present.* A *GhostWest* excerpt is embedded in "Kingdom, Phylum, Class, Order." Like the rest of my *GhostWest* essays, it ponders how the historic past dictates our sense of the present, how we westerners respond to places and to stories so intimately connected.

Personally, I've arrived in a desert filled with energy and life. After the green-treed, glaciated mountains of the Pacific Northwest, after the narrow canyons of graduate school, my own personal waterway has opened into a terrain of pages and words and playas and wilderness so extensive I'll never be able to explore the full range. Like the Truckee River, I guess. The little girl who read by flashlight when her parents thought she was asleep has become the college professor whose enthusiasm for literature and landscape will never diminish. *Reader of the Purple Sage* maps the route from there to here—from the mountains to the desert, from an intellectual interest in sense of place to a personal commitment to write about the land, from Zane Grey to *Earthtones* to *GhostWest* to whatever lies ahead in the purple sage.

CHAPTER THIRTEEN

Environmental Journalism

The "Preliminary Notes" to Edward Abbey's latest collection of essays include two paragraphs that have triggered my imagination well beyond his immediate context. Abbey explains that *Down the River* contains several selections which "deal with unpleasant and ungrateful subjects—the damnation of another river, the militarization of the open range, the manufacture of nuclear weapons, the industrialization of agriculture." He sees the creation of such essays springing from a "sense of duty," comments ironically on "the easy money" they bring, and emphasizes his preference for "sweeter, funnier, happier themes." Then he concludes with a telling line— "Environmental journalism is not a cheerful field of work."[1]

Perhaps environmental journalism is not a happy vocation, but it nonetheless has become a significant writing form—and force—in contemporary twentieth-century America. A look at its shapes and its subjects, along with an examination of the art of its key practitioners, reveals a scope that encompasses the world and spans more than a hundred years. Chiefly, however, its focus has been the landscape of the American West.

Just what *is* "environmental journalism"? When I began thinking about this paper, I perceived the genre as propagandistic, conservationist writing about the out-of-doors. Abbey's nonfiction, of course, would be a prime subject for discussion. *Slickrock* seemed an obvious book-length example, while an essay from *Down the River* titled simply "MX" would serve as a shorter, more compact, and perhaps more forceful piece for analysis. As I read further, however, my definition began to stretch. Digging into the dusty annals of old *Audubon* magazines and *Sierra Club Bulletins,* the energetic essays of John Muir, then the ageless work of Henry David Thoreau, I found new subtle distinctions. As a result of all this, my own essay has become an exploration quite different from the one originally launched by Abbey's provocative words and my notion of the art form somewhat changed.

"Environmental journalism," as I understand it now, is a form of nonfiction prose that centers its attention, and ours, on the land around us. While it most often expresses a preservationist bias, or at least a conservationist slant, it also can be steadfastly neutral or even mildly prodevelopment. In tandem with its environmental focus, it raises profound issues about the quality of our existence, exploring how we live in our immediate surroundings and how we perceive our need for a wilderness just beyond our grasp. Significantly, environmental journalism pleads for a reappraisal of values in a contemporary world, one that its practitioners, sadly enough, find valueless. At any rate, it makes us think—about the landscape, about the land, about ourselves.

Obviously part of my definition sounds like a paraphrase of Henry David Thoreau. As you will recall, he questioned the quality of those "lives of quiet desperation" he saw his fellows leading, while he trumpeted the importance of untapped wilderness and personal solitude for each and every individual. He set a tone, too—the straightforward conversational style that marks the prose of so many of our best twentieth-century nature essayists. For example, he tells us in "A Winter Walk" how

the clouds have gathered again, and a few straggling snowflakes are beginning to descend. Faster and faster they fall, shutting out the distant objects from sight. The snow falls on every

wood and field, and no crevice is forgotten; by the river and
the pond, on the hill and in the valley. Quadrupeds are con-
fined to their coverts and the birds sit upon their perches this
peaceful hour. There is not so much sound as in fair weather,
but silently and gradually every slope, and the gray walls and
fences, and the polished ice, and the sere leaves, which were
not buried before, are concealed, and the tracks of men and
beasts are lost. With so little effort does nature reassert her rule
and blot out the traces of men.[2]

This potency of nature reasserts itself in page after page of
Thoreau's prose. He is most concerned, in his world, with the human ability to recognize that power, to coexist harmoniously with
it, and to elicit a personal renewal from the natural milieu.

Sometimes, however, circumstances prevent Thoreau from ven-
turing into the wilderness. Like so many of us a century later, he
must instead draw strength from his intellect alone. In the opening
pages of "A Natural History of Massachusetts" I found a strong
indication that, although he doesn't use the term, Thoreau was
aware of the power to be gleaned from environmental journalism.
"Books of natural history make the most cheerful winter reading,"
he observes. "I read in Audubon with a thrill of delight, when the
snow covers the ground, of the magnolia, and the Florida keys, and
their warm sea-breezes; of the fence-rail, and the cotton-tree, and
the migrations of the rice-bird; of the breaking up of winter in Lab-
rador, and the melting of the snow on the forks of the Missouri;
and owe an accession of health to these reminiscences of luxuriant
nature."[3] By 1842, then, the impact of the landscape upon man already had provided essayists with fresh materials and had struck the
minds and hearts of such embryonic conservationists as Henry
Thoreau. As a matter of fact, one can retreat even further into
America's past, to the botanical observations of William Bartram on
his southern explorations or the more philosophical ruminations of
Virginia's Thomas Jefferson, and find men pondering the spiritual
importance of the natural world.

To a twentieth-century reader, though, these writers are curiously one-sided. Thoreau, for example, shows far more dismay at the encroachment of civilization on man's spirit than he does at the impact of machines on the environment itself. He writes admiringly of those voyagers, loggers, settlers, and hunters who make "The Maine Woods" their home, and actually respects the logging process itself. That same paradoxical coupling, love for the wilderness paired with a curiosity about the men who tame it, appears in *Walden* where he eagerly watches the ice-cutters at work, "ploughing, harrowing, rolling, furrowing, in admirable order."[4]

The point is clear. By the middle of the nineteenth century, America had not yet fully cannibalized herself (although she had already begun gnawing on her extremities). So Thoreau and his contemporaries were freer to concentrate on the intellectual, emotional, and spiritual sides of the environment. Concern for the land's very existence had not yet become a necessity.

Only a few decades later, the story was quite different. The frontier was closing, the wilderness diminishing, and philosopher-explorers like John Muir were beginning to realize the insufficiency of American environmental policy. I think it was with Muir's articulation of specific threats to the California landscape—destruction of its redwoods, its Yosemite Valley, its mountain meadows, its wild rivers—that environmental journalism, as we know it today, was born. An account of that birth appears in Stephen Fox's fine study, *John Muir and His Legacy: The American Conservation Movement* (Boston: Little, Brown, and Company, 1981). There Fox describes the friendship that grew between Muir and Robert Underwood Johnson, editor of *Century* magazine for many years, a friendship that first led to the campaign for Yosemite National Park and then continued to argue for ever-increasing wilderness protections, a friendship that brought environmentalism into America's living rooms.

An examination of *Century*'s pages shows us exactly how John Muir's writing, under the influence of Johnson and the pressures of their campaign, changes with the passing years. Muir earlier had published travelogue essays in the old *Scribner's Monthly, Century's* predecessor. "In the Heart of the California Alps," for example, was an 1880 article describing those "glorious" Sierra, "with their thousand peaks and spires dipping far into the thin sky, the ice and snow and avalanches, glad torrents and lakes, woods and gardens, the bears in the groves, wild sheep on the dizzy heights, . . . the love-work of a whole life."[5] For ten pages, Muir paints a rhapsodic word-portrait of the beauties of the California scene. He does not, however, mention a word about preservation, conservation, or environmental protection.

But ten years later he goes on the offensive. Two articles about the Yosemite Valley appeared in *Century* in 1890. The first, "The Treasures of the Yosemite," sounds rather like the California Alps essay in that it describes the landscape pictorially and effusively, but it differs in that it contains many more statistics and concrete details. Muir is laying the groundwork for a second-stage attack. Then, in September, he launched phase two, "Features of the Proposed Yosemite National Park." There he not only catalogues the scenic elements of his favorite California wilderness—the mountains, waterfalls, wildflowers, creatures large and small—but he ends with a straightforward declaration of purpose.

> Unless reserved or protected the whole region will soon or late be devastated by lumbermen and sheepmen, and so of course be made unfit for use as a pleasure ground. Already it is with great difficulty that campers, even in the most remote parts of the proposed reservation and in those difficult of access, can find grass enough to keep their animals from starving; the ground is already being gnawed and trampled into a desert condition, and when the region shall be stripped of its forests the ruin will be complete. Even the Yosemite will then suffer in the disturbance effected on the water-shed, the clear streams becoming muddy and much less regular in their flow. It is also devoutly to be hoped that the Hetch Hetchy will escape such ravages of man as one sees in Yosemite.[6]

John Muir, for the first time, is writing as an environmental journalist. He concretely and specifically has moved his point of view away from the purely spiritual benefits of the wilderness and positioned himself nearer to the land. He is fighting for environmental efficacy in its own right.

Robert Underwood Johnson joined the debate too, creating a chorus of voices calling for scenic protection. Unsigned editorials appeared in *Century* to underscore the importance of Muir's arguments. "The articles by Mr. John Muir in the present and preceding numbers of *The Century* on the Yosemite Valley and the proposed National Park will have failed of their natural effect if, in addition to exciting the wonder of the reader at the unique beauty of waterfall and cliff effectively portrayed in Mr. Muir's picturesque descriptions, they do not also stimulate the pride of Californians to an active interest in the better discharge of the trust assumed by the State in its acceptance of the Yosemite grant."[7] This broadside, throwing the force and prestige of a major magazine behind the cause, lends credence to the whole notion of environmental protection and strengthens Muir's own voice and vision. And even if his Hetch Hetchy pleas went unheard, Muir's wishes for a protected Yosemite led finally to an entire National Park system.

Did environmental journalism make a difference? It would take a much longer paper than this one to answer such a complex question, for sometimes such writing is effective and sometimes it is just so much verbiage. Muir's battles probably were won or lost more because of economics and political power bases than because of the persuasiveness of his prose. But it took voices like his and Johnson's to galvanize the public outcry necessary to make gains for environmental protection. In so doing, John Muir set a pattern for environmental journalists to follow, meshing human needs with environmental needs in a network that tries to salvage both the human spirit and those disappearing natural resources. Edward Abbey calls it "the rediscovery of our ancient, preagricultural, preindustrial freedom . . . a sort of Proustian recapture."[8] He, and all the other environmental journalists writing after Muir, speak in much the same way.

I make that generalization after sitting beside dusty piles of old magazines and opening issue after issue. One tattered copy of the *Sierra Club Bulletin* can serve as a microcosm of all the rest; the table of contents for the May 1947 issue is typical. Of the sixteen short essays included, almost half describe personal adventures in the wilderness or else document ascents of various peaks and domes. The remainder sound as though they had been written either by Thoreau's or by Muir's direct descendants. One in particular, "The Problems of the Wilderness," argues much as the master might have done—"The benefits which accrue from the wilderness may be separated into three broad divisions: the physical, the mental and the esthetic."[9] Indeed, Bob Marshall synthesizes a kind of experiential transcendence. "One of the greatest advantages of the wilderness is its incentive to independent cogitation," he writes.

> This is partly a reflection of physical stimulation, but more inherently due to the fact that original ideas require an objectivity and perspective seldom possible in the distracting propinquity of one's fellow men. It is necessary to 'have gone behind the world of humanity, seen its institutions like toadstools by the wayside.' This theorizing is justified empirically by the number of America's more virile minds, including Thomas Jefferson, Henry Thoreau, Louis Agassiz, Herman Melville, Mark Twain, John Muir and William James, who have felt the compulsion of periodical retirements into the solitudes. Withdrawn from the contaminating notions of their neighbors, these thinkers have been able to meditate, unprejudiced by the immuring of civilization.[10]

Marshall's article, first published in a 1930 issue of *The Scientific Monthly*, explores those spiritual and physical values induced by the natural world. As his paragraphs proceed, though, his tone changes. The transcendental implications disappear, replaced by a militancy unheard at Walden Pond. With brisk words, Marshall attacks the establishment and argues, not for civil disobedience, but for outright rebellion. "There is just one hope of repulsing the tyrannical ambition of civilization to conquer every niche on the whole earth. That hope is the organization of spirited people who will fight for the freedom of the wilderness."[11]

These sentences sound remarkably like John Muir organizing the fight for Yosemite, and even more like the conclusion to *Slickrock*. There Edward Abbey agrees, "We have submitted to the domination of an insane, expansionist economy and a brutal technology . . . which will end by destroying not only itself but everything remaining that is clean, whole, beautiful and good in our America. Unless we find a way to stop it."[12] So it would seem that the faster modern man devours the wilderness, the angrier environmental journalists have to become. No longer have they the luxury of leisure, writing about man's esoteric needs, while the pantheistic source behind those needs quietly disappears. Instead, they have had to sound a battle cry. We need Thoreau's "tonic of wildness," but we also need to conserve the wilderness itself.

The other environmental journalists writing in the May 1947 *Sierra Club Bulletin* argue just that way. A quick listing of essay titles suggests the breadth of their concern—"Protecting Mountain Meadows," "Sierra Packing and Wilderness Policy," "Kings Canyon National Park." The most comprehensive broadside comes from the pen of Bernard DeVoto in a wide-ranging attack called "The West Against Itself." He traces a historical pattern of plunder and rapacity that began with the fur barons, the cattle kingdoms, and the lumber industry, and that shows no signs of slowing down. DeVoto reports, "at the very moment *when the West is blueprinting an economy which must be based on the sustained, permanent use of its natural resources* [DeVoto's italics], it is also conducting an assault on those resources with the simple object of liquidating them. . . . The West as its own worst enemy. The West committing suicide."[13] Nearly four decades have passed since DeVoto penned that elegy, but his words are prophetic.

By the nineteen-seventies, environmental uproar had exploded throughout the country, across the oceans, even into space (witness the NASA equipment left on the moon), and environmental journalism led with a barrage of words. Even the once-staid *Audubon* added a section called "The Audubon Cause" to its issues, printing such essays as "Redwood Park: costly, sorry abortion," "Phosphate fate will determine Idaho high country's fate," and "Huntington Beach: disaster waits impatiently in wings."[14] *Audubon*'s longer articles also bear an argumentative tone quite unlike the zoological and botanical offerings heard half a century earlier. The May 1971 issue, for example, contains an overt attack on the establishment— "It's About Too Late For Tahoe." Using such diction as "avalanche of development," "total commercial exploitation," "scruffy casinos," "urban mess," and "lack of vision," the author traces damages wrought by man and concludes, "The final hard truth about Lake Tahoe . . . is that without tough federal action and the leadership to bring it about, we will proceed to corrupt Tahoe beyond the economic and technical ability of this generation to redeem it. What is happening here is a stark reflection of the extent of our own corruption."[15] And this is the official magazine of the Audubon Society.

Clearly the thrust of the twentieth century has altered forever the nature of environmental writing. To be sure, our contemporary essayists have not forgotten Thoreau's admonitions about the spiritual necessity of solitude and space, but their task is complicated by a heartfelt need to warn us about an ominous future. Edward Abbey's essay, "MX," exemplifies that new breed of prose—a happy/sad combination of sacrality, prophecy, and despair that moves beyond the most radical of John Muir's conceptions. Writing about the "Missile Experimental," Abbey laments an omnipresence that "casts a long shadow over the American West, and across most of Western civilization, for that matter. A shadow that extends from Tonopah, Nevada, to Vladivostok, Kamchatka, Siberia."[16] At the same time, Abbey praises "interludes of illusion. I drive on, indulging the reveries of a solitary wanderer, keeping one eye peeled for topaz, amethyst, opal, beryl, tourmaline, obsidian, agate, crystal-loaded geodes."[17] Such a cataloguing, in Abbey's world, is but a prelude to a feeling, almost transcendental, about the land. In this essay, however, Abbey's affinity for the desert is sidetracked by a cause celebre—the government's plan to install missile sites across the Great Basin.

Abbey begins by outlining the Pentagon's proposal. Then, following a scheme familiar to his readers, he describes a personal tour of the area under siege and concludes with a plea for its preservation. "We drive on into the shimmering April afternoon. Grand, arid, primeval country opens before us, range after range of purple mountains, each separated from the next by a broad open basin."[18] Exploring a wildlife refuge, an abandoned Pony Express Station, a sleepy Utah village, an isolated spring, Abbey contemplates the possible effects on each of environmental encroachment. Needless to say, he favors leaving the landscape alone.

> Contrary to the apparent belief of the military, this region is fully inhabited. It is not empty space. Wide, free, and open, yes, but not empty. The mountains and valleys are presently occupied to the limit of their economic carrying capacity by ranchers, farmers, miners, forest rangers and inspectors of sunsets, and by what remains of the original population of Indians, coyote, deer, black bear, mountain lion, eagles, hawks, buzzards, mice, lice, lizards, snakes, antelope, and wild horses. To make room for MX, its thirty thousand construction workers, and its glacier of iron, steel, cement, and plastic, many of these creatures, both human and otherwise, would have to be displaced.[19]

Here is environmental journalism in microcosm. Here is where Thoreau, Muir, Marshall, DeVoto, and others, in turn, have led.

Turning away from a gentle New England landscape, they have sought the open spaces of the West. There they have articulated the fight for preservation of a precious landscape. There, too, they have projected a fearful vision—a "glacier of iron, steel, cement, and plastic"—that may well replace the wilderness they love. But despite the changes in substance, the increased horror and dismay at the twentieth century's appetite for land, they have remained faithful to their heritage. They still draw spiritual strength from the earth's

READER OF THE PURPLE SAGE

178

preserve; they still draw literary strength from their past. "Thoreau becomes more significant with each passing decade," Abbey summarizes. "The deeper our United States sinks into industrialism, urbanism, militarism—with the rest of the world doing its best to emulate America—the more poignant, strong, and appealing becomes Thoreau's demand for the right of every man, every woman, every child, every dog, every tree, every snail darter, every lousewort, every living thing, to live its own life in its own way at its own pace in its own square mile of home."[20] Like most other nature essayists for our age, Abbey has not forgotten the century-old lessons of the man from Concord.

So, while contemporary times call for new strategies, human beings still cry for the same needs. Muir knew this; so did Marshall and DeVoto and all the other writers whose goal is preservation of both spirit and space. The legacy continues, as Abbey concludes. "Wherever there are deer and hawks, wherever there is liberty and danger, wherever there is wilderness, wherever there is a living river"—wherever there are environmental journalists—"Henry Thoreau will find his eternal home."[21] No longer "a cheerful field of work," the genre he gave us, refined by Muir and his followers, is now a major denomination in our Western literary heritage.

NOTES

1. Edward Abbey, *Down the River* (New York: E. P. Dutton, 1982), p. 6.
2. Henry David Thoreau, *The Portable Thoreau* (New York: Viking Press, 1947), p. 73.
3. Thoreau, *The Portable Thoreau*, pp. 31–32.
4. Henry David Thoreau, *Walden* (New York: Norton & Co., 1962), p. 195.
5. John Muir, "In the Heart of the California Alps," *Scribner's Monthly*, 20 (1880), 345.
6. John Muir, "Features of the Proposed Yosemite National Park," *Century Magazine*, 40 (September 1890), 667.
7. "Amateur Management of the Yosemite Scenery," *Century Magazine*, 40 (September 1890), 797.

8. Edward Abbey, "Thus I Reply to René Dubos," in *Down the River,* p. 120.

9. Robert Marshall, "The Problem of the Wilderness," *Sierra Club Bulletin,* 32 (May 1947), 45.

10. Ibid., p. 46; in this passage, note that Marshall quotes from Thoreau's *Journals.*

11. Ibid., p. 52.

12. Edward Abbey, with Phillip Hyde, *Slickrock* (New York: Sierra Club/Charles Scribner's Sons, 1971), p. 77.

13. Bernard DeVoto, "The West Against Itself," *Sierra Club Bulletin,* 32 (May 1947), 38.

14. See *Audubon,* 79 (March 1977), 121 ff.

15. William Bronson, "It's About Too Late for Tahoe," *Audubon,* 73 (May 1971), 80.

16. Edward Abbey, "MX," in *Down the River,* 83.

17. Ibid., p. 91.

18. Ibid.

19. Ibid., p. 89.

20. Edward Abbey, "Down the River with Henry Thoreau," in *Down the River,* p. 36.

21. Ibid., p. 48.

CHAPTER FOURTEEN

Western Literature and Natural Resources

Three main currents of intellectual investigation came together in the nineteenth century and produced what is called American nature writing. Explorer/adventurers like Lewis and Clark or John C. Frémont reported in narrative form their unique experiences in the frontier West, while scientist/observers like Alexander Wilson or John James Audubon added descriptive details to the reports they made. Meanwhile, transcendentalists like Ralph Waldo Emerson and Henry David Thoreau began musing on the more philosophic implications of man's place in the natural world.

After mid-century, the genre seemed defined, as numerous essayists continued expressing their personal experiences in nature—adventurous, scientific, philosophic: narrative, descriptive, contemplative. John Muir, writing as the century came to a close, perhaps epitomized in his work the genre's possibilities. Such essays as "A Near View of the High Sierras" and "A Wind-Storm in the Forests" reveal his enormous curiosity. In the latter he lashes himself to a treetop just to feel the wind—exhibiting his courageous capacity for wonder; in the former he climbs Mt. Ritter by a difficult although scenic route. Combining a zest for new adventure, a keen eye for detail, and an abiding love for his environment, Muir produced a body of essays that exemplified the genre. Even so, American nature writing was already in transition.

When Muir was a young man, the high Sierra stood in relative obscurity, their peaks and valleys known only to a few pocket hunters, sheepherders, and stray pioneers. At the time of Muir's death in 1914, however, the California mountains had—in his mind—been ravaged. Carriage-drawn tourists crowded Yosemite Valley, while base camps housing as many as a hundred hikers at a time replaced the sheep in Toulumne Meadows. Worse yet, outside political and industrial forces had discovered the profit to be made from wilderness exploitation. If San Francisco could condemn the singularly beautiful Hetch Hetchy Valley as a cheap source of power, Muir argued, nothing was sacred.

John Muir's fight to preserve the Hetch Hetchy, although a losing battle, was monumental in its long-range ramifications. It drew the Sierra Club into what turned out to be only the first of an untold number of environmental confrontations between ordinary citizens and a techno-industrial bureaucracy. Moreover, and most crucial to my discussion here, it gave the American nature writer a new topic to explore. Conservation and preservation versus the developers' will to alter the landscape overrode all other concerns. After Muir's crescendo, no other theme has so dominated essays about the natural world.

At first, though, the sounds were muted. Ironically, some of the major mid-twentieth-century voices were themselves, in the decades before, exploiting their surroundings. Scientists like Olaus Murie, Robert Marshall, and Aldo Leopold all held jobs that hastened environmental imbalances and then, after observing the results, turned to roles as public spokesmen. The former two founded The Wilderness Society, while the latter wrote eloquently about his change of heart. A single Leopold essay demonstrates both the man's transition and the genre's.

"Thinking Like a Mountain" (pp. 129–33) begins "full of trigger itch," when a pack of boys fires into a pack of wolves, kills the mother, and maims the pup. "We reached the old wolf in time to watch a fierce green fire dying in her eyes," Leopold reports, a fire that becomes for him a symbol of the force that must be left undestroyed in a natural environment. He goes on to describe what happens to a mountainside when man kills so many predators that their victims proliferate. "I have seen every edible bush and seedling browsed, first to anaemic desuetude, and then to death. I have seen every edible tree defoliated to the height of a saddlehorn. Such a mountain looks as if someone had given God a new pruning shears, and forbidden Him all other exercise."

Then Leopold extrapolates, "So also with cows. The cowman who cleans his range of wolves does not realize that he is taking over the wolf's job of trimming the herd to fit the range. He has not learned to think like a mountain. Hence we have dustbowls, and rivers washing the future into the sea." *A Sand County Almanac and Sketches Here and There* asks readers to think like the wilderness itself, to acknowledge the interrelatedness of all its inhabitants, and to understand the destructiveness of tampering with one segment at the expense of another. The decimation of predators, Leopold insists, leads to an unnatural imbalance that in turn destroys the land itself.

At the heart of his argument is a thesis first proposed in 1864 by George Perkins Marsh. "Man is everywhere a disturbing agent" (p. 36), Marsh wrote in *Man and Nature*. "The ravages committed by man subvert the relations and destroy the balance which nature had established; . . . and she avenges herself upon the intruder, by letting loose upon her defaced provinces destructive energies hitherto kept in check" (p. 42). As a result, Marsh continues, "The earth is fast becoming an unfit home for its noblest inhabitant, and another era of equal human crime and human improvidence . . . would reduce it to such a condition of impoverished productiveness, of shattered surface, of climactic excess, as to threaten the depravation, barbarism, and perhaps even the extinction of the species" (p. 43). Such unpopular statements caused this scientist's words to remain out of print for almost a hundred years.

Indeed, most writers who point out the irreparable destructiveness of man's impact on the environment find little popularity. John Wesley Powell lost both his job and his reputation when he spoke of water rights and irrigation practices in the arid West. The dust bowl of the 1930s proved him correct, but his peers unanimously rejected his conclusions fifty years before. Rachel Carson found the same kind of rejection when she wrote *Silent Spring,* although now her theories about insecticides and pesticides are accepted as fact.

A catalog of similar writers with similar experiences would take up the remainder of my article, so let me add to my observations about this facet of contemporary American nature writing by examining a single perpetrator. In 1984 Philip L. Fradkin published a history of man's unhappy relationship with the Colorado River, *A River No More.* He opens his analysis with a personal experience, describing his search for the Colorado's source at the headwaters of the Green.

> There were countless glints of warm light on water and ice as I walked toward the rising sun. To the right was a waterfall splashing down in stages from the small tarn holding the meltwater from Stroud Glacier. The minute, intense reflection of the sun in the tarn almost brought my perception of the source down to a single radiant drop.

Then, as the sky darkens from bright sunshine to ominous cloud, Fradkin's mood changes from exuberance to contemplation. "The mountains were weeping this day; the river's growing salinity, like tears, threatened to stifle its life-giving force; and my overall feeling of what had happened to the world's most-used river was one of muted sadness" (pp. 36–37). Three hundred pages later, *A River No More*'s conclusion proves what he feels. Trying to locate the Colorado's mouth, Fradkin instead finds the "ultimate despoliation"—shallows bogged down in cracked mud flats. "I withdrew hastily," he announces, "after sinking to my knees in the ooze" (pp. 338–39).

Between the outset of his exploration and the ignominious experience at the end, Fradkin engages his readers in a series of human machinations along the river's length. Cows eat grass, erosion cuts deeper arroyos, mines unearth coal and natural gas, farmers irrigate fields, cities and states demand water rights regardless of upstream or downstream users, dams reshape the channels, silt and salinity build proportionally, and evaporation occurs. Each event scars the environment; each temporizing solution is one further abuse. What little remains, the author describes as "a turgid, algae-choked remnant of a river" (p. 304).

Cautioning that we should learn from those who preceded us, Fradkin outlines the Anasazi demise. He explains that at the beginning of the twelfth century Chaco Canyon held a large civilization that denuded its surroundings—cutting as many as five thousand trees to build a single pueblo and leveling the fields for agricultural purposes—a civilization whose crops were fed by an intricate, sophisticated irrigation system. Rains, not drought, quickly turned the dream into a nightmare. Within a hundred years, Chaco Canyon lay abandoned. "Its meteoric rise and fall," Fradkin warns, "comes close to approximating the time constraints of the speedier twentieth century" (p. 21).

Although praised by other essayists and environmentalists for its forceful insights, *A River No More* has to date had little impact on political practice in the 1980s. As Edward Abbey preaches, however, it is the writer's duty to rouse the moral consciousness of his readers. Therein lies the challenge that Philip Fradkin and his predecessors answer. Their branch of contemporary American nature writing exposes the permanent damages wrought by human notions of progress. Tending to be more journalistic than literary—Fradkin won a Pulitzer Prize for newspaper coverage of the Watts riots—it directs reportorial barbs toward tangible, palpable ills.

The other branch sounds far more esoteric. "We need the tonic of wildness," Henry David Thoreau wrote more than a hundred and thirty years ago.

At the same time that we are earnest to explore and learn all things, we require that all things be mysterious and unexplorable, that land and sea be infinitely wild, unsurveyed and unfathomed by us because unfathomable. . . . We need to witness our own limits transgressed, and some life pasturing freely where we never wander. (pp. 209–10)

Essayists today have heeded Thoreau's predication and have gone on to explore its dimensions in the twentieth century. Less concerned with how we cause disjunctures in the natural chain, these writers worry more about ills perpetrated against the soul.

A transitional figure was Bob Marshall, a Washington, D.C., bureaucrat who, before his untimely death at age thirty-eight, served first as director of forestry of the Office of Indian Affairs and then as chief of the Division of Recreation and Lands. His 1930 essay, "The Problem of the Wilderness," rephrases Thoreau's words by explaining three intangible benefits that accrue from the wilderness—"the physical, the mental and the esthetic" (p. 142).

In physical exertion, he finds ways to unfetter society's chains; in mental freedom, he enjoys both excitement and repose; in the esthetic, he takes pleasure in detachment from all temporal relationships. "Any one who has stood upon a lofty summit," he writes,

and gazed over an inchoate tangle of deep canyons and cragged mountains, of sunlit lakelets and black expanses of forest, has become aware of a certain giddy sensation that there are no distances, no measures, simply unrelated matter rising and falling. . . . In the wilderness, with its entire freedom from the manifestations of human will, that perfect objectivity which is essential for pure esthetic rapture can probably be achieved more readily than among any other forms of beauty. (pp. 144–45)

Despite occasional otherworldly abstractions, most of Marshall's essay sounds more down to earth. At its close, he calls for a thorough, "radical" study of the wilderness needs of the nation. "It ought to be radical," he argues, "because it is easy to convert a natural area to industrial or motor usage, impossible to do the reverse" (p. 148). Marshall looks into the future, foreseeing not only a growing force of backpackers, campers, and hikers, but also a bonding together in the service of environmental causes. A generation ahead of his time, he lists concrete steps that must be taken to preserve "the tonic of wildness."

Thirty years later, Wallace Stegner was repeating a similar theme. In 1960 he wrote (and later made public) a letter to the Wildland Research Center at the University of California, Berkeley, in which he argued for the wilderness *idea* as an "intangible and spiritual" resource in itself, as a force that has shaped the "strenuousness and optimism and expansiveness" of the American character. He explains,

> We need wilderness preserved—as much of it as is still left, and as many kinds—because it was the challenge against which our character as a people was formed. The reminder and the reassurance that it is still there is good for our spiritual health even if we never once in ten years set foot in it. It is good for us when we are young, because of the incomparable sanity it can bring briefly, as vacation and rest, into our insane lives. It is important to us when we are old simply because it is there—important, that is, simply as idea. (*Sound,* pp. 146–47)

Indeed, Stegner concludes his letter by insisting that those without the strength and youth to explore what little genuine wilderness remains should "simply sit and look." Even if they cannot get to a single roadless place, "they can simply contemplate the *idea,* take pleasure in the fact that such a timeless and uncontrolled part of earth is still there" (*Sound,* p. 153). And so he refutes the axiom that wilderness access ought to be available for everyone. Some contemporary essayists would go even further, suggesting that even if we are physically able to enter the wilderness world, we ought to hold back. "Perhaps a few places are best left unexplored," writes Edward Abbey, "seen from a distance but never entered, never walked upon" (*Road,* p. 119).

On the other hand, most nature writers (including Abbey himself) sound a lot happier when meeting the wilderness head-on. *"We love the taste of freedom. We enjoy the smell of danger,"* he writes elsewhere. "We take pleasure in the consummation of mental, spiritual, and physical effort; it is the achievement of the summit that brings the three together, stamps them with the harmony and unity of a point" (*Journey*, p. 215, Abbey's italics). Such was the clarion call of Muir and his contemporaries, too. After noting that Mt. Ritter was a mountain "savagely hacked and torn . . . a maze of yawning chasms and gullies," Muir proceeded directly to the top "without effort, and soon stood upon the topmost crag in the blessed light." He reports, "How truly glorious . . . this noble summit" (p. 65)!

One result of directly confronting any wilderness challenge is a more personalized kind of nature writing—the only legitimate kind of nature writing, Joseph Wood Krutch would argue (p. 13). Both Abbey and Stegner, for example, go beyond the confines of either philosophy or science by experiencing firsthand and then describing a changing landscape. Essays by each show Glen Canyon before and after its obliteration by Lake Powell. While Abbey's "Down the River" in *Desert Solitaire* is perhaps the better known "before" piece, Stegner's "Glen Canyon Submersus" reveals the more poignant "after." Abbey remembers,

> Down the river we drift in a kind of waking dream, gliding beneath the great curving cliffs with their tapestries of water stains, the golden alcoves, the hanging gardens, the seeps, the springs where no man will ever drink, the royal arches in high relief and the amphitheaters shaped liked seashells. A sculptured landscape mostly bare of vegetation—earth in the nude. (*Solitaire*, p. 187)

His words call to mind a place that now exists only in the imagination.

Motoring two hundred feet above an Anasazi ruin, searching for wildlife that no longer frequents the water's edge, seeking forgotten canyons and passageways, looking for a campsite against a vertical wall, Stegner sees something quite different.

> The old masked entrance is swallowed up, the water rises almost over the shoulder of the inner cliffs. Once that canyon

was a pure delight to walk in; now it is only another slot with water in it, a thing to poke a motorboat into for five minutes and then roar out again. And if that is Hidden Passage, and we are this far out in the channel, then Music Temple is straight down. (*Sound*, pp. 129–30)

The lake looks spectacular, Stegner acknowledges, but he remains dissatisfied.

Vast and beautiful as it is, . . . democratically accessible and with its most secret beauties captured on color transparencies at infallible exposures, it strikes me, even in my exhilaration, with the consciousness of loss. In gaining the lovely and the usable, we have given up the incomparable. (*Sound*, p. 128)

In retrospect, these words carry a bitter irony. During a 1955 effort to save Echo Canyon—where the Yampa and the Green rivers converge—Stegner edited a slender volume called *This Is Dinosaur*. His successful plea for preservation of the national monument was an early expression of his belief in the abstract value of wilderness.

It is a better world with some buffalo in it, a richer world with some gorgeous canyons unmarred by signboards, hot-dog stands, super highways, or high-tension lines, undrowned by power or irrigation reservoirs. If we preserved as parks only those places that have no economic possibilities, we would have no parks. And in the decades to be, it will not be only the buffalo and the trumpeter swan who need sanctuaries. Our own species is going to need them too. It needs them now. (*Dinosaur*, p. 17)

Our public officials concurred, or at least they agreed that irreplaceable fossils ought to be preserved. Heeding a groundswell of public opinion against the proposed dam, Congress rejected the United States Army Corps of Engineers' plan. Then, in its place, they authorized Glen Canyon's demise. Because Glen Canyon held no tangible treasures, it had few defenders. In less than a decade it was gone—a loss David Brower calls the single greatest mistake of his lifetime. "Glen Canyon died," Brower opens the Foreword to Eliot Porter's *The Place No One Knew,* "and I was partly responsible for its needless death. So were you. Neither you nor I, nor anyone else, knew it well enough to insist that at all costs it should endure" (p. 5).

Despite the irony, this example shows that twentieth-century nature writing embraces activism. Few practitioners—whether pointing out human destruction of the natural chain or simply insisting upon man's philosophical needs—isolate themselves from political indignation. Some, like John Graves canoeing down the ill-fated Brazos, incite little overt action, but many lend their time, their pens, and their wholehearted energies to environmental causes. Some go still further. "I see the preservation of wilderness as one sector of the front in the war against the encroaching industrial state," says one activist. "Every square mile of range and desert saved from the strip miners, every river saved from the dam builders, every forest saved from the loggers, every swamp saved from the land speculators means another square mile saved for the play of human freedom" (*Journey,* pp. 235–36).

Starting from this premise, Edward Abbey not only writes polemics directed at specific ills but also suggests some rather extraordinary undercover tactics. He means war. The rhetoric of *Slickrock* and of *The Monkey-Wrench Gang* attacks, counterattacks, sputters, shouts, and snarls. While neither Hayduke nor his creator actually blow up Glen Canyon Dam—at least they haven't yet—their plans invite covert applause from sympathetic readers. Actually, Thoreau even contemplated a crowbar raised against a dam he loathed and dreamed of nature leveling the structure's heights (p. 156), so this subversive thesis cannot wholly be claimed by the twentieth century. But it signals where several contemporary nature essayists seem headed. Believing singlemindedly in the writer as ethical activist, Abbey leads the way. "Why settle for anything less?" he asks. "Why give up our wilderness? What good is a Bill of Rights that does not include the right to play, to wander, to explore, the right to stillness and solitude, to discovery and physical freedom?" (*Road,* p. 137).

In order to rouse public concern for the preservation of wilderness, however, authors themselves cause damage. Muir found that out when he lured too many people to Yosemite. Krutch may have repeated the same sin by popularizing the Sonoran desert. And how many more visitors, after enjoying *Desert Solitaire,* have been attracted to Arches? Just as an exploded Glen Canyon Dam would perpetrate ugliness, so a wilderness loved to death is a wilderness destroyed. How to write about wilderness without simultaneously destroying its very nature is a real conundrum confronting essayists today, a conundrum most of them choose not to address. Abbey himself says, "Come on in. The earth, like the sun, like the air, belongs to everyone—and to no one" (*Journey,* p. 88). He does not articulate what might happen if everyone were to answer his invitation.

So extolling the virtues of wilderness in the twentieth century differs greatly from praising its efficacy in the nineteenth. Where nature writers once could describe pristine lands that apparently stretched forever, now they must recognize problems and paradoxes alike. Man's anthropocentrism alters the natural order of things; indeed, it has redirected the processes of animal, vegetable, and mineral evolution. Yet man has not been able to redirect his philosophical needs. The effective contemporary essayist recognizes our antithetical nature and exposes—either by scientific or philosophic or sometimes political means—the crosscurrents. Meanwhile, even as he or she writes of wilderness, wilderness ceases to exist. Somewhat isolated, pleasant to describe, those relatively untouched pockets only in the broadest sense can be called wild. Nonetheless, they are a natural resource worth protecting, as authors like Fradkin, Stegner, and Abbey, like Frank Waters and David Lavender, discovered when they explored the surface and subsurfaces of the Colorado River.

Suppose we consider the Colorado a natural metaphor of what was once wild and free and now runs perilously close to extinction, a moving reminder of wilderness loss at the expense of anthropo-centric gain. "Past these towering monuments, past the mounded billows of orange sandstone, past these oak-set glens, past these fern-decked alcoves, past these mural curves, we glide hour after hour, stopping now and then, as our attention is arrested by some new wonder" (p. 233), mused John Wesley Powell from imaginative depths. Now the wonder is that an untold number of diesel-pow-ered sightseers not only will never see what lies below but will never know the difference. Here, as elsewhere along the 3,000-mile flow, the functional has replaced the incomparable. Perhaps few boaters care, but it is the nature writer's duty to critique the exchange.

Suppose, then, we consider the Colorado's tributaries as em-blems for what natural resources still exist. One such unnamed place—unnamed because the author wants to protect its isola-tion—is described by Rob Schultheis.

> We went deeper, days, miles, into the earth. Side canyons
> choked with alluvial stone and timber led off into nowhere. We
> crossed places out of a vision. Crackled geometry of dried mud;
> a bed of cobbles; a pool of worn-out water glowing like fire.
> Juniper trees, a forest of hags, knelt in the dusk. . . . Our tracks
> across the dunes were erased by the wind even as we looked
> back: it was as if we had never been there at all. (pp. 41–42)

The way leads still deeper, until the cliffs rise at least two thousand feet and the streambed contorts beneath their feet. "Everything was broken down, suspended in the act of falling or shattered to pieces. . . . The canyon turned and turned on itself again, like a snake in death" (p. 45).

Finally Schultheis synthesizes the psychological schism of the experience. "There is a stage in every quest, every journey, when you seem hopelessly suspended between where you were and where you were bound" (p. 45). Speaking of a descent to the San Juan River, he might well be speaking for our contemporary nature writers. Suspended between past and future concepts of wilder-ness, caught by human aspirations, sometimes controversial, too often unread, they struggle to explain. "Wilderness is not a luxury but a necessity of the human spirit" (*Solitaire,* p. 192), Abbey tells us. No civilization can successfully cut itself off. So we are told by the contours of the Colorado; so we are told by contemporary American nature essayists.

WORKS CITED

Abbey, Edward. *Abbey's Road.* New York: E. P. Dutton, 1979.

——. *Desert Solitaire.* New York: Ballantine Books, 1968.

——. *The Journey Home.* New York: E. P. Dutton, 1977.

Fradkin, Philip L. *A River No More.* Tucson: University of Arizona Press, 1968.

Graves, John. *Goodbye to a River.* 1980. Reprint. Austin: Texas Monthly Press, 1984.

Krutch, Joseph Wood. *The Best Nature Writing of Joseph Wood Krutch.* New York: William Morrow, 1959.

Lavender, David. *Colorado River Country.* New York: E. P. Dutton, 1982.

Leopold, Aldo. *A Sand County Almanac and Sketches Here and There.* 1949. New York: Oxford University Press, 1981.

Marsh, George Perkins. *Man and Nature.* Cambridge, Massachusetts: Belknap Press, 1965.

Marshall, Robert. "The Problem of the Wilderness." *The Scientific Monthly* (February 1930): 142–48.

Muir, John. *The Mountains of California.* 1911. Reprint. Berkeley: Ten Speed Press, 1977.

Porter, Eliot. *The Place No One Knew.* Edited by David Brower. San Francisco: Sierra Club Books, 1968.

Powell, John Wesley. *The Exploration of the Colorado River and Its Canyons.* 1874. Reprint. New York: Penguin Books, 1987.

Schultheis, Rob. *The Hidden West.* San Francisco: North Point Press, 1983.

Stegner, Wallace. *The Sound of Mountain Water.* 1969. Reprint. Lincoln: University of Nebraska Press, 1985.

——. *This Is Dinosaur.* New York: Alfred A. Knopf, 1955.

Thoreau, Henry David. *The Portable Thoreau.* Rev. ed. Edited by Carl Bode. New York: Penguin, 1981.

Waters, Frank. *The Colorado.* New York: Rinehart, 1946.

CHAPTER FIFTEEN

Kingdom, Phylum, Class, Order
Twentieth-Century American Nature Writer

Is it possible to classify authors the way we classify butterflies? Pin them to a velvet cloth, perhaps, then label them in Latin? Offer a hierarchy of hagiographers? A taxonomy of titles? A nomenclature of naturalists? In *This Incomparable Lande,* Thomas J. Lyon suggests a quasi taxonomy for nature writers, but his seven categories pertain more to written content than to characteristics of individual writers: field guides and professional papers, natural history essays, rambles, solitude and backcountry living, travel and adventure, farm life, and man's role in nature (3–7). If I understand the classical system of taxonomy correctly, such groups and subgroups should categorize plants and animals themselves, not their products. So a real taxonomy of naturalists should focus on authors rather than essays, on the postures and strategies that authors display.

The first part is easy. Kingdom? Writer. Phylum? Nature. Class? American. Order? Twentieth Century. Twentieth-century American nature writer. An author like Edward Abbey insists that he doesn't belong in any such category, but he's wrong, of course. "I am not a naturalist," he announces on the first page of *The Journey Home.* "I never was and never will be a naturalist. I'm not even sure what a naturalist is except that I'm not one. I'm not even an amateur naturalist." On the next page he adds, "Much as I admire the work of Thoreau, Muir, Leopold, Beston, Krutch, Eiseley and others, I have not tried to write in their tradition. I don't know how" (xi, xii). I disagree. Not only did Abbey understand the tradition well, but he built upon it. His work actually defines the standard for contemporary American nature writers, especially for naturalists writing during the last two or three decades. He showed all of us how to combine a keen observer's eye and a pictorial sense of place with an understanding of the fragility of ecosystems, a commitment to biocentrism more than anthropocentrism, and an abiding respect for the land, for the landscape, and for the natural resources that remain. All these characteristics are Abbey's and are characteristic of the prose that we today call nature writing—the work of naturalists.

So my taxonomy begins simply enough, with a set of characteristics that includes everyone from Aldo Leopold and Joseph Wood Krutch and Loren Eiseley to Edward Abbey, from Gary Paul Nabhan and Rick Bass and John Janovy Jr. to Ann Zwinger and Terry Tempest Williams and even to Ann Ronald. When we write essays about the natural world, we're all in the same kingdom, the same phylum, the same class, the same order. But are we members of the same family? Of the same genus? Of the same species? Perhaps not.

Let's start with family. Modern-day naturalists are a well-educated group. Most have college degrees; many have masters and doctorates. Of those I just mentioned, Leopold majored in forestry at Yale and taught natural resource management in the College of Agriculture at the University of Wisconsin. Krutch was an English professor at Columbia; Eiseley, an anthropology professor who specialized in paleontology; Janovy, conservation biology. Abbey studied philosophy; Bass, petroleum geology. Nabhan holds a Ph.D. in ethnobiology; Zwinger, an M.A. in art history. Williams, with a masters in ecology, has spent many years as the naturalist-in-residence of the Utah Museum of Natural History. Every one of these writers has a firm disciplinary grounding in some specific academic field that strongly informs the way in which that author perceives, interacts with, describes and draws conclusions about his or her own corner of the natural world. So they're all part of an academic family, though they might hate to hear me say that. Nonetheless, they do approach their subjects with different intellectual mind-sets, mind-sets that inhere naturally from their own undergraduate and postgraduate training. In my neoclassical taxonomy, then, each one belongs to a slightly different familial subset.

Abbey, for example, looks at the land with a philosopher's eye. A complex thread of epistemological inquiry weaves from essay to essay and binds his work from book to book. Attempting to locate a large generic mankind in its proper place in the natural world—or a smaller Ed Abbey in his—he seeks to understand the metaphysical mysteries within and beyond his own special terrain, the American Southwest desert. "What is the peculiar quality or character of the desert that distinguishes it, in spiritual appeal, from other forms of landscape?" he asks in a defining chapter of *Desert Solitaire* (270). "Where is the heart of the desert?" (273).

A more literal writer might try to answer in concrete terms, but Abbey the philosopher knows better. "I am convinced now that the desert has no heart," he concludes, "that it presents a riddle which has no answer, and that the riddle itself is an illusion created by some limitation or exaggeration of the displaced human consciousness" (273). From the 1968 publication of *Desert Solitaire* until his death in 1989, Abbey kept revisiting his own ontological questions about the meaning of the desert, advancing ideas and then backing away from precise pronouncements, weighing alternatives, realizing the insufficiency of any answer he might give, preserving the Sphinx-like "riddle which has no answer."

> The desert says nothing. Completely passive, acted upon but never acting, the desert lies there like the bare skeleton of Being, spare, sparse, austere, utterly worthless, inviting not love but contemplation. In its simplicity and order it suggests the classical, except that the desert is a realm beyond the human and in the classicist view only the human is regarded as significant or even recognized as real. (270)

His classical training leads Abbey to write "bare skeleton" analyses, to contemplate the desert as "a realm beyond the human," to speculate in metaphysical terms.

If we read the sections from his personal journals published after his death as *Confessions of a Barbarian,* we find the same conundrums repeating themselves again and again. Various entries query the nature of science, the guise of the desert, the "paradox of life and death," and the role of the philosophical anarchist in the contemporary world. One youthful excerpt, predating *Desert Solitaire,* shows Abbey's philosophical musings at an early age. "In the desert one comes in direct confrontation with the bones of existence," he wrote in the early 1960s, "the bare incomprehensible absolute *is-ness* of being" (185). Later journal entries share his thoughts on romanticism and naturalism, transcendentalism, and existentialism. The "completely homocentric obsessive self-obsession" of the latter, in fact, leads Abbey into an angry tirade against the "egocentric anthropocentric view of life" that he believes responsible for the twentieth century's treatment of the environment (351). Clearly his early intellectual training directs a great deal of his mature thinking, and his prose intrinsically reveals his intellectual grounding. He looks at the land with a philosopher's eye; he asks essential questions.

Let me contrast that way of looking with Ann Zwinger's. Trained as an artist and, later, as an art historian, she draws her landscapes on a small canvas carefully framed. Her eye focuses on exactly what is before her; her pen sketches artistically rather than philosophically. Two desert descriptions—one from the first page of her 1989 book, *The Mysterious Lands,* and one from the last—are characteristic. Each paragraph could proceed in a philosophical direction, but doesn't. Zwinger's is a purely visual point of view, her paragraphs a gallery of shapes and colors and details.

> Narrow clouds stripe the horizon pink, violet, and cream, a
> pousse-café of a sky. Over a cusp of rock, one spot of color
> glows royal rose, deepening and broadening, turning the pink

stripe ruddy, the cream to gold. The silhouettes of the Chi-
huahuan Desert take on interior shapes and color but the mes-
quite holds jet black, its thorny zigzag branches drawn in India
ink by a tense hand incapable of either a gentle curve or continuous straight line. (3)

Where Abbey might muse about the nature of the inscrutable
"tense hand," Zwinger does not. For her, the term functions only as
an image, not as an epistemological inspiration. I don't mean to
imply that Zwinger's writing is shallow, because it isn't. I mean to
say instead that she has her eye on other matters, and those matters
are visual in nature.

Her North American desert book concludes with "a single thin
cloud" poised over the mountains, "a molten spear illuminated
from beneath." She watches it incandesce, "the curve of a bow arc-
ing between two distant points. Then it fades. The ends still glow
while the middle darkens to match the mountains beneath." Given
an opportunity to contemplate humankind's relationship to what
she sees, however, Zwinger chooses not to draw profound connections. "The relationship shifts," she concludes, "the cloud, like a
spear thrown from an atlatl, flies to the next mass of mountain,
burying its head in the mountain flank" (297). Her examined life,
having little to do with first causes, stops with the pictorial.

Am I drawing a sweeping conclusion from just a few examples? I
think not. While it is clear that one could write an entire book
about this topic, detailing how academic habits of mind are reflected in writers' habitual attitudes, it is equally clear that one can
randomly turn to individual essays and find substantiating evidence. That is, one can construct a familial argument brick by brick,
or one can simply look through the windows of the building. In
these pages, I'm looking through the glass—or, in the following
example, through a scientist's glasses.

John Janovy Jr., the Nebraska biologist and nature essayist, has
written two books about his special landscape, *Keith County Journal*
and *Back in Keith County*. A selective look at the two tables of con-

tents spells out a worldview quite distinct from either Abbey's or Zwinger's. Termite Country. The Snail King. Two Wrens. Swallows. Grasshoppers and the Ackley Valley Ranch. The Lady Whitetail. Painting Birds. Game Fish, Trash Fish, Chubs, and Shiners. Orioles and Banjos. Tigers and Toads. Wings. Owls. The Experiment. Janovy's prose is as straightforward as his chapter titles. His diction and syntax zero in on plants and creatures analogous to the ways in which Abbey's words approach first principles and Zwinger's adhere to the rainbow.

Here's what Janovy, "back in Keith county," has to say about burrowing owls.

> They had a way of scrunching up their wings as they'd run back into the hole. They had a way of looking out through the sunflowers with the wariest of high curiosities. . . . They had a way of making you think they could see the *whole big* world just beyond their own flightlessness and could not wait to get out there in it, standing up on that hot burrow sand lip just flapping their little wings as hard as they could, determined flapping, hinting at the grace of an owl's wing, with imagined liftings of a little owl's body raised on toes with talons. (144)

Individual phrases like "scrunching up their wings" or "high curiosity" or "little owl's body" may sound excessively romantic, but when you examine the whole chapter, you find that Janovy's literary prose overlays a Darwinian worldview. His purpose in describing the personified burrowing owls is not to show cute critters but to ask hard questions about the ways humans affect natural selection.

The parent owls selected a burrow too close to a highway. Death by death, Janovy documents the demise of their young as each chick ventures onto the pavement and into a vehicle's path. Ever the scientist, Janovy brings the corpses to the laboratory table, analyzes them, photographs them, paints them, then puts their bodies where ants can consume them and without embellishment remarks that the ensuing skeletons will be useful for teaching purposes. At the same time, he fits their deaths into an evolutionary continuum. He concludes that the owls' choice of a burrowing hole too close to a busy highway was "a stunning lesson in the fragility of wilderness" (149). He wonders, too, what we as humans have cost ourselves as well as what we have cost the owls. Ann Zwinger, who also details physical behavior, does not ask such evolutionary questions. It is the conservation biologist who considers the real impact of a highway red in tooth and claw.

John Janovy is an example of a scientist with a literary flair. His antithesis on my academic writer's spectrum is Chip Rawlins, an English major and one-time Stegner creative-writing fellow who holds a job as a hydrologist-technician. In a strategy just the opposite of Janovy's, Rawlins specifically veers his nature writing away from scientific conclusions. Sampling water from the dark depths of a high mountain lake, night-dreaming, he eschews a biological summation for visual description, literary allusion, and personal contemplation. "I'm not ready," he states, "to bow to my meters and flasks. . . . I like this silence, in which there is hunger but no greed" (278). Such a leap of the imagination, I must admit, is typical of an English major in the wild.

Let's not dissect English professors quite yet, however. Instead, let's switch back to another scientist, ethnobotanist Gary Nabhan, watching rains fall on a dry Tohono O'odham terrain. "Desert arroyos are running again," he reports, "muddy water swirling after a head of suds, dung, and detritus. Where sheetfloods pool, buried animals awake, or new broods hatch." He's fascinated by the biotic community that suddenly appears: "dark egg-shaped clouds of flying ants," toad ponds "wild with chanting while the Western spadefoot's burnt-peanut-like smell looms thick in the air," a yellow mud turtle with "no memory of how many days it's been since his last swim" (3–5). Listen to Nabhan's cadence, heed the toad pond diction and syntax, spot the egg-shaped clouds on a burnt-peanut horizon. Such lively extrinsic details differ enormously from Rawlins's solemn pronouncements and melancholy introspection.

Naturalist Terry Tempest Williams says, "It is time for us to take off our masks, to step out from behind our personas—whatever they might be: educators, activists, biologists, geologists, writers, farmers, ranchers, and bureaucrats" (84). But I think she's mistaken in imagining that we can so easily "take off our masks." Such masks are not easily removed, for nature writers necessarily rely on their educational training. Whatever their undergrad or graduate specialty might have been, they not only "talk the talk" but they "think the think." That is, they look at the natural world, they describe the natural world, they analyze the natural world, they think about the natural world in terms grounded in their academic disciplines. More than simply technique, neither mask nor disguise, it's an entire way of thinking, a habit of mind that informs vision, cognition, interpretation, and metaphoric analogues. Separate academic attitudes situate each writer in a particular family of twentieth-century American nature writers.

Within each family, there must exist a number of different genera, or genuses. Each genus, I would suggest, is equated with the distance the narrator stands from his or her subject. That distance opens or closes the text for the reader and tells the reader whether or not the writer's words are to be believed, whether or not the writer's judgements are to be trusted. Narrative stance influences objectivity and subjectivity, intimacy, passion, and even reasoning about a subject. In short, narrative stance is at the heart of one's writing posture. It codifies how an author, and hence the reader, understands and interprets a particular natural milieu. A sometimes slippery sliding scale, my generic taxonomy includes these categories: residents, emigrants, immigrants, sojourners, travelers, and tourists.

The two extremes are the easiest to delimit. One genus is comprised of the resident essayist who stands wholly inside his or her materials. That genus is easy to discuss because so few contemporary essayists belong in such a category. Though lots of writers have lived or currently do live in the landscapes they describe, few have spent both childhood and adulthood in a single spot. An exception is Linda Hasselstrom, who grew up in rural South Dakota, left for a time, went to college, married and divorced, taught English, married again, and then returned to the family ranch where she still lives and works today. *Windbreak,* written in diary form, traces a typical year on a cow/calf operation in prose that is picturesque but hardly romantic.

> *December 5 Low -10, high 15; wind blowing, and lots of drifting.*
> . . . We chopped the ice and let the cattle in a few at a time to drink so they didn't crowd out onto the ice and break through. After we'd fed, they'd churned up the slope so much the pickup just sat and spun. We tried a dozen times, and were just beginning to face the prospect of walking home—ten miles in snow to our knees, with a cold wind and a chill factor the pickup radio said was close to thirty below zero—when we finally got enough traction to get out. (54)

Not all of *Windbreak*'s 233 pages are so miserably cold, but they're just as contextually vivid. Sometimes her words are eclectic. "I saw a dozen brilliant orange butterflies perched on a cluster of purple cone-flowers today. The purple and orange were wonderful, a change from the usual gentle greens and browns. Prairie punk" (174). Sometimes her words are parched. "Pasture trails ripple with heat on the horizon. The sky seems bleached by the sun, boiled to a pale uniform blue. The grass is brown, shattering as we walk on it" (193). Such descriptions are not paintings to hang on a wall. They're a three-dimensional film rolling twenty-four hours a day. The reader, who both holds the camera and rides alongside Hasselstrom in the moving celluloid pages, connects emotionally with the land because the author's projected images so closely contour around it. But the reader must also be wary. Sometimes Hasselstrom stands too close to her land to see it with objectivity. Then her South Dakota sounds parochial, and maybe not very appealing. "Bombed prairie dogs all morning, then again after 6 p.m. when it cooled off" (164).

If someone tries to write about an environment he or she sees only in haste, however, the result is far more problematic. The reader perceives neither objectivity nor subjectivity, feels no connection whatsoever. I don't want to belabor a kind of writing I find superficial, but here's an example of a New England biologist passing through eastern Oregon. Diana Kappel-Smith writes well enough, but she certainly doesn't see playa the way I see it. "I scuff my feet on a graveled shore as if I can't believe," she says. "I finger succulent needle leaves of greasewood, wishing blades of rush. I kick a rabbit-brush, which tosses, hissing like a wave. Dumb. The land is dumb, silent, flat forever. I take my chances now and turn up north on an unmarked road that is two wheel ruts through silence, dust, immense plain" (206). Listen to her words. Scuff. Can't believe. Kick. Hiss. Dumb. Flat forever. I take my chances. Dust. Dumb. While such hostile diction conveys the author's obvious discomfort in the high desert, it also discourages a reader from developing any sympathetic understanding of the country through which Kappel-Smith speeds. Just as the author feels alien, so she alienates the reader. It's hard, for me at least, to take a fly-by-night tourist very seriously.

Most naturalists locate themselves somewhere between Hasselstrom and Kappel-Smith, with different perspectives, different situations, different distances. Some belong to the traveler genus. Travelers are the writers who, like Kappel-Smith, move through a new landscape but more slowly. Confessing at the outset that they are outsiders, wearing their distance from their subjects on their sleeves, such authors pretend no inside knowledge whatsoever. Instead, they cannily craft "otherness" into a studied, rational point of view. William Least Heat Moon is a master traveler. For his first book, *Blue Highways,* he crossed the country on secondary roads so that he might learn fact and fiction about those who live off the beaten track. Driving in a leisurely fashion from community to community, Moon would glean both firsthand knowledge and secondhand comprehension, then write explanatory vignettes. His second book, *PrairyErth,* closely focused on a single Kansas county, pursues the same end. First the traveler learns, then he educates others. Unlike Kappel-Smith's superficial viewpoint, Moon brings credibility to his writing by his in-depth methods of inquiry—investigating, interviewing, walking, talking, reading, and synthesizing. He touches the soil intellectually in order to understand a new terrain, even devoting an entire chapter to a single blade of grass. "The signature of the long prairie," Moon explains, "big bluestem, probably originated in the valleys of the Appalachian Mountains, although its character is better suited to the climate and land forms farther west; its migration recapitulates the grand plate movement of the crustal rock it comes from, and it's also an analog of human passages: red and white" (195). Although six hundred pages about Chase County may tell some readers more than they ever wanted to know about Kansas, the technique of the traveler/nature writer, the learner/educator who in this case seeks accurate information about big bluestem, grand plate movement, and human passages, is well modeled in *PrairyErth*.

William Least Heat Moon is a hands-on writer of one sort; Loren Eiseley, another. Eiseley's best-known collection, *The Immense Journey,* contains two essays that show how a pure academic type might try to touch the land more closely. In the first, Eiseley takes his reader into a body-width crack, where "the light turned dark and green from the overhanging grass" and "the sky became a narrow slit of distant blue." Eiseley reports that "[i]t was tight and tricky work," but his deep exploration pays dividends. What he finds is an entire creature's "skull embedded in the solid sandstone," and what he imagines is a profound connection with its evolutionary past and his own evolutionary future. "The creature had never lived to see a man," Eiseley asserts; and then he wonders, "what was it I was never going to see?" (4, 5). The experience propels him into an immense intellectual journey, during which he remains an outsider looking in but continually reaches out and touches those things at which he gazes.

To capture the immediacy of firsthand experience, for example, he floats himself out into the Platte River current.

I drifted by stranded timber cut by beaver in mountain fast-
nesses; I slid over shallows that had buried the broken axles of
prairie schooners and the mired bones of mammoth.

   I was streaming alive through the hot and working ferment
of the sun, or oozing secretively through shady thickets. I *was*
water and the unspeakable alchemies that gestate and take
shape in water, the slimy jellies that under the enormous mag-
nification of the sun writhe and whip upward . . . or sink indis-
tinctly back into the murk out of which they arose. (19)

As he italicizes, he *is* water, and his technique yokes the reader with
his sense of becoming "a microcosm of pouring rivulets and float-
ing driftwood gnawed by the mysterious animalcules of my own
creation" (20). Just as he did when he descended into the sandstone
slit, Eiseley extrapolates about human connectivity with the evolutionary process, first by putting the reader in touch with the earth
and then by sliding the reader through layers of rock, water, mud,
and intellectual speculation.

   Eiseley, it seems to me, has learned a lesson I've heard expressed
by Wendell Berry. Writing of the Red River Gorge some distance
from his own Kentucky home, Berry prophecizes how meaningful
intimacy between a visitor and a landscape might develop. "Slowly,
almost imperceptibly, the experience of strangeness was transformed into the experience of familiarity. The place did not become
predictable; the more I learned of it, the less predictable it seemed.
But my visits began to define themselves in terms of recurrences
and recognitions that were pleasant in themselves, and that set me
free in the place" (227). The more a nature writer learns firsthand,
the more time he or she spends somewhere, the more familiar and
at once more profoundly mysterious that landscape becomes.
Then, better able to articulate what he or she sees and feels, a writer
can seamlessly connect the reader to that landscape.

   Edward Abbey spent almost all of his adult years in the desert
Southwest. He returned again and again to those places he loved
the most, and he sometimes wrote more than one essay about a
single place. Glen Canyon, for example, appears and reappears as

he watches it drown. Ann Zwinger began her writing career with the 1970 publication of *Beyond the Aspen Grove,* a book of essays about their family summer cabin in the Rockies. Each of her subsequent books has involved countless visits and revisits to a chosen terrain—the Green River, the Grand Canyon, Trail Ridge Road in Colorado, Baja California. Abbey and Zwinger both have understood the importance of seeing a landscape under a variety of seasons, weather conditions, and personal situations. They have not, however, written in the way that Linda Hasselstrom does, eking a creative minute here or an hour there from more sobering toils and tasks. Should we trust them? I think so. Maybe not quite in the same way we believe in the intrepid South Dakota ranch woman, though perhaps with more faith in their impartiality. Abbey and Zwinger, like Eiseley, move into a landscape and unfailingly reach out and touch it. They are less intellectually remote than Eiseley, but they all use the same technique—intertwining a life of the mind with the embodied life of the land through which they move. They're sojourners. Not residents, not tourists, not travelers—they spend more time, more seasons, in a single place than do travelers—but sojourners in their adopted lands. As members of this sojourn genus, they pick flowers from the earth, then hand a landscape bouquet to the reader. We can hold their special places tightly; we can smell the flowers; but we don't necessarily get our hands dirty. Neither do they.

There is another genus which layers between the sojourners and the residents. I call them the immigrants. Geologist-turned-naturewriter Rick Bass has chosen to settle permanently in the remote Yaak Valley of Montana. He probes his adopted terrain through various means—short stories, anecdotes about people and about animals, essays of the seasons. His book called *Winter* provides both rhythmic repetition and asymmetrical counterpoint to Hasselstrom's motifs. It also shows the differences between a long-time resident's and an immigrant's point of view. Like Hasselstrom's South Dakota, northern Montana is cold; unlike her existence, however, Bass's lifestyle doesn't require relentless confrontation with the elements. *"December 19. Forty below,"* he observes. "We're a little frightened. We're at the mercy of the cold. We hope for mercy." On the other hand, nothing requires the writer to go outside. "We hide in our sleeping bags" in front of the fireplace, Bass reports. "We read, we sleep. We can't get warm. But," he concludes, with a colon after the *but* to set off his summation—"But: this won't last" (123).

Hasselstrom's wind chill does last, and she doesn't have the luxury of hiding inside her house before a crackling fire. She can't write, "It was fun, carrying armloads of sweet hay from the barn across the road and into the pasture in the cold weather" as Bass can, when he helps a neighbor feed two horses once or twice (105). Hasselstrom has to do it every day, and it isn't sweet and it isn't fun. Yet because Bass lives a daily existence in his valley, he too is able to watch February turn into March and to craft descriptions that turn with the seasons.

> This sound: dripping. Running water coming off all the roofs, down all the downspouts, trickling across the paths and game trails in rivulets. Windy, with gusts and swirls from every direction, but mostly from the south and west, and purple skies, yellow weeds sticking up through the snow and blowing back and forth in the warm winds. A chinook: forty-eight, almost fifty degrees above. . . . Spring is suddenly here. . . . Winter is being routed in a single day. (154)

A sojourner might not see that single day, for a sojourner might still be in Missoula or Whitefish waiting for the roads to be plowed. Or for the mud to dry. A long wait, I would guess. Bass, on-site, can seize opportunities to watch the land in all its guises, perhaps even to see it more objectively than Hasselstrom does. But he doesn't need to go outside unless he wants to! That alone makes an enormous difference in perspective. He's an immigrant, not quite a real denizen of his chosen land, though he intends to be.

I think there's one more genus in the middle of this spectrum, that of the resident who emigrates away. He or she is an author who reconstructs a past that's no longer present, who images a landscape where the writer no longer holds a vested interest but who still cares passionately about memory and meanings and the passage of time. Mary Clearman Blew, who grew up in Montana, lives in Idaho now. She admits that her memories seem as "treacherous" as the river she knew as a child, and she wonders about the truth of what she writes.

> Is it possible, sitting here on this dry shoulder of a secondary highway in the middle of Montana where the brittle weeds of August scratch at the sides of the car, watching the narrow blue Judith take its time to thread and wind through the bluffs on its way to a distant northern blur, to believe in anything but today? The past eases away with the current. I cannot watch a single drop of water out of sight. How can I trust memory, which slips and wobbles and grinds its erratic furrows like a bald-tire truck fighting for traction on a wet gumbo road? (3–4)

I trust her memory, however, because she expresses it in such a down-to-earth way. The brittle weeds, the distant northern blur, the bald-tired truck fighting for traction on a wet gumbo road. These tangible images sound so very contrary to Kappel-Smith's dumb articulations, but they echo differently than Hasselstrom's words, too. "Soft, far away in the dark, unmistakable, unforgettable, a growing rumble, the bawling of cattle, and the yips of the riders," Blew writes on a later page. "A primordial sound, swelling closer, a sound I would hear in my sleep, hear again and again as I grew old enough to ride and taste dust for myself and smell cattle" (47). Blew's soft memories are dreamlike, mystical, removed in time from the here-and-now. They're not the thoughts of a visitor, they're more familiar than those of a sojourner, but they're no longer the impressions of a resident either. They're from a genus in between, the genus of the emigrant.

Let me summarize the six genera I propose. The two ends of the spectrum are the most obvious—the resident and the tourist, the ultimate insider and the ultimate outsider. The traveler uses his or her distance from the subject matter as an effective analytic and descriptive ploy. The sojourner, more intimately connected to a particular landscape than the traveler, nonetheless prefers to live permanently somewhere else. Then there are the immigrant and the emigrant, whose intimacy with a given place involves residency of a unique sort. Living on the land, either past or present, they do so in a bodiless kind of way. Rick Bass, penning many pages about sawing and chopping wood in *Winter,* laboring hard, working up a sweat, would disagree. But on any given day he can stop; he can go to his greenhouse study, and he can write when he chooses. He's of a genus apart from Linda Hasselstrom's, as is Mary Clearman Blew, her memories softly blurred. Together with my other examples, they span a set of possibilities for narrative posture. Whether resident or visitor, traveler or sojourner, immigrant or emigrant, where each writer positions him- or herself determines candor, veracity, objectivity, subjectivity, truth, and, ultimately, sense of place.

Have I stood the classical system of taxonomy on its head? I think so. I've allowed twentieth-century American nature writers to choose their own families, to select a genus as well as to be born into one. In my own defense I argue that family and genus in my writers' taxonomy are as much the result of temperament as of anything else, that they're inherent authorial characteristics. Intellectual interests determine family; emotional connections determine genus. But I do acknowledge the possibility of writers moving from category to category. In the real taxonomic universe, sagebrush can't decide to be aspen, coyotes can't opt for raptordom, and ichthyosaurs can't turn into cutthroat trout overnight. In my taxonomy, however, Janovy might cross literature with conservation biology; Eiseley, travels with sojourns. And Bass might live in Montana long enough to qualify as a genuine resident.

Can they select or redefine their species as easily? I'm going to say no. A species is too particular, too personal, too differential. So I'll conclude my essay with an examination of just a single species, the one I know best. It's a Nevada species found mostly in Reno. It belongs to the family called English professor; it's a member of the genus called sojourner. Using a prose style adapted from literature, it sallies forth from the city to the desert and back to the library.

Simile, metaphor, imagery of the senses, literary allusion, rhetorical flourish—all these literary devices enable this species to describe an ostensibly alien terrain in words that convey affection and wonder. This species—I'll call it Ann Ronald, for lack of a better term—has turned the Nevada desert into *Earthtones*. In that book, I had to make the kinds of decisions I've just been discussing. How much book learning? How much intellectual distance? How much emotional connection? In which family and which genus to pose?

You don't just sit down and start pounding away on your word processor. You start with a mind-set, of course. I'm an English professor, so I think in rhetorical terms. Like Chip Rawlins in the Wyoming mountains, I refer to other writers, and I turn analyses from side to side. A prism of words, reflecting landscape and thought both outward and in. I'm a sojourner. Like Edward Abbey, I return to the same desert again and again. Early morning, sunset, a March thaw, an October snowstorm, it makes no difference what day or which season. Then, like Ann Zwinger, I come home. I go to the library and look up facts about native peckings or cliffroses or lenticular clouds, learn more about anthropology or botany or atmospheric physics. Let me give you some brief *Earthtones* examples.

As an English professor, I recall a Keats poem in the silence of the Black Rock Desert. "And this is why I sojourn here, / Alone and palely loitering; / Though the sedge is withered from the Lake, / And no birds sing" (53). The actual dry lake bed and the poet's romantic projections blend introspectively for me. As a sojourner—and I admit to a Keatsian imagination with my choice of words for this genus—I stroll through a canyon where "licorice and chocolate give way to cherry and strawberry tones. . . . I can reach out and touch both orange-pink walls at once, or I can just step out of the narrow parts, into sage and rabbitbrush and brown dirt" (11). That is, I can move in and out of my chosen terrain. As a sojourning bibliophile, I look, I learn, I look anew. When I discovered that "the ichthyosaurs literally were beached and then buried by limey waters, rocks, lava flows, ash, and mud," I then extrapolated, and wrote that each preserved fossil piece "tilts downhill in the desert dirt, as if a school of fishlike reptiles were paddling toward deeper water when the hot sun toasted them into eternity" (82). I always look for new knowledge and new modes of expression. That way, pelicans at Pyramid Lake can fly together as "[a] curtain of northern lights, a drapery of shook foil, a pelican chandelier" (34).

Let me close now with a longer, more developed example. What follows is a combination of sojourning, library research, literary allusion, and word prisms. Just published in a collection titled *Western Technological Landscapes,* "Dust to Dust" shows clearly, I think, this writer's family, genus, and individual species. It's too awkward to analyze my own prose any further, so you'll have to do that as you read, as you remember my nature writer's taxonomy.

"Seen from a distance, desert playa resembles endless sheets of parchment paper, ivory pages unfigured by any known language past or present. Closer at hand, the illusion of emptiness does not diminish much. A single human being, walking alone on a grainy alkali flat, can circle endlessly under a hot sun. Spiraling away from landmarks, I can lose myself in a mirage of refracted time, lose connections with earth and space.

"Some of my friends like to make desert angels, throwing themselves down on the drifting desert pavement, swinging legs and arms back and forth in corporeal angel designs. Disembodied even as they touch the snowless ground, they enshrine a scattered circle of desert spirits under a sun-white cathedral sky. I used to laugh when we would play this schoolyard game. I never dreamed that real phantasma might rest just beneath the surface of a desert floor.

"Far from tire tracks and boot prints and even angel wings, a lost tribe lies buried in the alkali cement of time. Tucked into a womb of blowing sand and dust, a gathering of bodies surfaces slowly from the playa. First the tip of a skull, followed by a jawbone, six teeth, a hip socket, a long thigh bone, slivered fingers, spine chards, radius and broken ulna rubbing side by side. The pace of emergence varies, as does the sequencing of the bones. But emerge they do, these long-lost partial skeletons rising from a long-lost, only partially definable past. The unnamed corpses slowly percolate up from where once they were interred. If not rescued by the hands of modern tribal members and trained archaeologists, the bones disintegrate into fragments and blow away.

"Most of the recognizable remains curve into the fetal position. Facing west, knees tucked beneath their chins, their bones are frayed by the wash of wind and dirt. Some of the burial mounds are marked by worked rocks, grinding stones and dull primitive points. Others are decorated with artificially arranged gastropods, delicate spiral shells that blow away when brushed by my fingers. Still others scarcely seem like burials at all—a bone here, a piece there, a scatter of bones strewn by the wind, ragged edges, long slivers, a fragility of bones.

"Three wet years in a row flooded one Great Basin playa with the overflow from a river that normally evaporates as it reaches its sink. When a summer without much precipitation followed the floods and dried out the waters, more than just blowing dust rose from the arid expanse. A 1988 archaeological report reveals that '144 relatively complete skeletons and 272 incomplete skeletons or single bone elements' were found. Nearly a decade later, even more relics have dusted themselves into the parched sunlight.

"Dry 'osteological analyses' report some interesting facts. More males than females were counted, though archaeologists were unable to determine the sex of many of the burials. The males tended to have large, high cheekbones with prominent nasal bones, large brow ridges and square-shaped eye sockets, massive jaws. The smaller females, whose heights ranged from 5'2" to 5'7", tended to have medium high cheekbones, median brow ridges, and medium-sized jaws. The pathologies and anomalies suggest there was no marked change of occupants over the course of time—little in-migration, little out. These playa natives generally stayed put.

"Most of them suffered from arthritis. Not only do their bones show the normal stresses and strains that would come from gathering food and carrying loads, but they also display osteophytic growths on their joints. While this small skeletal sample may distort the 'high eburnation frequencies'—anthropological jargon for the disintegration of cartilage that results in bone-on-bone contact, thus wearing, grooving, and polishing the bones involved—archaeologists generalize that alkaline water or fungally contaminated food or a combination of the two contributed to the skeletal abnormalities. Or perhaps a lifetime of constant bending and kneeling and scraping and toting exacerbated the skeletal wear and tear. Whatever the causes, and without modern drugstore remedies to alleviate pain, the shoulders, elbows, wrists, and knees of the older natives must have ached constantly.

"I like to think that those bones studied by scientists in the late 1980s rest more easily now. They have been respectfully and privately reburied somewhere, in accordance with modern Paiute tribal wishes. Meanwhile, new skeletal pieces surface each season. The last time I walked through the ancient graveyard, four were visible. One entire skull shadow rested above a folded femur and scapula. Another skull simply sat naked on the playa, unearthed and unprotected. Two other burials were scarcely discernible, one with its eggshell bones already scattered, the other mostly remaining underground.

"That particular November day felt properly autumnal. A schizophrenic wind blew cold and warm, while the overhead sky looked washed-out, a flat watery blue. The lowering sun gave my body an elongated, unnatural shadow, and my boots crunched a hollow sound on the empty playa. Empty? Not really. Underfoot, a silent cemetery of bones. How many more burials lay below my feet? How many more skeletons could rise from their ghostly graves? While I tiptoed across the uneven contours, I found myself remembering Emily Dickinson's hymnal phrases:

> *There's a certain slant of light,*
> *Winter afternoons, . . .*
> *When it comes, the landscape listens,*
> *Shadows hold their breath;*
> *When it goes, 'tis like the distance*
> *On the look of death.*

"Once this playa was alive with people. A group of men, flaking and chipping rocks; others, farther away from the camp, hunting, throwing darts, and shooting arrows. Some women sewing skins together or weaving plant fibers; others, carrying water from a distant marsh or cooking alongside a smoky fire. If I read the landscape correctly, a spot to my left was the kitchen. Charred bones— the long, spiny teeth of a fish jaw, two fragile skeletal wings, a burnt rabbit leg, a half-buried fin, two dozen clam shells, a tiny spine—are strewn across a fifteen-foot radius. The shifting winds, subtle erosion, flood, and drought have covered, uncovered, covered, uncovered them countless times. Right now they are half buried, half revealed.

"So are the mysteries of this isolated Great Basin playa, where so much life—so many years ago—has so quietly departed into a desert slant of light" (87–90).

So are the mysteries of the twentieth-century American nature writers, half buried, half revealed, in the hands of a literary critic today.

WORKS CITED

Abbey, Edward. *Confessions of a Barbarian*. Ed. David Petersen. Boston: Little, Brown, 1994.
——. *Desert Solitaire*. New York: Ballantine Books, 1968.
——. *The Journey Home*. New York: E. P. Dutton, 1977.
Bass, Rick. *Winter*. Boston: Houghton Mifflin, 1991.
Berry, Wendell. "The Journey's End." *Words from the Land*. Ed. Stephen Trimble. Reno: University of Nevada Press, 1995. 226–38.
Blew, Mary Clearman. *All But the Waltz*. New York: Penguin, 1991.
Eiseley, Loren. *The Immense Journey*. New York: Vintage Books, 1957.
Hasselstrom, Linda. *Windbreak*. Berkeley: Barn Owl Books, 1987.
Heat Moon, William Least. *PrairyErth*. Boston: Houghton Mifflin, 1991.
Janovy, John, Jr. *Back in Keith County*. Lincoln: University of Nebraska Press, 1981.

Kappel-Smith, Diana. *Desert Time*. Tucson: University of Arizona Press, 1992.

Lyon, Thomas J., ed. *This Incomperable Lande*. Boston: Houghton Mifflin, 1989.

Nabhan, Gary. *The Desert Smells Like Rain*. San Francisco: North Point, 1987.

Rawlins, C. L. *Sky Witness*. New York: Henry Holt, 1993.

Ronald, Ann. "Dust to Dust." *Western Technological Landscapes*. Reno: Nevada Humanities Committee, 1998: 87–90. This essay was reprinted as "Buried Bones," chapter 8 in *GhostWest: Reflections Past and Present*. Norman: University of Oklahoma Press, 2002. 109–112.

——. *Earthtones*. Reno: University of Nevada Press, 1995.

Williams, Terry Tempest. *An Unspoken Hunger*. New York: Vintage Books, 1994.

Zwinger, Ann Haymond. *The Mysterious Lands*. New York: E. P. Dutton, 1989.

CHAPTER SIXTEEN

Raising the Bar

A vertical line runs from Henry David Thoreau, past John Muir and Mary Austin, alongside Aldo Leopold to Edward Abbey. Our contemporary nature writers inherit a genre shaped by their predecessors—Thoreau's seasonal and cyclical structure, Muir's loquacious effusions, Austin's meticulous observations, Leopold's judicious twentieth-century land ethic, Abbey's energetic and engaging narrative voice. Would-be Thoreaus and Abbeys inherit, as well, an abiding human concern for the land itself and a determination to understand man's place in relationship to the natural world. Against this vertical yardstick, *even if we don't mean to do so,* we instinctively have measured each new writer and every new book.

During the last decade, this axis has spun to the horizontal. New nature writers cluster all along it now, holding the parallel bar steady by the sheer weight of numbers. So many dozens crowd the field that it is sometimes difficult to distinguish among them, often problematic to sagaciously determine which authors to read. And if we use the traditional Thoreau/Abbey yardstick to make our judgments, we calculate feet and inches in an increasingly metric field. The traditional measuring tape is old-fashioned, the computations too easy, the numbers necessarily skewed. Recent innovations in the field of nature writing spin the axis in new directions. So rather than measure a group of new authors against touchstones from the past, I want to test them against themselves. At the same time, I want to make some guesses about how and why nature writing is changing these days. I might even try to predict where the bar may be located in the future.

I'll begin with Terry Tempest Williams's *Desert Quartet* because that slim volume is the most daring of the books piled beside me. Its prose bodily integrates human and earthly sensuousness—an "erotic landscape," as it were. "I dissolve. I am water," Williams writes. "I receive without apology" (23). Her words spill on the page like riffles in the stream. She is trying to turn sensory experience into erotic onomatopoeia and to see how far she can extend the senses. "The fire explodes. Flames become blue tongues curling around each other. My eyes close. I step forward" (41). So Williams shakes off the constraints of the traditional tape measure.

Also distancing himself from the conventional crowd is Bernie Krause, whose journalistic prose invites the reader to make musical connections with the natural world. *Into a Wild Sanctuary,* subtitled *A Life in Music and Natural Sound,* combines autobiographical details of Krause's musical background with an explanation of his training in and fascination for bio-acoustics. He sculpts natural sounds in traditional symphonic form by using the natural world as a biophonic orchestra. I'm familiar with Krause's Nature Company CD series but, before reading *Into a Wild Sanctuary,* I knew nothing about the process of capturing and comparing the songs of old and new growth trees, for example, or the conversations of gorillas or of frogs. Unlike *Desert Quartet,* this book makes no attempt to echo emotion. Rather, it pragmatically explores the aural acuity necessary to be a bio-acoustic sculptor. Like Williams, however, Krause manipulates the senses in new and apperceptive ways.

At the opposite end of the playing field are writers who consider nature more intellectually than intuitively. Neither Paul Shepard, in his posthumous *Coming Home to Pleistocene,* nor Michael P. Cohen, in *A Garden of Bristlecones,* lacks passion for his subject, but each man brings a lifetime of learning and thinking to his work. Each ponders connections and continuities between science, history, and the human condition. The former author, in a series of gracefully analytic chapters devoid of personal vignettes, addresses the ways in which evolution has shaped our human minds and bodies and speculates how we might reconnect our lives with our generic roots. The latter interlaces the scientific with the personal and speaks as directly to the general reader as to the specialist.

A Garden of Bristlecones seamlessly weaves history with geology with biology with plant science with philosophy with literature. In its pages, Cohen seeks successfully the language of bristlecones, the articulations and cross-pollinations between the world's oldest living organisms and ourselves. "The bristlecone stands before an observer like an object before the senses," Cohen writes at the end of chapter 7, "an idea before the mind, and a presence to be reckoned with" (180). He then begins chapter 8 by saying, "Dressed in thought and expressed in language, the bristlecone pine has come to mean many things beyond itself" (181). In effect, Cohen deconstructs the generic individual tree, its history, the men and women who have studied the bristlecones, and a wilderness of human interstices and implications. An incredibly erudite book, gracefully written and profoundly inquisitive, *A Garden of Bristlecones* models what a writer can accomplish by bringing a wealth of objective and subjective facets together in a single book. Sketches and drawings by Valerie Cohen contribute integrally to *A Garden of Bristlecones,* too, for her colors and shapes replicate both the physical convolutions of the trees and the twists of Michael P. Cohen's mind. Just as Krause sculpts the natural world's musicality, so Valerie Cohen sings its visual artistry on canvas.

Several recent books, in fact, contain drawings to enhance the texts. Terry Tempest Williams's *Desert Quartet* includes companion sketches and paintings by Mary Frank. Hilary Stewart's *On Island Time* not only describes her adopted island in British Columbia but illustrates its special treasures, while Ann Haymond Zwinger's newest collection of essays visually as well as descriptively documents plants and tiny animals encountered during her long career as a naturalist. One or more drawings accompany the prose on nearly every page of Hilary Stewart's book: a Stellar's jay, juncos, a fox sparrow, and towhee on driftwood; nootka rose and hips, plus bracken; a buck browsing, a raccoon, lupine, and an ox-eyed daisy. On-site, Stewart moves boulders, introduces new plants, hangs birdfeeders, cuts cedar boughs for the deer, leaves apple slices for the raccoons. She designs her circumscribed terrain not only inside the book itself but also on the patch of land where she has retired. Ann Zwinger pictures a much broader, and less managed, world. *The Nearsighted Naturalist* projects a lifetime of global landscapes, some in her own backyard, some as far away as the Yangtze's Three Gorges, all biocentric in their focus. Her drawings, her close-ups, are neither chapter-specific nor illustratively imperative. Rather, they suggest a singular lens through which, pencil in hand, a nearsighted naturalist views what lies before her.

Not only does this book bring together Zwinger's essays published during the last twenty years, but it also defines her personal sense of the profession she pursues. "Classical natural history writing," she construes, "is based on three main principles: detailed and precise fieldwork; absolute scientific accuracy; and a graceful literary style that combines both" (285). She quotes Edwin Way Teale, who said that "nature writing is preserving a moment and place in time in the same intricate detail that a fly is preserved in amber" (273). Like Thoreau and his predecessor William Bartram, like Aldo Leopold describing his Wisconsin farm and Mary Austin characterizing her land of little rain, Teale and Zwinger believe in meticulous representation. Zwinger's exacting drawings and words echo and make manifest this particular vision.

Her representational point of view is instructive for our purposes because this artist/writer clearly sets herself and her classical predecessors apart from what seems to weigh down many of the books I've been reading these past months. I'm inclined to agree with Stephen J. Lyon's assessment. "This may be heresy," he wrote in a letter dated October 1998 to the editor of *Salon* that has been widely disseminated on various Web list-serves, "but how many times do we need to wade through some introvert's musings on his or her latest tramp into unspoiled wilderness" (http://www.salonmagazine.com/mwt/lamo/1998/10/cov_15lamo.html)? Although Lyons exaggerates in the service of truth, he rightly summarizes a current tendency toward egocentric meanderings. Many writers are changing the rules of the natural history game, cashiering closely observed phenomena in favor of compound psychological interest. This is not to say, of course, that men like Thoreau and Abbey weren't themselves egocentric. Rarely, however, did their quirks hold center stage for more than a nonfiction paragraph or two, and never did they immolate themselves. Of today's writers, I cannot say the same. I hope I'm not one of them, but my critical responses to the next several books certainly reveal my own idiosyncratic tastes.

Patricia C. McCairen's *Canyon Solitude* describes a solo raft trip through the Colorado River's Grand Canyon. Colin Fletcher's *River* does the same, although his more ambitious solo journey begins where the Green River rises in Wyoming and continues all the way to the Gulf of Mexico. Both books highlight their author's emotional interactions with their riparian surroundings. McCairen's incessant introspection goes no further than the canyon walls; Fletcher's observations do have serious environmental overtones, but also dwell on the personal. When he enters the string of reservoirs that bead the lower Colorado, he says the river seems "caged." And when the current slackens, he decides "that the river had, like any living entity that endures, moved into the autumn of its days" (310). Political insights aside, Fletcher devotes too many pages to housekeeping tasks, campsite discomforts, ill health, and his own personal autumn.

David Petersen troubled me for a slightly different reason. In *The Nearby Faraway* he invokes his muse as if Edward Abbey were riding in his pack and as if Petersen were incapable of seeing the landscape without his mentor's help. Abbey isn't really necessary at all, for Petersen is very astute when he relies on his own powers of observation. Petersen alone tiptoes through his landscape without leaving permanent footsteps, he pays close attention to details, and he rarely lets his own personality intrude. "[A]t the leeward base of an umbrella-line old-growth spruce, I find a big oval of cushy duff scraped clean of ground litter," he writes. "And dry as Noah's socks. My nose confirms it: wapiti. I gratefully claim the earthy ark for my own and settle in for the duration of the storm" (54). Petersen should trust his own talent; he need not share his ark with Abbey.

A writer who does trust her own stories is SueEllen Campbell. From Roland Barthes and from choreography, she borrows the word "figure" to characterize "a momentary attitude of the body or a fragment of a dance" (x–xi). *Bringing the Mountain Home* maps specific figures that lure Campbell outside and that express her "own landscapes of desire" (xii). Unlike Terry Tempest Williams, however, Campbell shares events rather than emotions, episodes rather than effusions. She takes the reader on the trail with her— relishing a Grand Canyon vista, cowering during a Colorado thunderstorm, watching bald eagles soar, questioning the logic of bears— and lets her reader intuit the appropriate visceral response. More personally present than some authors, Campbell nonetheless avoids unwholesome self-interest.

Mobility and sociability distinguish the narrator of *Wide Skies,* too. As a representative of the National Endowment for the Humanities, Gary Holthaus has criss-crossed the rural West and learned the stories of people he met. In *Wide Skies* he tells those tales with affection and insight. "Until we get our stories straight," Holthaus explains, "we will never find the West as home" (20). He describes Sherm and Mary, eking a living from a dryland farm; Springdale, a little town divided by civic strife; Smitty's death from cancer and his wife's reaction. Holthaus narrates his own stories as well, seeking both a sense of community and personal roots in the American West. Like Campbell, he eschews the classical tradition in favor of a more modern, more culturally inclusive, approach to his surroundings.

Bruce Berger, also a storyteller, cultivates roots in an adopted landscape. *Almost an Island* investigates what its author calls "the peninsula of my obsession" (103). Berger explains: "I had begun combing Baja California with the notion that because it was a single shaft of desert, finite, framed by the sea, after sufficient exploration it could finally be amassed inside and held in one vast, composite, visionary thought" (170). It could not. But if the whole is less than the sum of the pieces, Berger's individual stories of bird watching and people watching are extroverted, replete with lively human interactions, and interesting to read.

Another colonialist, Reg Saner, wants to make sense of the Anasazi Southwest. He metaphorically titles his new book of essays *Reaching Keet Seel,* and directs his readers to a variety of New Mexico, Arizona, and Utah Anasazi sites. Although Saner does convey sensitivity to Native beliefs, he explicitly omits introducing contemporary Native Americans into his travels. *Reaching Keet Seel* expresses one man's lonely philosophic musings in a natural and personally exclusive setting. No one else seems important there. The same is true of Paul Gruchow's *Boundary Waters* and its attendant isolation. Where Saner revisits desert trails and tribal walls long familiar to him, however, Gruchow paddles into terrain where he had never before ventured. In those alien Minnesota and Canadian boundary waters, he affirms and embraces his own uneasiness and discomfort. "We confront in wild places evidence of powers greater than our own," Gruchow writes; "this evidence humbles us, and in humility is the beginning of spirituality" (201). Testing his own boundaries along with the waters', Gruchow might be an apt companion for Patricia McCairen. Both dwell too intensely, I think, on interior passages. I must confess that I personally recoil from such introspection.

Barry Lopez seeks interiors and boundaries and horizons, too, but less insistently. *About This Life,* subtitled *Journeys on the Threshold of Memory,* takes him in directions both outward and inward—to northern Hokkaido, to metaphors of flight, to the Grand Canyon, to the language of hands. Gathered primarily from previous publications, Lopez's collection, like Zwinger's *Nearsighted Naturalist,* summarizes years of achievement. Like Zwinger's, too, Lopez's book is uneven, printing some outstanding pieces alongside some less successful ones.

My favorite *About This Life* selection brings together Lopez's exquisite flair for the English language, his natural philosophy, his knack for keen observation, his tempered objectivity.

> In a treeless, winter-hammered landscape like Alaska's north slope, the light creates a feeling of compassion that is almost palpable. Each minute of light experienced feels like one stolen from a crushing winter. You walk gently about, respectful of flowering plants, with a sense of how your body breaks the sunshine, creating shadow. You converse in soft tones. The light is—perhaps there is no other word—precious. You are careful around it. (122)

Stephen Lyons's *Salon* letter opines that "we already have enough nature books to keep us spiritual into the next century." Barry Lopez's considerable talent suggests otherwise.

Just as light prophetically illuminates Lopez's prose, so a laser beam passes above and below my collection of writers. A modern measurement, the laser beam, marks the line my authors either toe or step over or lag behind. If Zwinger represents the classical nature writer and Lopez the philosopher, then Cohen is the one who outdistances them in a cross-country ramble through biological and intellectual terrain. Despite Cohen's strong finish, however, he neglects a critical turn in the road. That breachable boundary is one of environmental activism.

As the twentieth century draws to a close, many contemporary writers worry about human interactions with the natural world in ways that Thoreau and even Muir might not have imagined. Robert Schnelle's *Valley Walking* projects an activist's voice, one that will not compromise and one that grows more cantankerous as the book progresses. "I guess I am an elitist myself if that means preferring clean air, stillness, and unscorched earth," Schnelle writes (101–2). Pointing to pollution problems and uncontrolled growth within central Washington's Kittitas Valley, Schnelle looks to the future instead of the past. "Young people," he believes, "are the new growth on our blighted, national terrain" (119). His projection reminds me of a debate I once heard between Ann Zwinger and her daughter Susan. Two generations of nature writers; two diametrically opposing views of their craft. The older, classically restrained; the younger, determinedly political. *Valley Walking,* racing toward the twenty-first century, is not a book Edwin Way Teale would have written or admired.

Neither is Katie Lee's retrospective *All My Rivers Are Gone: A Journey of Discovery through Glen Canyon.* Unlike McCairen's and Fletcher's river books, Lee's narrative situates the self in a dialogue with environmental change. Plunging down a wondrous "Rabbit Hole," Glen Canyon and the Colorado River of the 1950s, Lee emerges into "Cesspowell, the Stool of the Colorado" at the end of her book (28, 247). With a connection to the land as erotic as Williams's and a political viewpoint as definitive as Schnelle's, the author of *All My Rivers Are Gone* honors "River Gods and lost loves" and makes no apologies for her resentment and rage at "the asphyxiation of Glen Canyon" (237). Her love she proclaims exuberantly: "You must feel the textures with your own bare feet and fingers, steep in the sun's heat after a cold slap from the pools, watch the tattered blue ribbon of sky diminish between the walls" (189). Her anger she wears "like a crown" (238)!

Lee's impassioned words, and this growing trend toward activism, belie the fact that many nature writers cling to a gentler model. Two recent meditations tell us that environmental pacificism is still possible for some observers. Barbara Drake's title says so directly, *Peace at Heart: An Oregon Country Life.* Her down home book fits the contours of the land, molding itself to the greens and golds of a rain-soaked West Coast landscape. Linda Underhill's *Unequal Hours: Moments of Being in the Natural World* plows its tranquillity on the opposite side of the continent, in upstate New York. Both books nicely reflect the recent surge of regional nature writing—the specificity, the heart-felt sense of place, the profound attachment—though neither unveils any clouds. Both also are indicative of the fact that university presses currently are encouraging and supporting this emergent field.

Is regional, or bioregional, nonfiction the playing field of the future? Are we chalking the lines in a narrow ballpark, its stands filled with expectant fans whose scorecards insist upon Thoreauvian rules? As I project an answer, I find myself half in bounds, half out. Or, to return to my original metaphor, I find myself stumbling against a bar that wobbles unpredictably.

Nancy Lord's *Fishcamp: Life on an Alaskan Shore* measures a contemporary cadence with phrases found in an old book of rules. "I like to retreat from the world as most of us know it," she writes,

> the worldly version that's almost exclusively involved with humans and human wants and desires—and live within one that is at once both broader in scope and simpler, quieter. If I don't quite embrace a doctrine of souls, I still think that the creatures, objects, and phenomena of the natural world have values in themselves, completely aside from their usefulness to people, and that these values are most closely seen by a person who has separated herself to some degree from the din and domination of her own kind. (210)

The most Thoreauvian of books, *Fishcamp* turns out to be my favorite of the twenty I've reviewed on these pages. Apparently my tastes were defined at an early age. I have been indoctrinated by a tradition that not only situates a thoughtful narrator in a unique locale but also asks significant philosophical questions. So I find that I prefer books with identifiable subjects—Lord's Cook Inlet, Krause's musical sculpture, Cohen's garden of bristlecones, Lee's remembered canyon. When I read a book of nature writing, I want more than an effusive "eye." I want to learn something.

Nancy Lord is well versed in anthropology, fascinated by linguistics, knowledgeable about native plants, possessed with keen powers of observation, and a skillful salmon harvester besides. She reads widely; she harvests ideas. I like Lord's sense of herself and of her surroundings. *Fishcamp* is a book to be read more than once, a text to be taught, a genuinely vertical piece of writing that steps easily and gracefully over the parallel bar where so many others horizontally cling.

Thus the reviewer cracks her shins. I began this essay by saying that, *even if we don't mean to do so,* we habitually measure writers and books against a yardstick Thoreauvian at one end and Abbeyesque at the other. And I suggested that we ought to be replacing such old-fashioned touchstones with twenty-first-century values and evaluations. Twenty books later, I find myself tripping over my own words. *Fishcamp* wins the gold medal awarded by this particular judge. *A Garden of Bristlecones* is just a centimeter behind.

Despite its traditional focus, *Fishcamp* foreshadows a future also predicted by *Bristlecones*. Each exercises the intellect, each insists upon interdisciplinary discourse, each balances the human perspective with a natural one, each models energy and eloquence. If neither is as insistent about political and environmental issues as some readers might like, each nonetheless displays ecological intricacies well worth understanding. These two books, along with parts of several others reviewed here, do indeed raise the bar: Zwinger collecting moths, Lopez exploring Alaska; Campbell's figures, Petersen's animals; Krause and Lee and Schnelle for the ways their minds stretch my own. Michael P. Cohen and Nancy Lord. A laser beam, not a ruler, measures such successes.

WORKS REVIEWED

Berger, Bruce. *Almost an Island: Travels in Baja California.* Tucson: University of Arizona Press, 1998.

Campbell, SueEllen. *Bringing the Mountain Home.* Tucson: University of Arizona Press, 1996.

Cohen, Michael P. *A Garden of Bristlecones: Tales of Change in the Great Basin.* Illustrations by Valerie Cohen. Reno: University of Nevada Press, 1998.

Drake, Barbara. *Peace at Heart: An Oregon Country Life.* Corvallis: Oregon State University Press, 1998.

Fletcher, Colin. *River: One Man's Journey Down the Colorado, Source to Sea.* New York: Vintage Departures, 1997.

Gruchow, Paul. *Boundary Waters: The Grace of the Wild.* Minneapolis: Milkweed Editions, 1997.

Holthaus, Gary. *Wide Skies: Finding a Home in the West.* Tucson: University of Arizona Press, 1997.

Krause, Bernie. *Into a Wild Sanctuary: A Life in Music and Natural Sound.* Berkeley: Heyday Books, 1998.

Lee, Katie. *All My Rivers Are Gone: A Journey of Discovery through Glen Canyon.* Boulder, Colo.: Johnson Books, 1998.

Lopez, Barry. *About This Life: Journeys on the Threshold of Memory.* New York: Alfred A. Knopf, 1998.

Lord, Nancy. *Fishcamp: Life on an Alaskan Shore.* Washington, D.C.: Island Press, 1997.

McCairen, Patricia C. *Canyon Solitude: A Woman's Solo River Journey through the Grand Canyon.* Seattle: Seal Press, 1998.

Petersen, David. *The Nearby Faraway: A Personal Journey through the Heart of the West.* Boulder, Colo.: Johnson Books, 1997.

Saner, Reg. *Reaching Keet Seel: Ruin's Echo and the Anasazi.* Salt Lake City: University of Utah Press, 1998.

Schnelle, Robert. *Valley Walking: Notes on the Land.* Pullman: Washington State University Press, 1997.

Shepard, Paul. *Coming Home to the Pleistocene.* Ed. Florence R. Shepard. Washington, D.C.: Island Press, 1998.

Stewart, Hilary. *On Island Time.* Seattle: University of Washington Press, 1998.

Underhill, Linda. *The Unequal Hours: Moments of Being in the Natural World.* Athens: University of Georgia Press, 1999.

Williams, Terry Tempest. With drawings and paintings by Mary Frank. *Desert Quartet.* New York: Pantheon Books, 1995.

Zwinger, Ann Haymond. *The Nearsighted Naturalist.* Tucson: University of Arizona Press, 1998.

CHAPTER SEVENTEEN

Afterword from *Words for the Wild*

Whenever I've written about a Western writer, I've tried to follow his or her trail. Zane Grey led me along the Mogollon Rim for miles, Edward Abbey drew me to Organ Pipe and the Superstitions and the Sonoran desert and a lot of other Southwest country, a cluster of pioneer women taught me about Tonopah, Nevada, and the list goes on. I think a reader knows Western writers better after tracking them awhile, and I think the same holds true for nature writers too. To really hear them, each of us ought to walk with them.

Obviously, though, trailing twenty-three authors across a continent in a single year (while putting this book together and holding down a full-time job) would be impossible. So I had to find another way to share the worlds of the writers in *Words for the Wild*.

My answer was simple—two week-long backpacking trips, one to the desert, another to the mountains. Along the way I would follow my own path, but I also would try to see the land as others did. Birds I would view through Audubon's eyes, bugs through Annie Dillard's. Desert plants I'd see as Joseph Wood Krutch saw them, the Sierra in the light of Muir. Even a drive to the trailhead would be part of the experience, for I couldn't cross Nevada's sagebrush expanses in any direction without thinking of Frémont's slow explorations back and forth across the West.

The first venture took me to the nearest available red rock. Not only is southern Utah just a day's drive from Reno, but its high canyon country yields more suitable June temperatures than lower desert terrain. I found a spot on the map I'd never seen, and headed east. I guess I'm still a purist at heart. Since we met only one other hiker in eight days, I hesitate to say exactly where we went.

By contrast, the second trip passed through Tent City. Because the Hoover Wilderness provides relatively easy access to the eastern Sierra and to a corner of Yosemite Park, and because it contains a myriad of trout-filled lakes, its trails are immensely popular. Californians and non-Californians alike camp side by side. A little cross-country travel, though, coupled with a little extra effort, took us well away from the hoards. In keeping with my philosophy of wilderness, we never spent a night in sight of another human being.

I like to think I always have my priorities straight. Before we started along the Utah trail, we drank the last two beers in the truck because otherwise they might spoil and because Edward Abbey would approve. Before we trudged into the Sierra, we did the same.

The Utah way led along a sandy creek bed and down a ridge to a stream that ran red with particled silt. That stream became our guide, as we splashed back and forth three or four dozen times a day up its rocky gorge and down again. Calf-deep and about fifteen feet wide, it felt deliciously cool. The side canyons were special treats, some steep-walled and forbidding, others sunny and flower-filled, still others squishy with quicksand and stagnant pools. Red rock was everywhere, but so were cottonwoods, oak, red blossoms, pink cactus, and creatures enjoying the shade.

Equally luxuriant were the mountain meadows a month later, as July flowers literally crowded the Sierra Nevada hillsides. I couldn't begin to count the kinds or even to catalogue the colors, but I know a botanist would have been delighted. The trip reversed a route I'd followed twelve years before, with conventionally beautiful mountain vistas and an excess of stream crossings, willow tangles, rock slides, snow patches, lake shores, and granite peaks. Not so very different from a hundred other jaunts in California's high country, it nonetheless was fun.

As I think about the two hikes now, in retrospect, I find my imagination stretched in two quite different directions. The canyon drew my eyes to what was near at hand. More intimate—perhaps because red walls, standing high on either side, block out a longer view—it was a place to examine pale golden butterflies, delicate seeps, hanging moss, the mottled colors of a baby rattler. This is not to say that I wasn't impressed by the big picture, for one side canyon led to an arch as high as I've ever seen and another to a waterfall as lovely as I could imagine, but on the whole I recall details rather than drama, specifics rather than spectacle.

The same is not true of my week in the Sierra. There a hiker crosses ten-thousand-foot passes and stares out over a landscape punctuated by peaks and clouds. One looks at one's feet only to keep from stumbling, as shapes and shades change on the horizon. John Muir coined a perfectly characteristic phrase, saying of the Sierra, "after ten years of wandering and wondering in the heart of it, rejoicing in its glorious floods of light, the white beams of the morning streaming through the passes, the noonday radiance on the crystal rocks, the flush of the alpenglow, and the irised spray of countless waterfalls, it still seems above all others the Range of Light." I agree.

I woke with a start in the Hoover Wilderness, the smell of smoke sharp in my nostrils. My watch told me it was nearly 5:30, but daylight was barely visible and a pall completely blocked my view. Since I know a modern forest fire brings an armada of planes and helicopters and since I could hear nothing but the riffle of a tiny stream, I knew we were in no danger. Nonetheless, the dim light cast an eerie shroud everywhere (even at noon, we couldn't see more than a couple of hundred feet in any direction), and we were conscious of filtered shadows all day long. Several uneasy parties left the area. We did the opposite, heading west into the smoke and the subtleties of light and dark, the ragged edges of just-glimpsed peaks, the blinking ray of sun that appeared and then was gone.

Friday's wind brought Saturday's fresh air, along with Saturday's storm. This time a light patter of rain on tent woke me. A downpour might soak through eventually, but this shower appeared short-lived. To my left Virginia Peak glowed orange in the morning sunrise while elsewhere, against the horizon, puffy clouds reflected the same amber tint. The black cloud directly overhead swept west, then east again, grew darkly ominous, then faded into a watery blue. For almost an hour the sky pulsed with shades of light, as John Muir's very words came true. I've read *The Mountains of California* perhaps a dozen times; I've never understood it as well as I did that morning while I watched the sunrise through the rain.

I think I understand Edward Abbey's writing better, too, every time I go into red-rock country. A description like my favorite one in *Desert Solitaire*—"great curving cliffs with their tapestries of water stains, the golden alcoves, the hanging gardens, the seeps, the springs where no man will ever drink, the royal arches in high relief and the amphitheaters shaped like seashells. A sculptured landscape mostly bare of vegetation—earth in the nude"—means more when I, myself, thread my way beneath a shadowed canyon wall. One Utah side canyon, called Beartrap, brought Abbey's words freshly to mind.

It swung sharply east from our mainstream route, a deep cut so narrow that the sky appeared a sliver overhead. An inch or two of water lapped from side to side—"No place to be caught in a flash flood," I remarked, craning my head in anticipation of nonexistent thunderheads. Obviously the creek ran deeper than a few inches a good many times each year. Dark caves scalloped the cliffs both high and low, polished boulders lay helter skelter in the way, clusters of ferns grew rampant. But even the ferns couldn't disguise the nudity of Beartrap Canyon, a stark cavern slashing a third of a mile into flesh-colored rock. "No place to escape," I kept my thoughts to myself while I eyed the slick steepness and listened to a growing undertone of sound.

Then I was reminded not so much of Abbey's words, but of John Wesley Powell's. "Down in these grand, gloomy depths we glide, ever listening, for the mad waters keep up their roar; . . . so we listen for falls and watch for rocks, stopping now and then in the bay of a recess to admire the gigantic scenery." A pool ten feet deep filled the dead end of Beartrap Canyon, a waterfall thirty feet high filled the silhouetting pool. It wasn't mysterious or frightening after all, this incredibly picturesque surprise, yet it was awesome. I could close my eyes and listen to the sullen crash of the falls; I could open them and see a royal amphitheater carved in high relief. In short, I could listen with Powell's ears, pretend to write with Abbey's pen.

Now, at home, I can read the words of either man and see not only the canyons of the Colorado but Beartrap Canyon, too. Their *Words for the Wild* mean more to me than they did three months ago, their voices speak more directly.

Other voices speak more directly also. I had selected most of the excerpts in *Words for the Wild* before setting out on my summer adventures, so I had my writers' visions well in mind. I intended to heed their cautions, to honestly attempt to see the wilderness from their points of view. This meant that I had to look at some new things in some startlingly new ways. After reading Joseph Wood Krutch's essays about the desert and then studying Annie Dillard's depictions of her creek, I was more than ready to view the wilderness kingdom with an open eye, to lie quietly, to look and listen, to watch the creatures lead their daily lives.

Every night at sundown, the Utah chorus—a cacophony of desert frog noise—began. Incredible tenors and bass emitted from voice boxes no bigger than thimbles. One evening I watched for an hour, as one lonely soul blasted the still air with an anthem of praise. The next day I took my lunch break alongside a snoozing rattlesnake—two and a half feet long, ten buttons proud. He was digesting a meal, gently burping a bulge down the length of his body. The state of inactivity suited me fine. I settled myself nearby, then tried to guess what animal had let itself get caught and how. When a second rattler prowled into view, I realized that, compared to the reality of reptile hunting, my imagination was feeble. Head high, tongue darting, it slid noiselessly through fallen oak leaves and disappeared. So did I.

Then, on Saturday morning, Darwin's world came closer still. We stepped onto a dusty battlefield just as the war had been decided. A striped whipsnake, clasping a flailing lizard in its mouth, wriggled victorious. We watched, then, as the snake delivered the final indignity. Carefully turning the unhappy victim lengthwise, the conqueror unhinged its jaw, gulped twice, and swallowed the lizard whole. We watched the little arms thrash, saw the lizard's body elongate to match the snake's shape, felt a sympathetic twinge when headfirst it disappeared.

On the spot I decided I should have majored in biology. Now I could understand long hours spent beside Tinker Creek waiting for the swift appearance of a muskrat's head or hoping to spy a water bug sucking his dinner meal. I could feel the clammy wrench of life and death enacted, the uneasy juxtaposition of pleasure and pain. Nothing in the Sierra matched the experience. A mother ptarmigan scolding her young was fun to watch—and I must admit I watched more closely than in my pre-Dillard days—but the interlude was benign. Four fluff balls skidding down a snowbank are hardly comparable to a striped whipsnake triumphantly lashing its tail.

As a matter of fact, I found the geographical and geological formations in my overpopulated part of the Sierra more fascinating than the few animals scattered here and there. Several *Words for the Wild* authors—John Muir, Clarence King, Joseph LeConte—first viewed these mountains in terms of available minerals, of volcanic activity, of glacial designs. While I can replicate neither a scientific purview nor a technical vocabulary, I can (and did) pay close attention to the rocks. The Hoover Wilderness exudes color—peaks of reddish orange, others of dull brown, dark walls of gray-black rock, occasional striations of green.

Past Summit Lake all that changes. Ahead lie granite domes rising from deep-cut valleys—Yosemite National Park. Even a neophyte can see the difference, but a neophyte who has just read about the California Geological Survey can appreciate it a little more. In the early morning, it still looks like this: "slant sunlight streamed in among gilded pinnacles along the slope, . . . touching here and there, in broad dashes of yellow, the gray walls, which rose sweeping up on either hand like the sides of a ship."

I could go on describing my two brief outings, canyon and clouds, for a good many more pages. Indeed, the longer I sit staring at my idle pen, the more details I remember. Some aren't wonderful, like the gnat attack that sent me into a personal-best sprint with thirty-five pounds on my back, or the day-long enforced march past an armada of cows placidly guarding the available springs. Most, though, are the sort that keep me going all winter—a mossy seep marked by tiny white petals, a battered yellow fungus clasping a fallen pine, a happy weasel with a mole in her mouth, a less happy chipmunk objecting to my tent, a shared shot of whiskey cut with unchlorinated water, a sunset (there's always a sunset).

"We need the tonic of wildness," Thoreau wrote more than a century ago. He was absolutely right.

CHAPTER EIGHTEEN

"Ghosts" from *Earthtones*

Tucked against the Schell Creek Range and looking across the Spring Valley basin, dinner eaten, dishes clean, cup of tea in hand, I was ready for nightfall. The setting sun cast soft alpenglow off the Snake Range to the east. The shadows deepened; the scenery and silence were vintage Nevada. When I spotted the tombstones, they seemed to belong. Three quarters of a mile away, what appeared to be a ghostly cemetery stood in silhouette. Maybe half a dozen markers half-buried in the sage, maybe a sagging wooden fence—it was hard to tell in the semidarkness and too late to investigate that evening.

The next morning I crossed the draw and pushed my way through the sagebrush. "N. L. Hughs a native of Missouri died Mar. 11, 1896 aged 63 years"; "James Doherty, died Oct. 21 1891 age 57 yrs"; "'T is finished! The conflict is past: The heaven-born spirit is fled." There, ninety miles from Ely and a dozen dirt road miles from pavement, stood a cluster of marble tombstones that would befit Virginia City. Elegant scrollwork bordered the names, forgotten memorials to a handful of men who died a century before. Apparently no women and no children were buried there, for I could find markers only for males. "M. Killian died Feb 4 97 Born in Penn July 4 1820"—the precise etching cut deep into the marble.

I spent most of the morning looking for clues. I was sure I would discover a ghost town nearby, a cluster of half-ruined buildings, the remains of some walls, or at least a clearing in the stony soil. Near the cemetery I stumbled on an abandoned well but found few other relics of past inhabitants. No trace of a street, no sign of a disintegrating dwelling, nothing that resembled a once-thriving community. Up the mountainside, an old mine shaft collapsed in on itself, rusted pipe and a few timbers, dirt leached turquoise-green, an unused road overgrown with brush. But the mine was far from the cemetery site, and surely could not have sustained the wealth that paid for marble carving. Closer to where my truck was parked, a couple of other mine shafts were more clearly visible. In fact, I had camped quite near some broken stone walls. Even these, however, appeared too insignificant to have fostered such a memorial display.

The library back home partially solved the mystery. Between 1870 and 1910, the eastern slopes of the Schell Creek Range first promised gold, then silver, then copper. The mines played out quickly, though not before boardinghouses, saloons, a blacksmith shop, a post office, a store, and a ten-stamp mill had been built in Aurum. Nearby Piermont also boasted a ten-stamp mill, and a population of about four hundred inhabitants at its peak. Today you find almost nothing except the cemetery. How many forgotten graves guard Nevada's memories? More than anyone can guess, I suspect. Everywhere across the Silver State, ghosts have left their trails.

Some of the first ghosts swam in the inland sea that sloshed two hundred million years ago. Reptiles as long as fifty feet from head to tail patrolled the shallow waters until equatorial temperatures turned the gigantic ocean to mud. The ichthyosaurs literally were beached and then buried by limey waters, rocks, lava flows, ash, and mud. Erosion and an inquisitive geologist named Dr. Siemon Muller finally unearthed their petrified bones. During the 1950s and 1960s, excavations by Dr. Charles Camp and Dr. Samuel Welles from the University of California, Berkeley, located forty separate specimens in just a few acres. A state park, established in 1970, shows off some of the immense ichthyosaur fossils. Its showpiece is a single quarry where nine partial skeletons lie exactly where they were found. There you walk around remnants of a twenty-five-foot tail, six-foot fins, the jaw of a badly crushed skull, ribs, shoulder bones, flippers front and rear. A single mid-body vertebra measures six inches in diameter, three inches thick. A row of them ridges the soil. Each piece tilts downhill in the desert dirt, as if a school of fish-like reptiles were paddling toward deeper water when the hot sun toasted them into eternity.

It's hard to believe that the nation's driest landscape displays a sea monster as the state fossil. Nevada legislators could have chosen any one of a number of other possibilities, for the state is littered with Paleozoic remains. Bill Fiero, in *Geology of the Great Basin,* describes a variety of small-size foraminifera, sponges, coral, trilobites, bryozoa, brachiopods, pelecypods, snails, crinoids, and cephalopods. You find them lodged in the most unlikely limestone places. Atop Cathedral Rock, 8,600 feet above sea level, I stepped on a perfectly fluted white shell, a "brach" the size of my thumb. Embedded in the same rock was a slightly larger but equally delicate veined leaf. These tiny fossils contrast mightily with the mammoth and bison bones found at both ends of the state. Archaeologists from the Desert Research Institute recently dug tusks and an intact skull from a dusty northern site that contains partial remains of four or five other enormous mammoths, some vertebrae of extinct camels and horses, and even one juvenile tooth of a saber-toothed tiger. Currently cleaning the findings with toothbrushes and stabilizing them with resin, the DRI team plans someday to display the remains for the public. Meanwhile, excavations continue.

It is unclear if these mammals died before humans arrived in the Great Basin or if the two coexisted for a time. Archaeologists tell us, however, that humans have lived in this desert for close to 10,000 years. An exhibit alongside the icthyosaur bones holds a Gypsum Cave projectile point found in nearby Union Canyon. Flaked in approximately 1300 B.C., the point is displayed next to notched and eared cherts dating from A.D. 500 to 1850. Ancestors of today's

Paiute and Shoshone peoples have inhabited this part of central Nevada for centuries. They left a tangible imprint on the land by chipping, pecking, incising, scratching, and painting symbols into the rocks themselves. When Robert Heizer and Martin Baumhoff published what they thought was a definitive study of rock art, they recorded 99 petroglyph sites in Nevada. Alvin McLane, the most knowledgeable petroglyph person in the state today, reports more than 150 sites somewhere east of Sparks—he won't say where—and hundreds more located throughout the basin and range country. So it is clear that the 1962 survey sorely underestimated what actually lies hidden in Nevada's rocks. Though they documented the yellow, red, and white pictographs of Potts Cave, Heizer and Baumhoff missed a Wheeler Peak site 13,000 feet above sea level. Though they detailed four figures in White Pine's Katchina Rock Shelter, they knew nothing of the 82 sites recently discovered near Battle Mountain. Though they reproduced many of the drawings found not far from Reno on the cliffs of Lagomarsino Canyon, they didn't mention the ones I've seen on a Peavine rockfall an hour's walk from my house.

Many of us would keep pictograph and petroglyph sites secret, but certain places are easily accessible and even visitor-friendly. Just off Highway 50, for example, the BLM manages the Hickison Petroglyph Recreation Area. There you see a series of interlacing lines, curves, crisscrosses, and scrawls that a handy brochure says "may represent hunting or fertility magic—or they may merely be prehistoric graffiti or doodling." No one knows exactly when the glyphs were drawn there, or why, but they remain a ghostly hint of past activity in the Great Basin. Neither extensive nor glamorous, the Hickison symbols show off unpolished work older than the more finished artistry found elsewhere in the state.

Not far from Laughlin, thirty-foot rock art panels guard the mouth of Grapevine Canyon. In all the years I have explored Southwest deserts, I've never found another site—not even Utah's "Newspaper Rock"—decorated with as many figures. Mythology tells us that nearby Spirit Mountain, sacred to Yuman-speaking Native Americans, is the site where their ancestors emerged from the earth. For generations, Indian people paid homage to the mountain's generative power by chipping symbols onto iron-stained walls, creating a gallery of forms and figures. Perhaps because of the canyon's proximity to Spirit Mountain and its ancient mythic heritage, prehistoric people incised more labyrinths and mazes than any other design. Some drawings circle and spiral concentrically inside themselves; others, square and rectangular, dead-end internally or else open either vertically or horizontally onto the rocks. Since anthropologists disagree about the symbolic meanings, I hesitate to suggest my personal interpretation. Yet it's easy for me to imagine the artists replicating labyrinthine passages between the underworld and fertile Grapevine Canyon, designing mazes between darkness and light.

Spirit Mountain invites such contemplation. The highest summit in what maps call the Newberry Mountains, it dominates the rest of the range. Spirit Mountain erupts from the earth. Giant boulders of irregular shapes and sizes spew down its sides in rugged disarray. Little greenery interrupts the brownness of the naked slopes. At sunset, but more especially just before dawn, the mountain glows with an inner transcendence. Ridgeline spires light up in a hazy interplay of light and shadow. If you sit and watch a sunrise, the raw power of the mountain compels you, not necessarily to climb to the top but to embrace its strength. I like to pretend that anyone who watches such daily and seasonal changes can appreciate Spirit Mountain's mythology.

It's easy for me to think I understand things about Grapevine Canyon too. Hunting symbols appear frequently. You'll find more atlatls incised into these walls than you'll see at the better-known "Atlatl Rock" in Valley of Fire State Park. One high panel shows several such throwing sticks side by side, each parallel hook etched deeply and precisely. Renderings of animals, however—especially the huntable desert bighorn—far outnumber implements of the chase. I couldn't begin to count the sheep that slouch, stand, prance, run, and leap up Grapevine Canyon walls, but I paid special attention to their poses. Long horns and short, curved horns and straight, heads tipped downward as if grazing, heads high as if running free, straight-bodied or sway-backed or possibly pregnant, legs stiff or bent, hoofed and hoofless, stances ordinary and imaginative, artistry simple and complex. One panel lines up five desert bighorn in a row, each in a slightly different posture, each dancing its way up the wall. Alive, eager, vibrant, they're the most sophisticated zoomorphs I saw in the canyon. And they're situated exactly where a hunter might have hidden in ambush, waiting for sheep and biding his time by figuring the rocks with magic.

Younger ghosts marked Nevada rocks in language more directly translatable. Where reddish cliffs point the way through High Rock Canyon, one pioneer chipped a permanent memorial to himself. "George N. Jaquith July the 16th 1852 Wis." I look at George's letters, and wonder whether he liked Oregon better than Wisconsin. I don't know the answer. Such is the tantalizing fate of most Nevada ghosts, for they rarely leave enough evidence to tell a whole story.

I like to shadow the pioneers, especially along the route of the Lassen-Applegate Cutoff, perhaps because it winds through some of the most isolated territory around. This so-called shortcut was the way chosen by forty-niners and their followers who either mistrusted the promise of all that gold in California or misjudged the rumors they heard. Fearing one desert crossing and therefore naively selecting another, a number of parties left the Humboldt River and struck out toward the northwest along a path blazed by Peter Lassen and Jesse Applegate. Some sought the fertile fields of southern Oregon; others, a supposedly easier route to the mines. J. Goldsborough Bruff, who chose this less-traveled way, reported in his diary: "Ravines, gulches, & dry stony beds of winter torrents run down in every direction. The trail follows up one of these dry conduits, along a sandy pebbly bed; White and yellow quartz, chlorite slate, iron conglomerate, and dust, with porphyritic pebbles, characterize the approach to the pass in the mountains. Passed, on road, since we left the river, . . . any countless wheels, hubs, tires, and other fragments of wagons; ox-yokes, bows, chains, &c."

Because little changes in a "land of little rain," the vistas across northern Washoe County still resemble what Bruff saw in 1849. As a matter of fact, recent volunteers who signed the Lassen-Applegate Cutoff at half-mile intervals past the Black Rock and on through High Rock Canyon used this diary as one of their guides. Bruff's descriptive detail and his rough accompanying sketches make people want to stand where he stood and walk where he walked. Fortunately, not all of his details resurface in the 1990s. Just past Rabbit Hole Springs, he "counted 82 dead oxen, 2 dead horses, and 1 mule;—in an area of 1/10 of a mile." Then he added, "Of course the effluvia was any thing but agreeable." When I first moved to Nevada, a friend teased me about the wagon trail past Rabbit Hole Springs. In Nebraska, he said, a depression in the grass marks an old wagon route; in Nevada, instead of looking for a depression you look for a line where the sagebrush grows taller. He pointed away from the springs and chuckled—all that fertilizer, all that vegetation.

A scene J. Goldsborough Bruff drew with special accuracy lies just west of the Black Rock Desert crossing, where a present-day dirt road touches Fly Canyon. Wagon ruts are still visible. At the bottom of a short steep grade, shattered pieces of wood testify to what obviously was a difficult passage. Here, where the pioneers so cautiously slid their wagons, the cliffs look just like Bruff outlined them. Perhaps the forty-niners took little time for sight-seeing— Bruff doesn't mention many side trips—but Fly Canyon is worth investigating. Climbing through the debris carried by high water, you circle past deep pools cut into the canyon floor. The largest is more than thirty feet in diameter; the smallest, less than a foot across. Some still hold water; some are dry. These potholes were carved by centuries of a powerful flow, which barely trickles now that drought has dried the upstream source. I've actually camped in the empty upper lakebed, once full, where grateful pioneers watered thirsty stock 150 years ago.

I try to imagine how a pioneer woman, trudging step by step across basin and range, might have judged the desert, and what, shading her eyes from the glare of an August sun, she might have seen. Weekends inside an air-conditioned pickup truck can't compare with a month of sun pounding on a faded sunbonnet. Crossing Nevada on foot must have been brutal. "The Dust!" exclaimed a doctor in 1850, "no person can have the least idea, by a written description—it certainly is intolerable—but that does not half express my meaning—we eat it, drink it, breath [*sic*] it, night and day, the atmosphere being loaded with it."

Nothing helped. "The river water which we have to use is detestable; it is fairly black and thick with mud and filth," wrote Henry Sterling Bloom, another emigrant that same year. But Bloom's sense of humor prevailed. "There is one advantage one has in using it—it helps to thicken the soup which would be rather thin without it." Laughter helped the pioneers keep their sanity.

Hospitality as well as humor helped ease the way for later travelers. The parents of Nevada essayist Idah Meacham Strobridge ran a stage stop where the Lassen-Applegate Cutoff forks away from the Humboldt River. Mark Twain must have paused there, though he doesn't mention the Meacham place by name. I sensed the sparseness of early travel accommodations when I visited Mormon Well Spring, a stop located not on a pioneer trail but along a busy horse-and-buggy route north of Las Vegas. Now listed in the National Register of Historic Places, the old corral still stands. Perpendicular poles hung together with barbed wire form an almost perfect circle that must be seventy-five feet in diameter. Standing alongside the weathered wood and looking at the long-unused roads and tracks and paths leading every which way, I imagined the corral filled with livestock, horsemen bustling around its perimeter.

The earliest pioneers would have been grateful for such a welcome. As the forty-niners successfully navigated the last dry reaches of the northern part of the state, their diary entries sound notes of ecstasy. "The first trees large enough to form a shade we had seen in 1,100 miles," Jasper Hixson eagerly observed. "Men were seen to rush up, half crazed with thirst and embrace these noble old trees and weep as children." Hixson was describing the climax of the Carson River Route, a diagonal that took him and his family thirty miles south of the Truckee River and on toward Carson Pass. Emigrant Trail Marker CRR 12-A identifies this pioneer route as it crossed a place where the U.S. Army would build a post eleven years later. I stood on Fort Churchill's deserted grounds at sunset and thought about ghosts.

More than three hundred men once lived in fifty-eight buildings. The fort, which cost $179,000 to complete, remained active for only nine years. It's been abandoned for more than a century. Only a few ruins rim the hollow square, their walls disintegrating until preserved as part of the state park system. Not far from CRR 12-A, a similar post marks the Pony Express route that also ran along the Carson River. I imagined a crossroads in the summer twilight— Indians, soldiers, pioneers, Pony Express riders, twentieth-century tourists. At Fort Churchill, as at many sites throughout the Silver State, ghosts come together.

Union Canyon, where ichthyosaur fossils and three-thousand-year-old projectile points rest side by side, was an 1863 ore site too. Although Union Ledge turned out to be the least important discovery in the region, it promised a path to nearby lodes—Ione, Grantsville, Berlin. Union no longer exists, except for some signs indicating where buildings once stood and a single adobe house that seems immune to the elements. Walking past the house, I thought I heard someone inside. A lizard scrabbled up the tar-paper roof; a scrap of canvas blew against the vacant back window; somewhere a tin can rattled. No one was there, except Mesozoic and Native American ghosts, and the shell of a house where a sign said the Josephs, then the Waites, then the Smiths once lived.

Berlin, two miles southwest of Union, like its predecessor has been adopted by Nevada as part of the Berlin Ichthyosaur State Park. The Berlin mill, coated with fresh preservative, boasts a new wall, a new ceiling, and new stairs inside. Shawn Hall's *Guide to Ghost Towns and Mining Camps of Nye County, Nevada* reports that it actually has been restored to "working shape." Some other buildings—the hoist shack, the stage station, the machine shop, the blacksmith's shop—remain relatively intact, while a few—Bob Johnson's saloon, Angela's brothel, Gregoria Ascargorta's boardinghouse—consist only of partial rock walls and piles of weathered wood. Although people visit Berlin each day, I've never seen more than a few at a time. On the whole, it's relatively quiet. Inside the machine shop, a board taps irregularly; outside, the tin roof lifts in the wind. A squeak of protective plastic rattles the empty window-pane of the blacksmith's shop. A door blows against its doorsill, while barbed wire scrapes the back wall. A sharp desert wind rustles the sage.

Gabbs, twenty miles away, is not a ghost town. Just last month I bought gas there. But the Premier Western Operations mine that dug into the nearby hillside is closed now, and Gabbs seems to shrink each time I visit. The mine buildings, red brick and skeletal concrete, remind me of the 1930s New Hampshire shoe factories, empty and forlorn, their facades layered with the grays of death. Which actually is the ghost town? Berlin, coated with fresh paint and functionally saved for tourists, or fading Gabbs?

Nevada Coates, who looks after the deserted remains of a place called Tybo, says there's no such thing as a ghost town. Some might call Tybo a ghost town, he grumbles, but it isn't. Nevada Coates lives there, he owns property there, and, as he says, he's not a 240-pound ghost!

Discounting the bearded caretaker's protests, Tybo houses genera-tions of ghosts. Its very name pejoratively means "white man" or "white man's district" in Shoshone. An 1870 silver discovery led to an 1874 boom, which, in turn, led to the 1879 failure of the Tybo Con-solidated Mining Company. Revivals in 1901, 1906, and 1917–20 failed too, as did a 1930s lead-zinc operation that finally closed in 1944. A newly placed sign says Alta Gold presently owns the min-eral rights, but they've done nothing near the site except hire a watchman. Two miles up Tybo Canyon, a pair of pristine charcoal kilns stand undamaged, their Italian-crafted rock walls hardly dark-ened with use. Nearer town, time has been crueler to the partial walls of a brick schoolhouse built on a foundation of stones. The only other brick structure, the Trowbridge Store, is crumbling too, although props inside and out keep it from falling over. A 1935 photograph in Stanley W. Paher's *Nevada Ghost Towns and Mining Camps* shows the hoist house, the head frame over the shaft, crushers, flotation mill, conveyers, the company general offices, the commissary, the superintendent's home, and the men's dormitory. Sixty years later, only the hoist and head frame are relatively intact, although mosaic rock sidings, concrete foundations, iron pipes, machinery debris, and piles of black charcoal scatter down the hill.

Somewhere else, I happened upon a miner's cabin slouched against a hillside. Its tin roof tipped sideways by winter snows and its sides bowed out, the shack nonetheless leaned upright, its contents untouched. Someone had painted the door a cheerful yellow and the window trim barn red. I stepped inside. Wallpaper made of flattened beer cases graced the interior walls; an empty Old Heritage bottle, dozens of rusted beer cans, and a stack of Prince Albert tobacco tins filled one corner. From the combination, I drew some conclusions about life here at the nine-thousand-foot-elevation level. The cabin's furnishings were timeworn and the kitchenware rusty with age, but I could see everything a hand-to-mouth prospector might need. A wooden bed frame, with springs intact; one large table, a smaller folding table, and a stool; a regulation cast-iron stove; two buckets, one for drinking water, one for bathing; a coffeepot, a skillet, plates, rusty silverware; an axe head; even a pair of boots and some torn khaki trousers. Only one window was broken, and the dirt floor looked almost clean.

A dugout behind the cabin would keep perishables cool. I wanted to go inside, but thought the dirt walls too unstable and feared what might live there now. A second cabin, higher up the slope, had fared less well than the one with the yellow door. More fully exposed to the weather, it had totally collapsed. Nearby tailings told the story of a mine long since played out—one large shaft fallen in on itself, a smaller shaft up higher, a few twisted rails. While snowmelt east of the mine was stained both brown and sickly green, a creek lush with saxifrage bubbled from a year-round spring beside the cabin.

I camped for two nights in the meadow just north of the shack,

where a panoramic view included snowdrifts still covering much of
the landscape. I could pretend a wintry existence in that long-de-
serted place. What seemed charming in summer must have been
hellish at other times of year. I imagined a temperature fifty, sixty,
maybe even a hundred degrees colder than my July weather, then
decided the men must have wintered elsewhere. This spot was too
isolated, and probably buried half the year by wind-driven snow.
Looking at the site—battered tin roofs, quaint red windowsills,
dirty tailings and rusted rails—I wondered why I find old mining
relics so abstractly romantic. I tested adjectives like "forlorn," "win-
some," "rustic," "picturesque," and "quaint," even as I rejected terms
like "pollution," "degradation," and "scars on the land."

Here was a two-bit mining operation launched with the same
spirit as a mega-mining operation today. A jackpot mentality drove
these prospectors, just as a strike-it-rich mind-set propels the corporations that work the Carlin Trend. This particular camp didn't
bother me, though, because it fit with the wilderness, its scope narrow, its intrusiveness focused. I liked this lonesome place. Today's
mines are different. At Goldstrike, less than two hundred miles
away, trucks haul 22,000 tons of rock every hour from a pit eight
hundred feet deep. For every gold bar, 125,000 tons of rock waste
must be dug, crushed, leached, and then left somewhere. Projections say the pit eventually will double or even triple in size. I don't
know exactly where the excavated earth will come to rest, but I do
know the landscape will look very different. It already does. Maybe
it's a matter of magnitude: small-scale digs, little lizards sleeping
benignly in the sun; monolithic operations, more like voracious
ichthyosaurs, wide awake and on the move.

You see a juxtaposition of old and new at Rhyolite, one of
Nevada's better-known ghost towns because of its proximity to
Death Valley. Rhyolite boomed in the early 1900s. In six short years
it grew to be Nevada's second-largest city, with as many as 12,000
men, women, and children living there. The boomtown had three
newspapers, two electric light plants, a hospital, an opera house, an
ice cream parlor, even a stock exchange. Then people left, and

Rhyolite began to fall back into the creosote and sage. Many walls still stand partially upright, so the deserted streets make a splendid photographic backdrop. Looking from inside one ruin through the walls of another to the desert beyond gives perspective to the decay.

Two well-photographed buildings remain almost intact. Perhaps the most remarkable structure is the bottle house built by Tom Kelly in 1906, with walls made from thousands of unbroken beer and liquor bottles. All that glass, and yet it's dark inside, almost gloomy. More ostentatious is the railway station, a neo–Southern California structure with green rococo ornamentation. Shabby, unpainted and unoccupied, the depot shows its age. A barbed-wire-and-chain-link fence protects the structure—from souvenir hunters, I guess. Parked in the depot's shadow for an hour one Wednesday afternoon, I counted cars from six different states. One family didn't speak English. Two others never got out of their cars. Perhaps they didn't notice the view.

A 1990s mining operation almost surrounds the ghosts of Rhyolite. Beyond the main street, a productive Canadian mine scallops the mountainside and exposes tons of raw earth. Three miles away, on the Death Valley highway, where drivers and passengers first glimpse an edge of the gargantuan excavation, a sign used to say proudly:

MINING AND RECLAMATION
IT WORKS FOR NEVADA.

Someone recently took the sign down.

The curmudgeon in me prefers the old ways. I also fancy ghost towns farther off the beaten track, where lonely spirits cast their spells. Imagine life in White Pine County's Hamilton—a population of 30 in 1868, 10,000 in 1869, 4,000 in 1870, 500 in 1873, empty in 1950, 75 in 1980, empty again in 1994. A seesaw of people instead of a bell-shaped curve. Twenty years ago I spent a weekend camped not far from the spot where a large sign now insists: PRIVATE PROPERTY NO CAMPING IN HAMILTON. Waking to a chilly dawn, I walked up and down streets where so many strolled before me, in and out of crumpled brick buildings where commerce briefly flourished. More walls were standing upright then, though intricate brick archwork still testifies to masonry's longevity. Today, new ghosts intrude.

Another Hamilton, just as deserted but much less picturesque, usurps the surroundings. Torn curtains flap from the broken windows of four abandoned prefab trailers. An aluminum storage shed, with a door the size of an eighteen-wheeler, sits alongside five substantial vats marked "Treasure Hill." Beyond the shed and a nearby heap of rusting pulleys, an abandoned leach pond stretches north and south. The place, deserted once again, looks haunted in a different way.

I'm not so naive as to believe that the nineteenth-century excavations weren't invasive—one look at the nearby denuded Treasure Hill proves their voraciousness—but the early prospectors left behind a mountain instead of an open pit, a township of brick instead of plastic, a cemetery with marble tombstones instead of a monument to engineering innovation. The same holds true in Rhyolite, in Berlin and neighboring Gabbs, in Tybo, in the landscape around that yellow-doored cabin and its antithesis, the Carlin Trend. Where prospectors once pockmarked the land and left behind what we characterize as romantic relics of the past, bulldozers now gouge the depths and leave behind almost nothing. In some places, even mountains disappear.

Like most Nevada ghost towns, Hamilton is guarded by a cemetery. Legible marble monuments and illegible wooden ones cluster together, memorials to women and children as well as men. "In Memory of Albert B. Charles, A Native of Plattsburg, NY, Died in Hamilton, Nev, Dec 6, 1869 Aged 43 years"; "I.H.S. In Memory of Mary Casey, Died June 13 1870, A Native of Cambridge Mass. Aged 19 years, Erected to her memory by her esteemed friend Isaac Phillips"; "Umberto Lani, Age 4 yrs 9 mos, Sweet be your rest." A spectacular view, extending every direction from the cemetery, includes playa, round-shouldered mountains, a town with a double life—brick and stone walls, turquoise and green trailers, wrought-iron fences and wooden pickets, a hundred-acre leach pond, plastic commemorative flowers and wild serviceberry in bloom. "Arthur Timson, Born July 27, 1873, Died Jan 6, 1898, Sweet be your sleep, Arthur, my darling boy." Miners are the phantoms of nineteenth-century Hamilton, but the landscape is the real ghost now. Mountains, crushed today and disappearing, are New Age Nevada ghosts, converging with the old.